#52- 2000   BK Bud   Aug. 2001

NORTH CAROLINA
STATE BOARD OF COMMUNITY
LIBRARIES
SOUTHEASTERN COMMUNITY COLLEGE

P9-CCR-767

.V 56
1998

How to Set Limits

SOUTHEASTERN COMMUNITY
COLLEGE LIBRARY
WHITEVILLE, NC 28472

Defining Appropriate Boundaries of Behavior for Your Children—from Infants to Teens

Elizabeth C. Vinton, M.D.

CB
CONTEMPORARY BOOKS

•Library of Congress Cataloging-in-Publication Data

Vinton, Elizabeth C.
     How to set limits: defining appropriate boundaries of behavior for
your children—from infants to teens / Elizabeth C. Vinton.
          p.   cm.
     ISBN 0-8092-3014-3
     1. Discipline of children   2. Child rearing.   3. Child development.
     4. Parenting   I. Title.
     HQ770.4.V56   1997
     649'.64—dc21   97-30756
                                                                   CIP

*To my husband, John, and our three wonderful
daughters: Sandra, Skyler, and Deborah*

Cover design by Scott Rattray
Cover photo copyright © Peter Cade/Tony Stone Images
Interior design by Mary Lockwood

Published by Contemporary Books
An imprint of NTC/Contemporary Publishing Company
4255 West Touhy Avenue, Lincolnwood (Chicago), Illinois 60646-1975 U.S.A.
Copyright © 1998 by Elizabeth C. Vinton, M.D.
All rights reserved. No part of this book may be reproduced, stored in a retrieval
system, or transmitted in any form or by any means, electronic, mechanical,
photocopying, recording, or otherwise, without the prior permission of
NTC/Contemporary Publishing Company.
Printed in the United States of America
International Standard Book Number: 0-8092-3014-3
18   17   16   15   14   13   12   11   10   9   8   7   6   5   4   3   2

Contents

13.45

acknowledgments

There are many people I want to thank who have helped me with the writing, editing, and publishing of *How to Set Limits*. Thank you first of all to my family—John, Sandra, Skyler, and Deborah—for your continued support. You have taught me a lot. Also, thank you to my own mother for her reassurance that anything I try to do is possible; that has always been a very powerful message. To my sister, Anne Hogeland, thank you for your insightful critiquing. To my friends, colleagues, and patients, I thank you all for your immeasurable contributions. Special thanks to my agent, Charlotte Raymond, for taking me on. To the staff at Contemporary Books, many thanks for your extensive counsel, especially with the revising and editing of my text. Thanks to my special friends Ann Parson, Eleanor Cochrane, and Joan Riley, who have knowingly and unknowingly contributed to my efforts. Thanks also to my friends in Wilton, Maine, where I did most of my writing.

To the reader: this book will give you guidelines and a very reasonable approach to setting limits for yourself and your children. Ultimately, the choices you make and the limits you set are yours, but I challenge you to be firm in those choices.

Finally, to our children with whom we are blessed, I say you are special and deserving of our best efforts.

How to Set Limits

what it means—and what it doesn't mean

Setting limits means defining the rules and regulations, the boundaries, that enable us to make decisions and act responsibly. Setting limits means drawing a line and then holding to that line. Limits provide structure—a framework, if you will—that guides and directs us in our daily living.

For parents, setting limits provides a means of maintaining control—you over yourselves, you over your children, and, ultimately, your children over their own lives. It does *not* mean imposing unreasonable restrictions, tethering creative or exploratory impulses, or bending personalities in contrary ways. Instead, what setting limits should do is provide parents with tools so they can skillfully guide their children—direct their children's energies to appropriate paths so they can fulfill their own destinies in a responsible way.

Our charge as parents is to raise our children—to "teach them well"—teach them right from wrong and good from bad. We are supposed to mold and guide our offspring into becoming decent citizens, caring individuals who will respect the rights of all people and who themselves are happy, independent-thinking, and self-assured. Our job is an enormous challenge and full of the unpredictable—with endless decisions. Make no mistake—parenting *is* a job, perhaps the most underrated, yet important, job we will ever hold. It is full of wonder, surprise, complexity—sometimes joy, but sometimes disappointment. The challenges of parenting—the struggles, the choices—are real. But how we parent will have an impact on future generations. And what greater legacy do we have than our children?

First, let's think about who or what runs our lives and our children's lives. In your house, who is in charge—who or what controls the decision-making process? What do your children see?

In this book, we will look at how we as parents can both guide and direct our children's behavior but still leave space for them to make decisions and choose for themselves. We will explore what kind of adaptations we as parents should make as our children grow and change.

Being a parent requires a delicate balance as we cast out the line but still hold the rod and reel. How much line should we give? And how does that change over time? Issues of lifestyle, choice, and responsibility are ever-changing and complicated, but given an appropriate framework of controls and limits, or standards, these issues and concerns can be successfully addressed. Setting limits is a process, a journey of selecting and then modeling, as well as expecting, preestablished standards of behavior.

Before we begin, it is important to recognize that households are not democratic institutions. Rather, there is a certain balance of power, with the parents definitely in the driver's seat. You, the parent, are the CEO, CFO, and chairman of the board, all rolled into one. You, at least in the beginning, are the decision maker. Children do not get equal votes. But over time, they can share in the process.

To illustrate, think of a pie or a circle representing "control." The pie is divided into slices or pieces colored in blue or white. As the parent of a newborn child the sections are colored for you—let's say blue—as you control your child's life. You're the boss—you hold the reins. But as your child grows, you loosen those reins as you allow him or her to participate more and more in decisions and choices and begin to color some of the circle in your child's color, the white. Over time the colors and control shift. By the time your child completes adolescence and emerges into adulthood, the pie will be shaded completely for him or her. Remember, this is a *process*—you set limits, maintain them, and then work over time to share control and, ultimately, to shift control to your child. You want to enable your child to reach his or her own potential, to do his or her very best. You fulfill your obligation as a parent as you empower your child to take charge, hopefully in a productive and responsible way.

We need to take ourselves and the job we are doing seriously. We need to recognize the importance of setting appropriate, consistent limits—to be fair, yet remain open to discussion. We know that we are not perfect—mistakes are human. We'll make not just a few but many, but we will adjust. Humility from a parent goes a long way—don't be afraid to share it. Furthermore, we have to recognize that what works for one child may not for the next. Each child is truly unique, with a different set of needs. We have to remain flexible, adjusting to each and every one.

As we parent, we recognize also that we are not always our children's best friends. Sometimes, in fact, they consider us their real enemy—and they may not like us at all! But being a parent is not a popularity contest. In setting limits, we *must* react to inappropriate or unsafe behavior. Kids don't always like that. But if our children act poorly—do the "unmentionable"—cross the line—we cannot ignore them. For what is a limit if not a boundary line? We do our children a great disservice by not calling them to task when we should. Remember, children acting out at home or in public are not cute. Fresh talk or screaming (at any age) is not acceptable. Throwing food, destroying property, lying, cheating, or reckless driving must not be permitted. Bad behavior is just that—bad!

There are definite norms for which we as adults are held accountable. Likewise, our children must be taught accountability—and taught correctly by us, with love and understanding—from the beginning. True love is unconditional, and whether we are called upon to reprimand or even punish our children, any correction or acknowledgment of unacceptable behavior must represent an act of that love. Hopefully, we can learn to exercise control and confidence as we deal with any wrongdoing or conflict. The old "spare the rod, spoil the child" does *not* need to be resurrected, however. Let me be very clear on this point. Physical or emotional punishment is not my intent in this book. We have no right to hurt our children, with words or fists! However, I think the pendulum has swung too far toward permissiveness, and many parents do not have control of their children or of their own lives. In fact, too often the children are running the show.

Furthermore, I feel very strongly that, by *not* setting limits (or not at least trying), we are dodging our responsibility as parents. Don't be fooled—children *want* and *need* order. And yet, on the flip side, they are incredibly smart and will take advantage of us (whether consciously or not) if we are unclear or vague about that order. Don't leave the door open. Children will push and push and make everyone miserable, including themselves, looking for boundaries. (They know our buttons.) Children need limits, structure—and that means rules and regulations. Otherwise, we have chaos. Children need to know where the line is drawn and that crossing it is not tolerated. Truly, this may be "easier said than done," but we must work purposely (with love and firmness) to establish that line.

Learn to say no and honor it. Don't be afraid of your child—don't be afraid of hurting his or her "feelings." Rather, look for fairness, consistency, and acceptable behavior. Don't back down. Children want affection, but not a pushover! It's true, some children are more compliant than others, and some are distinctly more difficult. But our assignment remains the same—to set and uphold reasonable limits. Furthermore, know that, when we are successful in maintaining control, we will not only gain the respect of our children, but also enable them to carry on in a responsible way, because there is no confusion about our expectations.

As a board-certified pediatrician and a parent of three grown children, I feel very strongly that we have a responsibility to organize our own lives, model appropriate behaviors, and then set clearly defined limits for our children. For that reason, I have written this book to offer specific guidelines—to help you, as a parent, with your parenting efforts.

To help facilitate your reading, I have divided the book into three parts. In Part I, I present a general plan, or blueprint, for our role as parents. I offer you an acronym, SECRET—the "secret" to setting limits. Truly, it can help you with your family. I challenge you to try it.

In Part II, I've examined each developmental stage, from the newborn period through adolescence, with a focus on age-appropriate expectations. The limits you set on your infant or toddler will differ from those you select for your teenager. Read about your child's stage, but don't forget to draw from other developmental stages. What's coming up? What might you do differently next time? SECRET will also be revisited in Part II as the blueprint for setting limits.

In Part III, I've chosen general areas of concern that affect all of us. Everything from grandparents to birthday parties, from the demands of ill children to the distractions of modern technology. There is a need for setting limits everywhere, as we confront common issues in the daily routine of raising a family. Again, we will revisit SECRET.

As you move along, remember to value yourself as a parent and to value your child. Take your role as a parent seriously, work hard at setting limits, and the world will be a better place.

PART I

SECRET

a guideline
for parenting

I

SECRET

The Keys to Setting Limits

What does it mean to "set limits," to "set controls"? It means designing a specific plan with rules and regulations, a framework that will enable you to parent well and wisely, with confidence, strength, knowledge, compassion, and, of course, love and patience. It means developing a set of tools and then keeping them in good working order always. Those tools—your parenting skills—need to be maintained, occasionally sharpened, and then—once in a while—reexamined. It's not always easy.

But what might that plan, or framework, be? What guidelines can we establish? For starters, I recommend focusing on four key concepts—"buzz words," if you will—four building blocks, for parenting. I want to prepare you, the parent, as best I can with a foundation upon which rules or limits can fall more easily into place. I will give you an outline—*you* can fill in the details. I want to empower you as a parent. It will take commitment and devotion, but the results will be worth the work!

The four keys are self, calm, respect, and time. And without being corny or simplistic, we can construct a mnemonic: SECRET. SE for *self*; C for *calm*; RE for *respect*; T for *time*—the SECRET to setting limits, the SECRET to more successful parenting. But let's look deeper. What does all this mean?

SELF

Know thyself. Before making rules or setting limits on others, you might want to look internally. Right from the beginning, you have to recognize that you are an individual, with your own set of standards, your own sense of fairness, of right and wrong. You have your own role models—your own ideals, codes of behavior. In addition, your temperament, your health, your energy level, your needs and expectations, and your interests are yours alone—and *will* all have an impact on your style of parenting. Over time, that style will develop—and it will reflect *you*!

Right from the very beginning—right from the "get-go"—I suggest looking at and taking care of yourself. Parenting is hard work—and complicated. It requires fitness—physical, spiritual, and emotional. We need to be in shape! How can we guide our children from dawn to dusk if we're not well—if we're not in working order? What kind of example do we set if we, you and I, are not a priority, just like our children. So, right from the beginning, *self* stands for you and for me. Take care of yourself. Eat, rest, work, and play.

> *Eat* well and regularly. Don't cheat yourself of calories, protein, or general nutrition. Eat balanced meals. Beware of dieting that robs your body and mind of basic energy.
>
> *Rest*—Do take time out to rest, nap, sleep. Put some balance in your day between busy and quiet time. It can't be go-go-go all the time.
>
> *Work* hard at parenting—work hard at any commitment you make. But also . . .
>
> *Play*—Yes, play! "All work and no play" makes you a dull parent. Take time for recreation, for *fun*—for sport and exer-

cise—for some reading—for laughter! Let your child join you or not, but let him see that your needs count.

Listen to your own body and mind. Do the best you can to keep them working at their best. Know that every second does not have to be given over to your child. You may need—and it's OK—time with other adults and, perhaps, some time away. Your ultimate goal is to be a good parent, and you will do that best if you are feeling well.

And then, slowly, over time, you can begin to figure out what works for you and your child, personally. Parenting is truly an individual thing.

Your style and your limits are yours to determine and exercise. Know that what worked for your neighbor doesn't necessarily hold for you. And likewise, what worked for your mother or for your father (or your doctor), again, is not necessarily for you. Through trial and error (sometimes lots of error), you will find your answers and develop your style. You will set the limits that work for your family.

For example, how much control must you maintain over your child—how tightly must you hold the reins? Where is your own comfort zone? How much of the decision "pie" will you share with your child—and when? This will come with time.

In the end, you have to be true to yourself in establishing limits that are appropriate for *you*. Gather advice, talk to people—ask yourself hard questions, be honest. You have to trust and believe in your own instincts and common sense. This is not always easy, particularly if you're a new parent. I mean, how are you supposed to know how you feel? How can you act responsibly when you're a first-time parent? The answer is, you have to devote time and energy—and lots of both—as you figure out what works best in your household. You work purposely, do some reading, solicit professional advice, talk to your spouse, listen to your own heartbeat.

And in the end, you must be willing to commit to certain standards of behavior—*consistently*—to draw and hold to that line. Remove any sense of conflict in yourself as best you can. Then your child can and will depend upon you.

Calm

As an extension of *self*—beyond taking care of ourselves, beyond figuring out what works—we need to look at the tone we set in our homes. This calls for *calm*.

We need to work in earnest at establishing and maintaining calm—keeping our composure.

Though none of us is perfect (Amen!), we need, as parents, to control—as well as care for—our own selves. Remember, our children are watching us. Do we present a picture of maturity, dependability, and serenity—or one of confusion and unpredictability? Are our lives too frantic, too busy?

Are we so overloaded that composure is impossible? Think about calm and patience. There should be no whining or complaining from us (or from our children). Try to limit your impulse reactions, "shooting from the hip."

More than anything, we need to take charge of *ourselves* in order to exercise control over our children. How better can we demonstrate limit setting to our children than by setting limits in our own lives? We need to feel good and confident about ourselves, and we need to control our own behaviors, emotions, and schedules. How else can we establish calm?

Limit setting begins at home—and with us. There are no shortcuts! Realize that we truly teach by example—which means that our chosen and established limits, whatever they are, have to be upheld by us, as parents, or our children will not abide by them. Know that it's not just the letter of the law, but the attitude that is important. It's not only what we do, but how we do it. Our children learn more from our doing than our saying. They learn by watching, and they see both our strengths and weaknesses. We are their role models.

As parents, we are responsible for laying down the law and then upholding it. How do we do that—with calm and composure? Think about the vibrations you're sending. Don't act out of temper, but out of love.

Are your children afraid of you? Do you react without thinking—unpredictably, without warning? Are you always changing your mind? Know that if there is no calm, then there is probably storm.

Is your home a nurturing place for you and your children? Know that this is not automatic but takes commitment and work. It demands looking at your priorities and making choices. An environment of peace and calm—where you are relaxed—sets a wonderful, favorable tone, where your children can concentrate on growing and conforming, rather than fighting against tension. Help your children by providing a warm environment.

Measure the atmosphere in your home. Permit no yelling or screaming from you or the children. Keep things in balance—in check.

Like it or not, we hold enormous power over our children—not just physical power, but emotional and spiritual power as well. Our power needs to be honored, never abused. We need to recognize our power and channel it appropriately with calm.

RESPECT

Respect all persons—yourself, your spouse (or the child's other parent), and your child. Know that each and every person is an individual with his or her own sense of purpose. Each is special, unique. Do we truly honor that? Do we give space to ourselves and to our children? Do we value each person for himself or herself and show respect? Do we *like* each other—ourselves, our child, our spouse? If not, we miss out on the beauty of our humanity. For we are a group of creative beings with gifts and talents of our own. We are all different.

Our child or someone else's child—it doesn't matter. Your first baby or third or the child next door, they are all one of a kind. Each deserves recognition. So do show respect for each other—model it—and then, demand it from your children. Be kind, be courteous, speak with love. Pay attention to the beauty inside of people.

Build your children up—support them—be there. But beware of building self-esteem at any cost. Respect your child's abilities—love him or her—but maintain integrity and honesty. Praise your child appropriately, but be careful about false praise. Don't tell your child he or she is terrific when it's not true. Share your disappointment in what he or she has done—the world will! And your child knows, anyway.

Allow for our differences as human beings; delight in our complexities. Allow your child to be himself or herself—not you or me. Open your heart and mind to your child's individuality.

Finally, know that, as each child is unique, each child has his or her own set of needs and will require a certain flexibility from you, the parent. But the flexibility is in the implementation of strategy—the "how tos"—not in the basic tenets. Kindness, respect for each other, courtesy—these things do not change. They are central. And they, too, like calm and composure, require commitment and hard work.

Time

Make time! Anything worth doing takes time. It takes twenty years to grow a child. It is not a quick fix. There is no magic fast track.

Do you *really* make time for your child, for your family? Do you truly honor the need your child has for your time with him or her? Is your time together too limited and/or too structured?

Does every minute have to count? Try turning the clock off. Go somewhere with no regard for time. Setting limits takes time—or, more to the point, being a parent takes time—and lots of it, more than you ever imagined. It is not a 9-to-5 job; it cannot be squeezed into a finite number of hours.

Whose time is it, anyway? Isn't your child's time as valuable as yours? Remember, we don't get time back! Don't let it slip away.

Parenting and limit setting take consistent, often repetitive work, delivered with commitment and love and patience. And that takes time. Rules and limits are to be set not out of frustration or for convenience but rather out of a sense of purpose. This takes time.

So in the end, I offer this framework: SECRET (sELf, calm, REspect, TIme) for you, the parent. Now we can begin to design a step-by-step approach for setting limits—the dos and don'ts, the rules for your household. You can take charge and develop strategies for your children. We can deal with issues of behavior, safety, choice, and control. I really believe that if we truly know ourselves, maintain composure, respect each other, and allow enough time, our ability to choose and set appropriate limits for ourselves and our children will be greatly enhanced. The balance we all seek in our lives will come more easily if we take the time required to sort things out. Our success as parents—our ability to guide our children toward self-fulfillment—will be greater.

But, of course, there is one major caution: I cannot promise completely smooth sailing. I wish that I could! Unfortunately, there are no guarantees—only guidelines and suggestions. It is important to recognize that with any child you, the parent, will hit some bumps somewhere along the way. As your child develops and establishes his or her own identity, there will be times for conflict or confrontation, even unhappiness. Storms do brew (remember we are all human), but how you weather them will depend upon the foundation you have laid as a parent. If you can hold the fort during the difficult times—keep yourself in check when challenged—you will meet the challenges of parenting more successfully. Remember that the next generation is learning from us. We need to do a good job. Know that help is available if you're struggling—be it friends, family, or professionals. Use this help if and when you need it.

Moreover, it is important to know that, even when we try hard and model good behavior for our children—when we *do* set limits—things don't always turn out as we hope. Some children are cut from a different swathe. They choose to follow a very different path from ours—to march to a different drummer. Some, for reasons never understood, have a more temperamental or just different disposition—and some are truly troubled. Some, if not quite a few, do require professional help to manage. It's not a matter of fault or failure, but simply a fact.

In addition, we work hard to help our children wherever they are, as much as we are able. We take and share responsibility for their outcome, but remember—only up to a point. Because somewhere along the line, as your child approaches maturity, he or she must take some responsibility for his or her own life as well.

PART II

How to Set Limits

guidelines for each
developmental
stage

• • •

Each developmental stage has its own special parenting demands and tasks. The infant demands more "hands on" than the toddler; the toddler demands caution and an ever-watchful eye. The school-aged child, as well as the teen, is expanding his or her boundaries and looking for space. We parent each child a little bit differently, according to his or her needs and abilities. And yet the issues are relatively constant. Issues of growth, behavior, safety, sleep, and diet are ever present. It's the how and what to do that are adjusted for the child's age.

With that in mind, I'd like to examine each developmental stage to see how each is distinct and then suggest appropriate limit-setting guidelines for each stage. We'll revisit SECRET (*self, calm, respect, time*) frequently, as it has application throughout.

• • •

2

The
Newborn

A newborn child is a gift, a very special present entrusted to our care. He is unique—truly one of a kind. And despite the infant's small size, he is complete—full of promise, but mystery as well. We will feed, change, and care for our infant with total and complete responsibility. This child is dependent upon us for all his needs! We will give him love and security—we will teach him that the world can be a wonderful place. We will help him develop trust in other people and keep him safe and warm. Everything this little human being needs, we, his parents, will provide.

But how can we do that? How can we be successful? How do we respond?

SECRET

For starters, let's remember the framework we developed in Chapter 1. Perhaps by honoring those four basic guidelines, we can begin to prepare ourselves better for the job of parenting. If we truly honor SECRET, then we can better direct and control our own behavior so that we can guide our child's behavior more adeptly, right from the start.

With regard to specific limits—the "rules"—these are less obvious in the newborn period. Yet even now, there is a place for limits, the "should dos" versus the "should nots." Who is in charge? Hopefully, you are. You color that control "pie" chart in your color—you're holding the deck of cards. It's you, the parent, who makes the rules—and make them you should. Boundaries do need to be set, even now.

So let's look first at the guidelines and piece together an outline for specific limit setting. Remember our key headings:

Self: Take care of yourself. Know what works for you.
Calm: Be cool.
Respect: Be nice to one another—give space.
Time: Allow time to parent well.

Self

Taking care of a new baby demands your being fit and able— physically, emotionally, and financially. You don't have to be an Olympic athlete, nor dripping in gold or diamonds, but you do have to be prepared for sleepless nights and be able to provide a safe and comfortable space for you and your child. Parenting, especially in the newborn period, is a rigorous job, with day- and nighttime demands. Are you up to it? Have you really taken stock in your own lives and limited your other activity so that you can do this job well? Have you taken time to recognize the value of what you are about to undertake?

Make no mistake about it, newborn parenting is hard work. It is not for the fainthearted. Taking care of a newborn is a twenty-four-hours-a-day, seven-days-a-week full-time job, with no days or evenings off. You are always on call, with no exceptions. Babies need to be fed and changed at 3 P.M. and 3 A.M.— day after day, night after night. Newborns rarely have parent-friendly schedules, and if they do, they often change them. Interrupted sleep for you, the parents—up once, twice, or even three times per night—is the norm. It's rarely easy, and sometimes it's not even fun. It can be isolating and lonely.

You are in a new role. There's no warm-up, no practice drill, no instruction manual. You didn't spend four years in college learning to be a parent. You may have had a kid sister or brother or some experience as a baby-sitter or day-care provider, but there is nothing like having your very own baby. Believe it or not, you will learn mostly through trial by fire—by "hands on." And that's a pretty sobering thought. No training for the most important job of your life! No corporate structure for parenting. You start out at the top.

So, with that introduction, to parent your best, you have to be in shape. You need to take good care of yourself, to preserve your well-being. Think about what you're doing. You are a priority.

You will want to be your very best and most happy self so you can reflect a positive and reassuring attitude to your baby. If you feel good, your baby will relish in your wellness. But if you're ill or sad or uncertain—suffering, for whatever reason—you make it harder for your baby as you signal those feelings. So the first few rules or limits deal with your own self-preservation. Recognize your own needs.

Get rest! Sleep when your baby sleeps. No one tells us—or maybe we don't hear it—how fatiguing being a newborn's parent can be. Well, I *will* tell you. Chronic sleep deprivation for months, loss of a day/night schedule, blending of hours and days—it happens. This is why it is so important that you make your rest a priority. Grab whatever rest you can. A good rule is to rest whenever the baby does.

Eat well! Eat regular meals and snacks—no dieting yet. Keep the fluids and nutrition coming. If you're nursing, know that you are really eating for two, and one of those is a newborn baby who is gaining an ounce a day. Keep the fluids and nutritious calories pouring in.

Preserve your energy! Take on no extra duties—just you and your baby. Use to your advantage the fact that you're a newborn's parent. Milk it for all it's worth. Say, "I can't, because . . ." Limit visitors to two per day, for fifteen to thirty minutes each. Tell family and friends that Dr. Vinton says to do this. Make me the bad guy, if you need to. Make sure your visitors come to help—and not to be your guests.

Limit phone calls. Use an answering machine to screen your calls. Even put an updated message on the tape for your family and friends: "We're very busy right now with Nicky, but everything's fine. Baby's feeding well, and we love being parents. Thanks for calling, but it's nap time for all of us, so please leave a message and we'll get back to you sometime soon—but maybe not today." These are all limits you will want to set!

Pretend you're in training—which is actually true. Get yourself in peak condition and maintain it as best you can so that you can address the challenges of parenting more easily. I don't know about you, but I'm no fun when fatigued or hungry or stressed. How can any of us do our best if we are not in good working order ourselves?

And then, slowly, if you're feeling well, you can begin to sort out and focus better on what specifically works for you. It's so much easier if you're feeling well.

As for the baby, except for providing nutrition, hygiene, and safety, there are very few absolutes, and even these have "how to" options. The fact is that you will be making choices all the time. But the choices have to feel right. For example, how you feed your infant (breast versus bottle—I hope you pick breast) and where you feed him and at what time are important decisions. Do you want to feed your baby on demand or by a fixed schedule—or both? Do you want your infant to sleep in your bed or his crib? Should you let your baby squirm or cry, even a little bit before you rush to him? What kind of diapers—what kind of doctor—how do the grandparents fit in?—there are all sorts of issues, some minor, some not. Do you want to hire a sitter to help out? What about a diaper service? How important is it to you to have easy access to your doctor? Try to address these questions. Be honest and write down your answers. Come up with a plan that feels right for you now—just leave some room for flexibility.

Know that there are no "right" or "wrong" answers—it's just a question of appropriateness for *you*. What do *you* want?

Remember that you make the choices. You control the decision "pie." You only have to feel comfortable with your choices. You have to recognize what is suitable for you. And for that, you have to know yourself. So think about your infant's feeding—how, what, and when. Think about sleeping places—all of you in one room or not. Discuss your options and your preference with your partner. And finally, try to be open to change if you find your initial plan not working.

Calm

Calm, composure, balance—they're heavy words and ever-present goals. We're all working on this one, forever. How can any of us, especially a newborn's parents, achieve just that? Most of us are anxious—if not at least a bit intimidated—by the awesome responsibility of newborn parenting. Bringing your very own child home from the hospital is wonderful, but it can be scary— there is so much to learn and do.

And, although we may be anxious and tired, hopefully, we're still in control. So here are a few more suggestions, even rules. In addition to the preceding, I encourage you to do the following:

Relax! Move slowly, with grace and control. No quick or jerky motions. Walk to your baby, never run. Approach him with calm. Pick him up gently. Caress your infant—never grab. Don't be in a hurry. Talk quietly and evenly, with no yelling, no whining. Tone is as important as (if not more so than) content. Listen to how your words sound. Make an effort to be smooth: in music, it's called *legato*. Sing, even if you can't carry a tune. Hum, and use words or not. Let your baby be soothed by your voice.

Breathe evenly. (Remember those breathing exercises from childbirth.) Control the in and out. Listen to your own heart-beat. Count to 10 or 20 or 100 if you need to regain your com-posure—if you're out of "sync." (I used to do lots of counting—almost like a mantra.) Count to 10 before picking up your baby if you feel stressed.

Laugh at yourself—and with your baby. Try not to take your baby or yourself too seriously. Remember to be a little light-hearted. Don't forget about a sense of humor—it can go a long way.

Composure can be an elusive thing. And it comes more nat-urally to some of us than others. But the more you can slow down your *own* pace in order to enjoy and care for your infant, the eas-ier your task will be, and the calmer your infant will be. There *is* a cause-and-effect relationship between action and reaction. A colicky baby may still be colicky even if you're relaxed but may be less so. An intense infant—and yes, they do exist—will still be intense, but less so if you can soothe him. Even the most mellow baby gets cranky—or worse, tunes out—if the parental signals are tense. Too *much* stimulation can be just as bad as too little. How can your infant learn his own calm if you signal tension?

Use a rocker, and keep yourself comfortable with lots of pillows. Play some music—make your home cozy and inviting. Take time to "smell the roses" and enjoy the day. Look around and acknowledge the ordinary but beautiful (the sunrise, the blue sky, a new snowfall). Don't be in a hurry for anything. Things get done; tomorrow will come, regardless. What's important is that you and your child greet tomorrow with composure.

And finally, don't forget to get help if you're struggling. Hire a sitter, call a relative, or call your doctor. If calm is impossible, seek support and help to bring it back.

Respect

Look at your baby and marvel at him—a birthmark, a curled toe, a sculptured ear. Count his fingers and toes. Notice how he is different—his temperament, his appetite, his sleep patterns. Listen to your baby's special sounds—the coos of conversation, the cries of hunger or pain, the settling sounds of sleep. Recognize that your baby is unique, with his own set of signals and needs. But at the same time, you, too, have your own signals and needs.

So here are more rules or suggestions. Remember, you are in charge. You have the power to decide what will be done and when—but in the context of recognizing that both you and your baby have needs.

Honor your child. Treat him with respect and courtesy always. He might be little, but nevertheless, he is complete. Honor each other—your spouse, other children, all people. Be nice to each other.

Respect yourself. Give yourself credit for tasks well done, for common sense, and for the ability to learn as you go. Have confidence. Recognize that you and your child might need some space and time apart. That's OK. In fact, some time "off" might lead to better time "on." Respect your own needs, as well as your child's.

Respect is actually quite straightforward. You either do or don't respect someone. Certainly your child deserves respect from you, his parents. How will he gain respect elsewhere if none is granted at home? Right in the beginning, practice respect.

Also be a role model of respect. Set the patterns now. Know that respecting each other within the household sets a very positive example. How do you treat each other? With kindness or not? Know that your baby is watching and learning all the time.

Be proud of your infant. Tell him he is wonderful. Celebrate his arrival. Share the news of his birth. And finally, remember that he is human, just like you. His schedule and his demands will vary day to day. Allow for flexibility and space. Allow for the human element.

Time

There are only twenty-four hours in a day—only so many hours of daylight. So much needs to fit into each day—and yet, so much can wait. There are choices to be made, particularly as you select out time for tasks and time for rest. You and your child need time for nourishment and sleep—time to feed the body and the soul.

Know that newborn parenting is very task oriented, particularly as the needs of your infant will fill both daytime and nighttime hours. The physical demands alone are very wearing—feeding, changing, washing. Sleep deprivation is real and can be very taxing, and we all handle it differently. (Youthful parents clearly have an advantage here.)

Here are a few more basic suggestions. Limit your schedule—put in no extras. Clean the slate. Put aside all your other professional and volunteer commitments—take on no new tasks. You're only setting yourself up for frustration and failure if you expect more. Remember, your time and energy have their own limits.

Leave extra time for everything. If feeding your infant usually takes thirty or forty-five minutes, count on more. Leave a time cushion for every activity—from feeding, bathing, and dressing to getting into the car. If you want to feel well and maintain control, keep time open-ended.

Don't fill every moment. Save and protect free time. Leave open spaces in your day. Either the time will fill automatically, or you will have a present of a few unclaimed moments to do with what *you* want.

Value time with your infant. This is so important! What did you do all day? You nurtured your child! That takes *time*!

So, in summary, setting the stage—preparing your home and your life for your newborn—really starts with *you*. You must look at your own life and your own world . . . and make room for your beautiful baby.

This is a time to really set limits on yourself. Focus on your baby, your partner, and yourself—nothing more. Eliminate as best you can any other demand, stress, or tension in your life. The stress of newborn parenting is quite enough. Make it clear to the world outside that your family is your focus. No cheating! There is no room for anything outside your immediate family in the newborn period. No time for new projects—or old—no extras. This is not a time to be extra busy and burdened—quite the contrary. You will be busy enough anyway.

So—no income tax preparations (get an extension), no committee work (pass it off to someone else), no painting the nursery (your baby won't notice), no cooking turkey dinner (someone else can do that), no holiday shopping (presents can wait), no anything else. Limit phone calls and visitors (as discussed previously), and limit your shopping. Keep your time *free*.

The more you do, the more tired you will be—and I promise you, that will affect your ability to parent. Most things can wait, if we only let them. Timelines and targets are our own doing.

Remember that you are beginning to set the stage, to develop an atmosphere in your home of peace and love. You can't do that if you're overtired, stressed out, and cramming, trying to be super parent. How you feel and act *will* affect your child. Remember his multidimensional needs—not just food and clothing, but love and security. He needs *you* at your best. The take-home message: You must take care of yourself and limit your own activity. You have to protect your time. Don't forget SECRET.

Where exactly are your priorities? Hopefully at home, with you and your family. Your responsibilities as a newborn's parent are enormous—try not to overload with anything more.

Now, a few specifics for your newborn. Indeed, even now there are issues of behavior, nutrition, sleep, and safety where standards can be set. Specific rules and limits can be made. So let's consider a few.

BEHAVIOR

As your baby feeds and grows, study him. Pay attention to his different sounds and motions. Get to know him. Begin, even over the first few weeks, to realize that every sound coming out of his mouth is not an automatic cry for "pick me up." Learn to discern little cooing sounds that are self-soothing, not "I need you." Don't be in a hurry to whisk your baby out of his bassinet every time he fidgets or makes a sound. Instead, check him visually and see if he really needs your intervention. Walk to his bedside, don't run. Remember SECRET, think *calm*. Check him out, but don't feel compelled to hold him for every minute of his waking hours. Talk to your friends who have several children and realize that they cannot pick up every child every second of the day. And yet their babies do not lack for love or security. Try to understand your baby's cues. Teach him to wait, but don't deny him your support. If you can be *almost* everything for your baby, instead of absolutely everything, he will develop more flexibility and tolerance for any changes or exceptions. Be there for your child, but don't be compulsive about your availability. Don't become a slave to your baby—rather, a loving, giving parent who recognizes your baby's sounds and needs.

Then as your infant grows and develops new skills, even in the newborn period, the demands and challenges to you will change. As he begins to spend more time awake (even in the first few weeks), you will want to make a different kind of time for him—time for play and conversation, not just time to feed and change; time to laugh, to do nothing in particular; time to build a relationship. Your newborn is a social person who needs more than just a feed. He wants and needs a play person, a companion. You have a responsibility for being there, for making and spending time. Even in the first few months—if not *especially* in these early months—you must spend time doing that "nothing" to build for the future.

Have conversations—hold, touch—get down on the floor—go for walks. Remember SECRET, especially the *calm* and *time* elements. Don't worry about a lot of stimulation or the "right" toys. The fact is, too much stimulation can be detrimental and backfire. The overstimulated child can become wired, out of sync, or agitated. Remember, it's the actual *being together* that counts. Again, it's the process. Build in *play* time to develop behavioral patterns. Spend unstructured time together.

Nutrition

When feeding your infant, especially in the newborn period, make yourself comfortable. Give your infant your full attention and spend this time quietly with him. Focus on him. He should be fed in your arms—never in a plastic infant seat with no body contact. He needs your body's physical presence as well as the liquid nutrition. Feel good about the time together, and your baby will be happy and calm. This is not a time to do two tasks at once. Yes, you can nurse and write thank-you notes or bottle-feed and dictate memos. But why? If you're "Type A," gear down a notch or two or many—let those notes wait, don't even think about any memos. Remember your limit: no extras! Just feed your baby—appreciate the time together and make it the very best quality time. Try to promote calm. The mood and process are as important as the actual food.

With regard to feeding, try *not* to put a nipple into your baby's mouth every time he cries. Know that he doesn't need to be fed immediately, every time he makes a sound. Nor does he need to eat all day long, with no gaps. He needs a break—and so do you. Feed your infant approximately eight to twelve times a day, and monitor his weight at your doctor's. (Not on a home scale.) Feed on demand and/or by schedule—that's your choice. But do leave space between.

If you're a list person, it's OK to mark down feeding times—but respect the fact that your baby is a person who will vary from day to day. Use those lists as a resource, but not as your primary focus. And if your child is thriving, my advice is to put those lists away.

SLEEP

Just as your baby must eat, he must also sleep—not just fidgety ten-minute naps—but some good breaks of one to three hours of real, honest-to-goodness sleep—a time when he or she is down! Sleep is important. We all need it: our infants do, just like us adults. Without it, we all suffer—even babies.

Sleep patterns are variable, and certainly, different babies will establish different schedules early on. Your newborn probably doesn't even know the difference between day and night—it's all the same to him. All he knows is that he is hungry, wet, or both. He may be up more during the night than the day—a kind of day/night reversal, reflecting his prenatal activity—not at all unusual. Remember that kicking fetus in the middle of the night?—this is the same baby.

You cannot, and should not, want to manipulate schedules too much. However, you can make minor adjustments like shaving or interrupting ten or fifteen minutes here or there. Resist long feeds and playtime during the late evening and early morning hours. Make those 2 A.M. feedings "business only"—a feed, a burp, a change, and back to bed. Signal sleep time. Likewise, encourage play and wakefulness during the daylight hours. You *can* influence sleep patterns bit by bit to effect better nighttime versus daytime sleep. Just go slowly and you will meet with success.

Teach your infant to settle himself to sleep in his own space, wherever that may be (crib, bassinet, or part of your bed). Try not to have your baby always fall asleep in your arms or on a nipple. Don't always put him down already asleep. Don't let him get used to always nodding off while being held or fed or rocked. Otherwise, over time, he will come to expect just that—your body contact for sleep as well as feeding. Instead, consciously work at putting your baby down for sleep when he is still a wee bit awake and letting him quiet himself. Allow him to stir—to fidget. You can pat or rock him briefly or cover him with a blanket, but try to let him be. Encourage him, even now, to self-settle. He can learn to do that! Then—and here's the payoff—as he gets older, he will be much more inclined to *re*settle himself when he wakens from light sleep, not necessarily from hunger. He and you will both sleep better. Know that your infant's crib or bassinet (or your bed) can be a place of warmth and security for your baby—help him to learn this. If you always put him to sleep in your arms—with whatever sort of ritual you establish—he will come to depend upon that routine for day, evening, and middle of the night—maybe for months and months. Beware! Set limits early by using his space, not yours. Let him get the message, "This is where you fall asleep and, hopefully, stay asleep."

Whether for nap or overnight time, remember to stay relaxed and not rushed when putting your infant down. Remember the principles of *calm* and *time*. Try hard not to hurry—do not give your baby the signal that you're anxious or tense or fatigued. Breathe slowly, speak slowly, sing that lullaby or soothing tune. Remember, always work on being relaxed; signal calm to your infant, and he will feel the same. As always, a baby is very sensitive to our nonverbal cues, so it is incumbent upon us to maintain our poise. We may not have all the answers, but we still can and must maintain our best self-control. Babies need to know we're OK—and then they will be happier.

Know that you do *not* have to maintain absolute quiet in the household while your baby is sleeping. In fact, have some sound or noise in the background so your baby gets used to that. It's perfectly OK to keep conversation going, play music, and/or keep the TV volume up to an audible level. Don't go around on tiptoe, whispering because the baby is sleeping. Your baby will adapt to whatever environment you provide, given the parameters of calm and peace. The more you expose him to, within reason, the more he will accept. A doorbell or telephone ringing, human voices, or background radio or music should all be very acceptable.

I find it truly amazing how much sleep can control our lives. Its lack has very real impact—it's not good for you nor your baby. Unfortunately, the newborn period is notorious for parental sleep deprivation. Night after night of feedings and changings at 2 A.M. and 4 A.M.—they are not fun. They can wear you down. But the fact is, your baby needs to feed frequently, day and night. Again, there are no nights off with a new baby, no holidays.

I don't know about you, but most adults tend to get cranky when deprived of sleep—and the newborn period is no different from any other. Fatigue is real, and exhaustion, even depression, can follow. So if your baby is a good sleeper, you fare well. Count yourself very lucky. Likewise, if your baby never sleeps, you don't either. More than any other task, training your baby to settle and stay settled will pay huge dividends. If your baby sleeps, you can, too. You will then have time to restore your own health and energy.

Finally, when you do put your newborn baby down for sleep, place him on his back or side—never on his tummy. There is a large body of evidence that points to tummy sleeping as a definite risk factor for sudden infant death syndrome. Don't let your baby become a statistic.

SAFETY

As your newborn begins to shift and roll, even before he learns how to crawl or toddle, look carefully at his space. Examine his room, your room, the kitchen, the living room, and any day-care environment. Really analyze your baby's world. Get down on the floor and check everything. Make sure it is completely safe. It is time to begin protecting your child as he begins to grow and explore. Respect his need for safety.

Believe it or not, your newborn will become more physical and mobile very quickly as he learns to sit, roll, and crawl. You need to control your child's space and realize that from now on, safety—as one kind of limit—will be a major concern. Only the specific issues will change.

So look at your beds, couches, countertops—your changing table. Are these surfaces well protected? Are your floors carpeted? Make sure you never leave your baby alone on the changing table or any raised surface, even if he can't roll over. How do you know when that first roll will come? Keep a firm grip on him wherever he is, always. Never turn your back on your infant when he's on a table or counter space, even for a fraction of a second. Do not trust him to stay put ever. You cannot rely on straps or belts. If your baby is a squirmer, change him somewhere safe—like the floor. Reexamine how you use the infant seat. By the time your baby is three months old, it's time to keep the infant seat on the floor—not on the kitchen counter or any other surface. (I treated one baby for a head injury, who fell from his seat that had been placed in a toilet bowl for presumed safekeeping while his parent "watched." Wrong! The seat moved and the baby flipped out.)

Consider a playpen and think about using it early. Start at four to five months, so by six to nine months your infant is comfortable with this new space. Teach him to be happy there, and he probably will be. Place him in the playpen for ten to fifteen minutes once or twice a day. Be with him in the same room. Talk to him, even play with him. Set up a mobile, shake some pretty rattles, place objects in his hand to explore. Make the playpen fun! Don't abandon your baby there—don't ignore him. Rather, make the playpen part of your day and part of his. This is not punishment—not a "play-penitentiary," to quote one of my parents. Then, when your baby is crawling and really moving about, if you need it you have a safe and familiar place for him. You have a "limited" space.

After all, where will you put your darling, curious infant when you have to use the bathroom, bring in the groceries, pour a cup of hot coffee, or do the laundry? You cannot expect your mobile, cruising baby to stay put while you attend to these normal activities of daily living. He is not a puppy dog that will "Sit!" In fact, he will tend to wander. So do get a playpen—and don't worry about depriving your child of open space for a few minutes. Instead, you are providing him with a familiar, safe, protected area. Just try to do it early on so he will accept it more willingly. By limiting his boundaries, you will ensure his safety.

As babies begin to sit and roll, baby walkers become an often-used piece of equipment. My advice is, *do not use a walker!* They are dangerous—really, an accident waiting to happen—and babies do *not* need that kind of exercise! It's true—babies tumble down stairs in their walkers and get all kinds of head injuries, some very serious. Brain surgery on a previously perfect baby is not a joke. It should never happen, but it does. Burns, scalds from pulling electric cords attached to hot, heavy appliances or tablecloths with cups of hot tea or coffee do occur. Your reaching, wandering baby, moving "innocently" in his walker, is *not* in a safe place. Even finger entrapment in the walker frame occurs. The bottom line is that walkers are risky business. You *cannot* watch your baby all the time, no matter how good your intentions. Life is unpredictable, and babies move fast. Things happen. A phone or doorbell rings, you get distracted, you thought your spouse had the baby. We've seen it all—and it only takes a second. I have seen many serious injuries caused by walkers. This is an easy limit to set—just never use one. Your baby will only benefit if he grows up without a walker. Tell your friends the same.

As your baby begins to explore more and more—starts to crawl, pulls to stand—it's time once more for you to really get down on your own hands and knees and see what he sees. What is it like to be on the floor in your home? Extension cords, plants, electrical outlets—protect your baby by removing or covering them. Know that anything dangerous is an automatic attraction to your baby. I don't know why this is—baby radar?—but trust me, babies know where they are *not* supposed to be.

Finally, make your home safe, but at the same time, do *not* make it your baby's playground. This is very important, because now you will begin to control and direct your baby's choices. Teach him right from the very start that not everything in your home belongs to him. Every place is not for his perusing. There are places that are "out of bounds" and items that are "off-limits." Hands off! Everything does *not* have his name on it.

Have his things *and* your things both out and available, and let him learn the distinction. *Do* leave your things (safe ones) near his—your books and his; your magazines and tapes, then his. Teach him there are a few no-nos . . . but also many yeses. Offer him substitutes, i.e., his things; have infant-appropriate toys ready for use and distraction. The child who learns right from the start that he can have some things but not all—that child is learning to respect property and the rights of others. He might be frustrated by the lack of total freedom, by having some denial. He might fuss—even shout or cry—but, wait a minute, that's life. A child who has absolutely free rein—who wants all and gets all—might become a bit of a "monster." And then when do you begin to restrict him? When do you change the rules, instead of maintaining them? When do you introduce the notion of "no"?

The child who has access to everything is a dangerous one.

He is also *in* danger, because he knows no bounds. In time, you won't be able to take him anywhere—your place, your neighbor's, Grandma's, they're all the same. If your child rules at home, he will try to do the same when out. What's the difference? Likewise, you will see when your friends visit what kind of parents they are. See what their children do to your place. A sofa is not a trampoline; your living room is not a gymnasium. Need I say more?

Your living room coffee table might have a few baby toys on top or underneath, but the adult book for display is not for him. Your TV and/or stereo knobs may be at cruising level—but they're out of bounds. Just have a toy with knobs and buttons close by. Divide a magazine rack in half. Fill one side with baby books, the other with yours. Sharp and breakable items should be removed for safety reasons—but nonbreakable treasures can stay. It sounds simple. Well, don't think your baby won't challenge the nos—he will. But your job is to uphold your decisions. Believe it or not, you are already laying the groundwork for future—and never-ending—limit setting. Teach your baby that you are in charge, not him. The crawling baby will become the walking toddler—and then eventually the driving teenager! Just keep the limits simple.

Teach your child, even your crawling baby, that he can't have or do everything he wants. You don't have to frustrate him completely—but maybe just a little. You can be clever by distracting his attention, removing him from the situation, and/or substituting a favorite toy, but with a little bit of effort (or maybe a lot), you can be successful with your teaching, as long as you are consistent. Ah hah! There's that word—*consistent.* It is key to your success as a parent, even from the beginning. We've said it before.

When you signal or tell your baby "this is a no-no," you are committing to doing so with consistency. Every time that object or situation is approached, it remains "no." Remember, you, as the parent, are supposed to be in charge. You choose what your baby may and should do, and what he may not. Then you must reinforce that directive with calm and confidence. You are the adult; you make the decision without consulting your infant child. What could be easier? He may not agree, but that's not the point. The decision is yours, and only yours, to make. Just make it reasonable and fair.

The hard part is the initial decision. Then the follow-up should be automatic. Make sure there are more "hands on" than "hands off" objects, but do include a few offs.

Finally, don't forget about an approved car seat for all car travel. Keep your infant in the backseat and facing toward the rear until he weighs twenty pounds. Don't forget that air bags can deploy and kill or maim children in the front seat.

ILLNESS

When your baby is sick, the rules have to change. No one would advocate ignoring an ill child in the middle of the night or any time of day. It would not only be mean and unethical but also unwise, even dangerous. What if something is really wrong? What if your baby is really sick? If your baby cries unusually or acts differently during the day or night, assure yourself that he is OK. Go see him, tend to him, and try to assess his needs.

If your baby is sick, pick him up, take his temperature if he seems warm, and make sure he's all right. Check him over, and call his doctor if necessary. Make sure he doesn't need immediate medical attention. If you're unsure, err on the safe side—call. Most illnesses do run their course, and usually there is no harm in waiting, but not always.

If your baby is newborn (less than eight weeks) and shows any unusual behavior or symptoms, I would advise calling immediately. For an older infant, use your judgment—but again, call if you're worried. React appropriately.

When your child is feeling better and back to his baseline, work to reestablish his previously good eating, sleeping, and behavior patterns. Feed him as you did before he was sick, rework self-settling for sleep, and resist picking him up. Try not to intervene too much with special attention during the middle of the night. Check on your child, but try to keep your hands off. If not, you might come to regret it. Despite previously good sleeping habits, your baby may now want more of you. And if your baby doesn't sleep, you won't either. And as always, fatigue will affect your ability to parent successfully.

If you've been unfortunate enough to have experienced a significant illness in your infant, do leave time for yourself as well as your baby to recover. Illness is draining, physically and emotionally, for the whole family.

Parenting Together

As a parenting couple, it is important that you and your spouse try hard to work together. For some, this is easy—for others, not so. But it is a very important concept and remains true forever—from infancy through adolescence. (We will revisit this idea often.) Unfortunately, this is easier said than done. But discussion between parents (assuming there are two) should take place. And because you are two individuals, you are not always going to agree. That's human nature. But you must listen to each other and come to some kind of consensus to promote a united front to your child. Otherwise, even from early on, he will play one of you against the other. (More about this later.)

Also make sure you are both willing to uphold the household rules, whatever they may be—always. Try to think through ahead of time and discuss what limits are to be set—and uphold them as absolute.

The Nine-Month Blip

Often at nine months of age, as babies become more active and independent, they also can become more wakeful at night. Whether this is behavioral—as a kind of separation anxiety—or the result of recent illness or teething, many previously good sleepers are no longer this. It is unlikely a response to hunger—there is no need to feed your baby at night. But suddenly, your baby might be more demanding, even a nighttime terror. What to do?

Again, as in the newborn period, it's time to reassure your baby that all is well and, at the same time, teach him that nighttime is sleep time. What do I mean? If your baby wakens in the night, do not feed him. Do check to see that he is all right, but don't offer bottles or breasts, not even a little water. Assuming he is well, try to ignore his cries. Pat him a little, but try to avoid rocking, walking, or soothing him back to sleep. If you do, you might be building habits that are hard to break. You risk giving him the wrong signal—"When you waken, I will settle you completely." Don't "reward" him for waking, or you might be stuck with a new middle-of-the-night back-to-sleep regimen for months. Remember, babies are not fools—rather, they're very smart. If your child learns that you will come running at any time, day or night, and then hang around for ten to thirty minutes while he drifts off to sleep, he's gotcha! Really, he is capable of drifting back to sleep himself. And you need your sleep, too. Are you playing into his hands? Who's in charge?

• • •

I see a lot of newborn infants in my pediatric practice. Calm, confident parents have a much smoother time. They feel better about themselves, and their babies sense that well-being. The parent who is feeding and settling his or her baby with ease probably has a happy infant. Likewise, the nervous, tense parent may very well have that pattern in his or her child. The very colicky newborn will still be colicky, as we mentioned above, relaxed parents or not—but usually with less intensity in a relaxed environment.

If you're having trouble enjoying your infant and are not able to establish easy (or even reasonable) feeding and/or sleeping patterns, talk to your baby's doctor. If despite your best efforts, you are not able to mellow out, talk to your pediatrician or family practitioner about calming techniques for both you and your child. Try using that rocker and putting on pleasant, soothing music. (Make sure *you* are eating and resting.) Try relaxation techniques. Of course, also make sure that your infant is well and growing normally, with no signs of illness or other problems.

Recognize that, if you need a little help or a lot, you are not a failure—rather, you are smart enough to realize that things are not what you imagined or hoped and that coping can be tough.

You're smart enough to reach out. You might need someone to spell you—a sitter or grandparent, just to give you some much-needed rest or simply a break. That's OK! Some babies are easier than others. You might need some professional help to sort out your own feelings. The important thing to know is that already, in the newborn period, you can begin to set little limits on your baby (and yourself) in the hope of establishing a healthy, workable routine that allows you to nurture your child, but not to become your baby's slave. And as you monitor your own behavior and emotions, you are beginning to be a role model for your infant.

In general, the first year of life is a time to love, nurture, and feed—but also to set some basic ground rules. You are the coach, the child your team. And like the coach, you design the plays—who and when. Your players (in this case, your child) will take direction from you. And like successful coaches, the successful parent will gain the trust and respect of his child, and consequently, that child should play the "game" of life at his best. By working hard to establish calm, setting limits on yourself, making time for your child, showing him respect, and being consistent—right from the beginning—you are doing the best you can for your baby. Who's in charge? Hopefully, you are! Remember SECRET—especially in this ground-breaking newborn period.

3

The Toddler

Are you ready for toddlerhood? The toddler is an active, high-energy dynamo—wonderfully innocent, anxious to learn. He is constantly on the go, both in mind and body, for practically all of his waking hours. He is a very busy person. He is trying, doing—and testing. The toddler is terrific—*not* terrible.

Perish the thought of the "terrible twos"—they are not so! In fact, toddlerhood is fun. Your bright, motoring toddler is not bad—nor is he malicious, violent, or malcontent. What he is, however, is curious and given to exploring more than ever. He does not understand danger—and that includes all hazards, from poisons to electricity to fire and swimming pools. His self-driven need to learn and test will prompt him to expand his boundaries and thus to challenge you, the parent. That doesn't mean the toddler period is unpleasant—only that it is demanding. It can and should be a time of glorious growth. But it does require complete dedication and supervision from you, the parent. Your toddler *will* claim enormous amounts of your time, your energy, and an eye—always—toward caution.

SECRET

The guidelines represented by the acronym SECRET can be applied for toddlers, as they can for every age group, to provide a framework for setting specific limits and rules. The rules will increase in number from now on as your child grows and spreads his wings. But the issues of behavior, choice, and safety remain serious and constant concerns.

Remember SECRET: SE for *self*, C for *calm*, RE for *respect*, T for *time*. Also, remember that control "pie." As the parent of a newborn, the pie was yours—the slices in your color only. Now, as your child enters toddlerhood, you can begin to share a few pieces with him as you allow him to participate in some decisions—though small they may be.

Self

Parenting a toddler, as with a newborn, demands a fit parent—physically and emotionally. Continue to maintain your physical fitness. Take time to exercise regularly yourself, in order to keep up with your toddler. His energy will rival that of a professional athlete as he learns to run, tumble, and change direction. If you're in shape, you can keep up with him. If not, you'll flag and then be more easily distracted, even lose patience. (Note: You *should* be tired after a day with your toddler—it's hard work.)

Go out for a brisk walk or jog at least three or four times a week. If you want, take your toddler with you. Purchase a sturdy stroller or even an expensive jogging stroller to outfit you both.

Eat well. Have nutritious meals and snacks. As in the infant stage, take in enough protein and other nutrients to meet your body's needs. Sit down when you eat. As you feed your child, fix something for yourself.

Sleep—and *nap*. Napping is a wonderful way to restore your own energy as well as your child's. Take time to do it. Rest when your toddler is down. Just as in the newborn period, don't ignore your own needs. Don't take quiet time to do more work—clean the house or fold the laundry. Instead, close your eyes or read for pleasure. Make quiet time your time, too.

Establish a routine for play and work. Make life somewhat predictable for your toddler and yourself. Make a routine, even a ritual, out of meals and the bedtime hour.

And then, just as before, figure out where you want to set limits. Figure out, for you, what is appropriate play space and what is not—whether it be a matter of safety, convenience, or privilege. Set boundaries. Do it together with your spouse. Determine which household items and areas are off-limits.

Calm

Comport yourself with composure, just as in the infant stage. Set a mood of comfort, calm, peace. The toddler needs to depend upon you to set the right tone. He might lose his temper, but hopefully, you will not lose yours.

Discipline yourself to use kind words and gentle body language. No swearing, no yelling; no hitting anyone. No threats, but rather, firm and controlled warnings. Follow through with *calm*. Be definite and clear.

Don't forget about laughter. Take yourself seriously—but not too seriously to enjoy your child.

Respect

Respect your toddler. Recognize his capabilities but also his limitations. Know that he is bright and curious—but much too young to be responsible for himself. His attention span is short. Know him!

Respect your toddler's need to explore—to test. Give him space and time for both.

Don't lose sight of your child's individuality. Know that his wants are his alone. His talents, personality, and inclinations are *his*. Recognize your child—now and forever—as his own being, and allow him space for expression.

Let your toddler share in making choices—be it a story at bedtime or the kind of sandwich for lunch. Introduce him to the notion of choice. Respect, even now, his ability to choose.

Time

Of all the guidelines, the one concerning time is critical. You *have* to make time for your toddler, or you will miss out. Give him the time he needs—and then plan for more. Plan extra time for *everything*—build it into your routine.

Leave room for unplanned events—for spontaneous play. Always have a time cushion for the unexpected—which, you will find, will become the norm.

Schedule less. Don't squeeze more into a limited amount of time. Instead, provide more time for less. Time will fill itself.

Now, let's look specifically at general areas of concern and apply those elements of SECRET.

Behavior

Just why are the toddler years so feared, so badly labeled? Why is the toddler's behavior thought to be so difficult? Probably because for the first time you, the parent, will come to realize that your child has a mind of his own, a will. He is a person separate from you, with his own set of wants and desires—which can be very different from yours. He may not choose or want to do what you want. But remember, that's normal! Your child is not your clone, but your offspring—with his own destiny.

Understand Your Toddler

The toddler is a born tester, as he is trying to define his own world, challenge you, and begin to establish his own independence. You don't want to crush his desire to explore, but you do need to keep him safe and work to establish certain codes of behavior. He will challenge you—lots! That's his job. And yours is to set the rules.

Toddlers are voracious learners—gathering information and storing knowledge all the time. It is really incredible. Their receptive powers are full speed ahead—they miss and forget nothing. They are constantly taking, taking—at all levels. They don't always understand the whys and wherefores—that's normal. All they know is what they want—even if they can't have it. Our job as parents is to channel their energy appropriately. But we are destined for a few blowups.

Remember, your toddler is only a couple of years old. His brain is still growing and developing. He is not capable of abstract thinking. The fact is, he's not even completely verbal. His receptive language (understanding) far exceeds his expressive language—so he's even trapped in his own head. He knows what he wants but can't always tell you. Furthermore, he does not understand the subtleties of danger, sharing, or priceless value.

So the toddler is set up for frustration—he wants but cannot always communicate and doesn't always understand. His brain circuits are not completely connected. He is too young to grasp all of what we are saying. And then, to make it more complicated, the brighter he is, sometimes the more frustrated and trapped he feels. So why are we surprised if he gets upset? This is normal.

What happens to an adult who is told, "No, you cannot have what you want"? Is it like water off a duck's back? No problem? Think how well many adults do when denied a want or pleasure—and then figure out how well they would do if fatigued or hungry. Then why are we so surprised when a tired and/or hungry preverbal child throws himself on the floor and screams bloody murder because he cannot have a bag of cookies or every magazine on the shelf?

So where is the problem? Is it really our toddler? Or are we as parents at fault? Are we expecting too much from a very young child, who has not reached the age of reason? Do we set our expectations too high for this child? How can we expect a two-year-old to handle denial or disappointment "like an adult"? Are we judging our toddler in adult terms of behavior, when even adults don't always shine? Do we truly believe a toddler can and should demonstrate adult control when crossed? I think not. Do we sometimes expect too much from toddlers? I think so!

Realistically, a toddler *should* have trouble dealing with any sort of limits that restrict his wants—be they physical, emotional, or physiological. A toddler is just that—a toddler, toddling on all fronts. He has limited resources for dealing with any restrictions, especially if they keep him from his goal. A natural response for him should be frustration—and this can be manifested by crying, tantrums, head banging, even biting. Why are we puzzled by his "acting out"? We shouldn't be.

Your toddler, by nature, *should* have trouble with denial. Remember, he has limited patience—if any at all. Patience is not his virtue—but it should be yours! After all, he is only two years old (or thereabouts), and what he wants, he wants now, not later. He certainly does not understand "not today," or "maybe tomorrow." He is at a very self-centered stage, with very immediate needs. Waiting and sharing are not yet in his repertoire of behavioral goals. Instead, it's "Me" and "Now!"

Provide for Your Toddler's Needs

So what do we do? To start with, think about creating an environment that is appropriate for your toddler—not one overloaded with nos and restrictions, but rather one structured around his needs. Make provisions for this developing child. Keep him active—use up some of that limitless energy. Go outside and run—lots! Climb on playground equipment—go for long walks.

And then, for quiet play, always provide your toddler (and this is so important) with something he likes and can have—whether it be at home or in the car or at Grandma's. Have ever ready a small set of stimulating (and ever-changing) play toys and items of interest. Just a few things to keep him busy and supplied. Keep it simple, however; don't overload him with choices.

At home, keep his things available—not hidden but out in the open. Make them pretty and attractive. Have an open box (with *no* lid, not a trunk) with books, blocks, "toddler" toys front and center. *His* things! Maintain a relative sense of order with these, as well as with yours. Keep a favorite toy—the new doll or the fire engine—close by. Just as we did with the cruising infant, provide appropriate resources. Your job is to help your toddler by giving him something to play with, to explore—toys that are right for him. Remember, toddlers don't really sit—they play.

Keep handy, and travel with (always), a bag of his favorite goodies—a book, a cuddly toy or blanket, a music box, even an emergency snack and a change of clothes. Keep a "Quiet Bag"— a collection of special things, such as large crayons, a note pad for coloring, a box of raisins, and a pad of stickers—for those *very* quiet events. Be prepared wherever you may be—dinner out, the airplane, or church. Don't be afraid to take your toddler anywhere, but recognize his toddler needs when you do.

Play with him—spend time *with* him—on the floor, in the yard. Don't just set him loose, or you are asking for trouble. Don't ignore him. Don't expect him to sit and wait like an adult. Channel him! Stimulate, but do not overstimulate him. And of course, keep him fed and rested.

If you really try to practice SECRET, setting limits doesn't have to be a chore. If you are in good health, are able to maintain calm, respect your toddler's limitations, provide for him, and give him the time and space he needs, your success rate with setting behavioral standards will be high—or at the very least, higher than it would have been otherwise. You are also likely to find that you enjoy your toddler!

Setting Limits for Your Toddler

We know, of course, that a toddler—or any child for that matter—cannot have everything he wants. This can be a very hard lesson, but that's life! Remember the cruising baby in Chapter 2? Even then, we talked about his things and yours. The same goes for the toddler. How can your toddler (or preschooler or adolescent) learn to appreciate anything if nothing is special? How will he learn to discriminate his from yours or his from other people's? Be specific about what he can and cannot have—what he can and cannot touch. *Guide* while you *provide*; mix in a few nos among the yeses.

Simply stated, your child—at any age—does *not* have to play with everything. Quite the contrary—there really *are* his things and then your things. Your job is to help your toddler by providing alternatives—appropriate resources—at home and away. Then it will be easier for your child to keep his hands off the "forbidden fruit." He will learn.

Teach your toddler respect for property, be it your possessions—the antique piece of furniture, the piano, the remote control, your purse—or someone else's. Teach your child that a living room is not a playground, but a place for quiet time. Reinforce, constantly, with calm and control (yes, there they are again) the can dos and the cannots. Make time to work constructively with your toddler. Exercise patience and demonstrate composure. He *will* get the message, just not necessarily right away. No one said parenting would be easy! No one said your toddler would always go your way.

Have your toddler's things *next* to yours—just like with the baby. Teach him to distinguish between yours and his. *Your* knobs on the stereo receiver—*his* on the busy box or puzzle board. Your picture books—then his. It isn't difficult to understand, but it does take a lot of commitment. Certain things are a definite no: the TV, the VCR, the computer. Those are your things—and they're high-ticket items. The remote control? Who is in charge? It probably should be "hands off" to your toddler.

What about Mom's purse and all its wonderful treasures? What happens when her purse and personal belongings become free game? Anything to keep your child happy? Wrong. A toddler playing with lipstick is not cute—he is a mess. And then why are we so surprised when it ends up covering our living room sofa? No to lipstick! The same for eyeliner, eyebrow pencil, and mascara. What about our loose change or loose jewelry? Where is it likely to end up? A dime in the stomach, a penny in the esophagus or, worse, the airway—a life-threatening event! Babies and toddlers *die* from aspiration. "Innocent" play with small objects is not innocent. Coins, pins, earrings, and paper clips are not for toddlers. Give them something else that is safe. Furthermore, what's to distinguish Grandma's purse, now with lethal cardiac medications or a potentially deadly hearing-aid battery, from Mommy's? They look the same.

When setting limits—and this is a tough one—try very hard to *prethink* those limits, to choose them ahead of time. Take time to define the household and behavioral rules. For example: no hitting, biting, or kicking; no throwing of toys or food; no ripping up of books; no stealing; and no playing with Mommy's makeup or Daddy's shaving cream. Be very concrete about rules and limits—avoid waffling. Make it clear to your toddler (and preschooler and adolescent) where the line is drawn—what is acceptable and what is not. And then, hold to it.

Be a role model of kindness, fairness, caring, and considerate behavior yourself. Be polite—say please and thank you. There should be no swearing, no foul language, and no shouting or screaming from us as parents. Share, and show your toddler how. As the parent, you need to be very clear about what you are doing and how.

Many parents have worked out clever ways to distract their toddlers when unacceptable situations come up. Think about alternatives, changing the scene. If necessary, you can always physically remove your child from a testy situation. But also know that there will be times when, despite your best grown-up efforts, your toddler will be unhappy—even explode. Then, let him fuss or cry—let the storm pass and pick up the pieces afterward. Despite our best efforts, we need to be prepared for a few, if not many, full-blown tantrums. They happen. So don't be afraid of them. Don't be afraid of damaging your child—you won't. Let tantrums pass—they will. Give your child space. Allow him to diffuse his temper, because he probably needs to let go once in a while, anyway. After all, don't adults occasionally lose it, too? Realize that your toddler is a small child, one who has lots of feelings but, again, is still too young to control them all. He may not be happy with restrictions. But that's OK. Know that over time you will help to direct those feelings, but sometimes the roof will blow. Also, know that toddlers are very resilient and bounce back after tantrums, often with acceptable behavior—almost like the calm after the storm.

Correction

If your toddler continually challenges you, respond with control. Try not to be frustrated about any lack of compliance—rather, admire your child's persistence. Know that it will carry him far in later years. But remember, you are the adult who must guide and steer him. Maintain your calm, give him time and space, and you'll do fine. Be prepared for *many, many* repetitions—and I mean thousands! I can promise you that it will take much more than one caution or warning to convince your toddler that an area or object is off-limits. (Remember, he's a born tester.) Be prepared for lots of hard work on this one.

"Johnny, dear, you cannot play with the electrical cord or outlets. They are no-nos." Well, Johnny, may approach those cords and outlets twenty times in the same hour. You, the parent, must remove him each time—try the old distraction trick—take him to another space. But be consistent in reinforcing your original command. This one is actually easy, because it is not so much a matter of establishing "I'm in charge," but of safety. But you are still the boss, the commander-in-chief.

It's the "gray" areas that are tough. When it is not necessarily a matter of safety, but rather one of preference or convenience, again, try to decide ahead of time what the rule is. Be reasonable—don't expect adult behavior from your toddler—and then, stick to your guns. If the rule is no crayoning in the living room, then stick to it. If it is no eating in the playroom or on the run, then don't allow it.

Then, when correction is necessary, criticize or reprimand the *behavior*, not the child. Of course, you must follow up on any warnings—any no-no—and do so with calm and assurance. But remember, it is the *behavior* that is wrong or bad, not the child. Say "Coloring on the walls is *bad*." "Urinating on the porch is unacceptable!" Don't say "You are a bad boy." These behaviors require an immediate and appropriate response. Take the crayons away. Bring your child inside to urinate in the toilet. But don't label your child as *bad*. Work to avoid a repeat of behavior that is unacceptable, and try to figure out why your child did this in the first place. Is this a cry for more attention? Is your child tired or unhappy? Work hard to praise good behavior—a job well done. Know that, as parents, we rarely praise enough.

Make sure that, when you are forced to react, you do so *swiftly*. If a toy is to be taken away, or a child removed from an activity, do so immediately. If you warn a child about potential discipline, you *must* follow through if he persists with the unacceptable behavior. Give one or two warnings at the most, no more. For example, if you warn your toddler not to throw his toys and he does, you must take them away for a time. If he rips the pages of the books and you have told him not to do so, take them away. If he climbs on the furniture, remove him from the room. Let your toddler help you clean up a mess that he caused—let him help you wash the crayon marks off the wall or help pick up the cards or puzzle pieces that he dumped. Your child can share in the repair, as well as the destruction. But don't forget to provide him with his own "bag of tricks" to keep him busy and happy. As described earlier, do provide him with an acceptable alternative wherever you are. We can't expect a toddler to sit quietly with nothing to do. Again, toddlers don't sit!

When it comes to a reprimand or a reaction from you, the punishment should "fit the crime." Remember, toddlers are only one or two years old. They need to be told no and separated from the scene where unacceptable behavior takes place and perhaps be given a few minutes of time out (although the toddler is young for this) or have a toy removed. But no huge punishment should be imposed. Don't threaten no Christmas or no circus if he doesn't stop. Do you really mean that? Are you really prepared to deny your child a share of Christmas or another special holiday because *you* are losing control?

Also know that there are different ways of saying no—like "Not today—how about this. . . ?" Save your nos so they will mean something—so you will be willing to follow through on them. A very definite no leaves no room for misunderstanding. Try hard not to overuse it. Make "no" mean something for now and the future. Learn different ways of redirecting behavior. And, of course, do not hit or spank. Even if you were spanked or hit as a child, don't do it! Use calm, firm words and appropriate actions instead.

Sometimes, in spite of your best efforts, you may begin to lose control of both yourself and your child. When this happens, immediately check yourself. Step out of the situation (mentally, or even leave the room if necessary and safe for your child) and calm yourself. Once you are again in control of yourself, resolve the situation with your child appropriately. Apologize to your child if you have screamed at or hit him, while still enforcing the rules. For example, say, "I'm sorry I lost my temper and yelled at you [or hit you]. I shouldn't have done that, and I'm working on not doing it anymore. But it *is* against the rules to throw your toys [or whatever the child has done], so you will not be allowed to play with these toys now [or whatever the consequence is]." Then redirect your child to an acceptable activity. Do not tell yourself you are a bad parent but that you have made a mistake and are working hard on improving your parenting skills. If you still feel out of control, take action to help yourself as soon as possible. Call a supportive friend or family member, your spouse, or an organization or professional who can work with you.

Don't be afraid to apologize to your child when you have genuinely wronged him (but do not apologize when he just doesn't like the limits or consequences you have set). Apologizing when you are truly in the wrong will reinforce rather than endanger your child's respect for you as well as make it easier for him to trust you in the future. It also models appropriate behavior for your child. If your child sees that you are willing to admit when you are wrong and work to change your behavior, he will be more willing to do the same. You will also give your child a clear message that it is indeed wrong for *anyone* to yell at or hit another person.

It goes without saying that you must never punish a child for having a tantrum. Quite the contrary! After he blows and then quiets, assure him of your love. Toddlers and young children are often quite submissive, even exhausted after a good scream. (So are we!) It can be a good time to regroup. Try to reconstruct what led to the tantrum—perhaps you can avoid or divert a future repeat. Tell your toddler—even if you think he doesn't understand—that you know he was mad or frustrated. Tell him those feelings are OK, and that you will help him deal with those feelings in a better way. Tell him the screaming or biting and/or hitting or spitting—commonly seen at this age—are things you can work on. Know that they are not necessarily malicious, but acts of frustration. Explain that these actions are unacceptable. Tell him some things he *may* do when he is angry—tell the person he doesn't like what he or she did, ask you for help, or go to a quiet place until he feels better. Again, don't call your child "bad"—it's the behavior that needs work.

Toddlers' tantrums come and go. And how you handle them will set the stage for the future. Maintaining calm despite your child's behavior is very important, because it models appropriate behavior for him.

Try to look at the bigger picture. What happened, why did it happen, and how might you handle such a situation differently? Recognize that you are setting patterns as well as limits.

Your toddler might get very unhappy when denied a want or when reprimanded for inappropriate behavior. He may cry, scream, and kick. (So might your ten- or sixteen-year-old!) Your responsibility as a parent is to lay down the foundation of rules and limits—to draw that line. Don't let your child scare you off. Don't give in to bad behavior, even though this is sometimes the "easier" way out. Instead, look at what you are building for the future.

CHOICE

Choice is a complicated issue. There are so many choices to be made, for many different reasons: choices as parents, choices by your toddler, choices about safety, diet, fun, and play—the list is endless.

As you begin to involve your toddler in choices, think first! Work hard to determine as best you can, beforehand (before saying a word—before opening your mouth), whether your child has a choice in the matter at hand. It's a kind of limit on yourself. (This will be true forever—for your toddler and your adolescent.) Does your child have a say? If not, don't offer it; direct, but don't ask. But if there *is* room for choice, then, and only then, offer it—and, of course, honor your child's decision. This is one of the hardest rules for parents. Let me say it again: Allow your child the opportunity to choose when appropriate, but do *not* give him choice when there is none and/or your mind is already made up. If you give a child of any age a choice and then take that choice away, you are not being fair. In fact, you are really being deceitful. That hardly shows respect for your child.

For example, if your driveway is unsafe—sloping into a busy

street—then no! a child may not play on it. And your child certainly may not ride toys down into the road, risking impact with a moving vehicle. Or your child may not go outside into the snow wearing summer clothing. You don't reason or leave room for choice in these matters. This is obvious. Instead, you tell him what he may and may not do. It's not a question of being nice or polite to a toddler, but rather being *honest*. When you are definite—and you must be—he will learn to respect that.

Car seats often become a source of struggle—toddlers often protest and then decide they will sit in one no more! Well, who is in charge? If your child resists the car seat, even climbs out of it, stop the car and then demand and reestablish restraint, even if crying or screaming persists. Don't arrive at the emergency room with an unrestrained victim of a car accident. Riding in a car seat is nonnegotiable. (It's even the law.) And as with the infant, use an approved car seat placed preferably in the backseat. Never place a toddler in the front opposite an airbag.

The difficult issues are the gray ones: Do you really care or does it really matter if your toddler wears matching clothing? Is it sneakers or party shoes, grubby sweats or pressed cotton? Does it really matter if he eats some or all—or any—of his peas? Does he have to drink all of his milk? What do *you* think? Issues of dress and nutrition can escalate into full-scale wars. Watch that they don't. Here you can give your child some choice. But when you cannot give a choice—for example, no sweat suit as a flower girl for your sister's wedding—make that clear. (Or cancel being the flower girl.)

In my office as a pediatrician, I tell a toddler when I am going to examine him at the appropriate time of our visit. I do not ask—because what if he says no? If I ask to listen to his heart, and he refuses—then what do I do? I've set myself up for failure, because either I honor his answer, and then I have done an incomplete exam, or I ignore his response, and I am dishonest. I'm going to examine him anyway. I shouldn't have asked the question if there really wasn't any choice. This does not build trust. Also, there is much less confusion if I direct the child rather than solicit support that may not be there anyway.

When you do give a choice, limit the number of selections offered to a toddler. Don't overload his circuits with too many alternatives. Respect his limitations, while letting him share in the decision-making process. Offer a choice of two or three options at most. The toddler, and even the older child, often has trouble choosing between options—particularly when there are many. So help this young child by keeping him *under*whelmed. Make choices easy. Which pair of shoes to wear, which sticker for a reward, or which dessert? Keep the selection process simple. Which outfit—the gray warm-up suit or the green one? What about lunch—peanut butter and jelly or grilled cheese? Open-ended questions like "What do you want for lunch?" may be too difficult and may also lead to an unacceptable selection, like ice cream for lunch.

Choice can even bring on unhappiness, as when the "wrong" choice is made or when your child changes his mind. So guide your toddler into making the best choice for him—and then support whatever choice he does make. This is very important. Remember, he is doing the choosing, so let him. Give him the freedom of choice that he deserves. Try not to attach any value or judgment to a "right versus wrong" decision. Instead, praise him for being able to make a choice at all. Compliment him on his ability to think and act on his own—his ability to make that decision. After all, what you are really doing is laying the groundwork for independent thinking—with confidence—for later years. (If he doesn't like the choice he's made, remind him that he will have another chance to choose another time.)

You also want to help your toddler make decisions in a reasonable amount of time. For example, in many doctors' offices stickers are given at the end of a visit. Patients are given the opportunity to choose one. Hopefully, the choice is from only a few—not hundreds. But nevertheless, the concept of "one only" from a group can be difficult for a toddler. Sometimes we have to limit the time allotted, or the kids would ponder their choice for hours and never make it home. For example, with many of my patients, after a full sixty-second minute, when choice still seems a long way off, I will give a ten-second warning, count slowly to ten, and then make the selection gently myself for the child who is unable. Next time around, hopefully the child will have more success in making the choice. However it works out, choosing should be a fun, low-pressure experience. Don't make choice an anxious time for your child. Rather, work with him slowly and gently to build confidence in making choices. Whether the issue is getting dressed in the morning, selecting cereal at the grocery store, or buying a birthday gift for himself or a friend, watch your child's cues and guide him into making workable choices for himself. Give him time, respect his choice, and be calm.

Transitions

Transitions can be tough for anyone. And some people, by nature, adjust more easily to change than others. With that in mind, it is important to recognize that for many toddlers, in particular, transitions can be very hard. It is our job as parents to smooth them over and to keep them simple.

When making a change, like leaving the playground or nursery school, be definite. When it's time to go, do it! Don't play games with your child and give him a mixed message. Is it or is it not time? Give him fair warning so he can prepare himself— "We have to leave in three (or five) minutes." Then when your three (or five) minutes are up, leave. Help your child learn that what you say is true.

Go when you said you would go, not after another three or five or ten additional minutes. Don't drag it out. Rather, gently guide your child away at the appointed time, even pick him up if he resists. Ignore fussing and don't respond to whining (who's in charge?)—but go. And don't *you* get caught up in distractions or conversations on the way out. If you want to chat with other adults before leaving, do so before you tell your child it's time to go. Remember, patterns set now will reward or haunt you later. You're building for the future.

If the transition requires getting dressed or cleaning up, let your toddler help. Here you can let him share in the process. But be very concrete. For example, instead of saying, "Let's help clean up the mess," say, "Let's put the blocks away." Or instead of, "What do you want to wear today?" say, "Do you want to wear the red socks or the blue ones?" Keep the questions and the choices (see the preceding section) very simple. Focus them clearly—this will make the transition easier for your toddler, and for you.

Those early-morning drop-offs at the sitter's or day care can be a nightmare if your two-year-old clings and screams every day. Work with your day-care provider calmly to establish a dependable brief routine (five minutes at most), and then hold to it. Don't prolong the separation process, it only makes it more stressful for your child. Say good-bye to your child, tell him truthfully when you will return, and then leave. Peel him off your body if you must. Phone in later as your own follow-up if you wish, but be consistent with the routine. Your child will learn to adjust. Despite the scene they may make at their parents' departure, most children are playing contentedly a few minutes later.

SAFETY

As always, your toddler's environment needs to be safe (just as for the crawling infant). And just as you did before, it never hurts to reexamine your child's world. Check around and under the stairs, behind doorways, and in cabinets and closets for safety hazards. Make sure all electrical outlets have safety covers. Set physical boundaries—do not allow your toddler to play anywhere unsupervised or unsafe. No playing near a street or close to water (two inches can drown), no playing with toxic plants, no lamp cords. No small toys, especially if they are round—nothing that can choke or plug an airway. No sharp edges. Really inspect toys; pretend you are a toddler determined to break or undo everything. Put all current medications and cleansers out of reach, and throw away the rest. Those pretty green iron pills—they look like candies—are poisonous. Put them high and away. (We lost a toddler to an iron ingestion when I was a resident—his mother's pills eaten "innocently" on the car ride home from the drugstore.)

Have poison control numbers on all phones, and consult poison control about any questions you may have. Have syrup of ipecac (used to induce vomiting) available, but use it only after calling poison control or your doctor first. Remember, toddlers seem to know intuitively where not to go (just like the crawling babies)—and then go there . . . and then go there again and again and again. They seem to gravitate to the wrong place, to seek danger rather than avoid it. Matches, scissors, spray cans, even dishwasher detergent (it is very caustic) all are no-nos. Put them away and out of reach. Hide them or get rid of them. And now, more than ever, *watch* your toddler always!

The toddler needs to be supervised all the time, not just some of the time. An adult's eyes must be kept on him for his every waking moment. Allow no playing, absolutely none anywhere, without supervision. And finally, do not assume that another adult is supervising your child—as in groups. Rather, assign supervision to a specific adult. "I'm watching Jimmy for now." "Now you're watching him." A group of adults in the general vicinity, presumably supervising your child, is worthless, because their eyes are on each other and only "sort of" on your child. "Sort of" isn't good enough. Periodic supervision is unacceptable. A toddler can disappear in the batting of an eye, and everyone be unaware, unless someone is really watching. You have to respect your toddler's innate curiosity and his ability to move fast. Mom thought . . . Dad thought . . . They thought. . . . Don't let that happen. It is your responsibility to protect your toddler against himself—just like the cruising infant. Make it very clear always who is providing the supervision—who is in charge. Sign on and off to each other, directly—leave no room for error. Then the likelihood of serious injury by ingestion or burn or fall—even death by drowning—is lessened.

And finally, when you are watching your toddler, make sure you are really doing that. Don't try to do two or three things at once. Watching (hopefully with some playing with your child) is all-consuming. You cannot also mow the lawn, work with power equipment, run on the treadmill, or do anything dangerous. You might be able to accomplish some small, quiet task (like paying bills, folding the laundry, correcting papers)—but don't count on it. Leave those projects and tasks for nontoddler time. This is a limit you must place on yourself. Respect your toddler's need for supervision—honor it—and make time for this lifesaving job.

I'm reminded of a toddler who wandered off during a thunderstorm. Mom thought the nanny was watching him—the nanny vice versa. Tragically, the child was discovered too late in the family pool, drowned. This was a good, responsible family with all the best intentions. A mistake cost them dearly. Truly, this was a preventable injury—but there are no second chances. So, please, watch your child. And be very clear about who is doing the watching. (By the way, if you do have a swimming pool, the best safety measure is a four-sided fence—one that separates the pool independently from your house and yard.)

CONSENSUS

When trying to set rules and regulations within the household, again, make sure as best you can that you agree as parents (see "Parenting Together," Chapter 2). You may find this a very difficult rule to follow, now or ever. Remember, parents are two distinct individuals with thoughts of their own. It is not uncommon to disagree, on minor as well as major issues. But as two intelligent, mature persons, parents should be able to discuss and come to a common corporate decision. We call it consensus—and consensus in the household is very important. You must decide together what your child may do and where your child may play and/or go—how his life is to be organized. Then, as before, you must uphold the rules or plan you have established. These are limits you have to place on yourself. You must present a united front. Leave a little room for flexibility if your plan doesn't work, but start somewhere.

Avoid giving your toddler the opportunity to play one parent against the other. It can begin early, or late, or anytime. It's called the "Mommy versus Daddy" show. Your child will learn to play favorites, if you let him, even as a toddler; they all do. The favorite can change—but watch out. Don't play into that! One parent is often the "heavy." That's OK, as long as you work together as a team. No matter who does "most" of the parenting, it is very important that each parent spend some time with each child individually. You must work consciously to share in parenting duties, even if one parent does more than the other or one is "at home." It shouldn't be a matter of one parent being more fatigued or more available than the other—probably both are tired and have other things they need or want to do. Days with toddlers are long, whether you are an at-home parent or not. Your days start early, and there are minimal, if any, breaks until bedtime. If mother is a full-time Mom, it often seems easier for her to follow through with parenting after Dad comes home. After all, she has the routine down. She's been doing it all day. This is a mistake! Dad must have hands-on time with his child, too. Take turns.

When Dad is in charge, your toddler may insist, "I want Mommy to read my story." Just say, "No, tonight is Daddy's turn. Tomorrow will be Mommy's." If your child cries, then let him. But keep calm, even when there's a ripple. Stand firm, or your child will rule—and won't that be a cheery time for all? If you're the "out" parent, your feelings may be hurt, but try to remember that your child's intent is not to hurt you. Recognize that maybe this is a hint or indication that you need to spend more time with your toddler. Children will choose the more familiar person. Make sure both you and your spouse are familiar, and not strangers, to your own child.

But what if you and your spouse come to a real impasse, where agreement is impossible? There are two things you can try: further negotiation with compromise or professional help. There is no need for one of you to surrender to the other—no need to assign one parent all the decision-making or executive powers. Quite the contrary, this could become dangerous. You would lose a sense of "check and balance," which you need with each other.

Remember, both parents *do* have a responsibility to participate in decisions regarding child rearing. Abdication is really irresponsible. So work hard to come to an agreement. Know that lack of consensus will happen more than once. I suggest bending to the more conservative parent with safety issues—you never want to be in an "I told you so" situation. That will lead to trouble and disharmony. Recognize that your small child will sense and exploit any ambivalence on your parts, so stick together, whether or not you have full agreement. Your toddler needs to know you stand and work as a unit.

Finally, know that disagreement by itself is not bad. In fact, it can be constructive and demonstrate coping skills for your child. Learning to work together, to give and take—particularly when you have disagreement—is a lesson in life. Let your child see how you parents agree *and* disagree—how you work together, sort things out, and respect each other.

TIME WITH YOUR TODDLER

We've discussed time before—it's part of SECRET. Hopefully, it will come as no surprise to learn that in the toddler period you really have to devote time to your child.

When planning to be with your toddler, it is so important that you leave room for extra time for almost everything you do. Let me say this again—plan on extra time for every errand and every activity. Don't hold to a full and/or strict schedule, with no room for flexibility. If you do, you're doomed from the outset. Life, and in particular toddlers, demands flexibility—and lots of it. That's the norm. If you're going to the park and it usually takes about thirty minutes, plan on an hour. If you have to go to the store and it usually takes you fifteen minutes when alone, count on doubling that when you bring your child. You've got to leave room to "smell the roses," because you will. You want to have fun with your child—so leave room to look at and enjoy whatever crosses your path. You will all be much happier if you do.

Time pressure is often our own doing and can lead to unnecessary unhappiness. Of course, sometimes the clock has to run our lives, but try to minimize that, especially when with your child. Time with your toddler should be enjoyed. If you're always paying attention to the time, looking at your watch, and trying to squeeze too much into too little time, you will be frustrated and your child will know that. Children sense our feelings and know where our focus is, even if subtle. Are you really focused on your child, or are you just patting yourself on the back for being a "good" parent? Again, who is in charge? You or your schedule?

Allow time for spontaneous play—don't make everything structured. Let things happen. Go to the zoo—even to the mall to window shop. Visit the playground and the library. Read to your child *lots* (see "Reading Together," Chapter 8). If your toddler is not ready for a full story, look at pictures and build vocabulary. Approach books with the sense of wonderment they deserve. Balance quiet time with active time. Encourage large motor, small motor, and cerebral activities. Take time and be mellow.

Keep life simple. Don't feel compelled to rush into anything and everything, be it special activities, group outings, or even preschool. There's no hurry. Just because everyone else is doing it is really not a good reason.

Your toddler does not need any formal, organized program yet. That time will come soon enough. At the same time, it may be a reasonable alternative—just not a must. (See "Preschool," Chapter 4.) What is important is that you and your child be together for natural, relaxed play—assuming *you* make time for him.

And finally, as you work with your toddler, play and learn together, you will also want to teach him to entertain himself. This is not abandonment, it's like the playpen. You want to build into your child an ability to do some things alone—with your supervision, but not always your hands on. Watch your child build a tower, put together a simple puzzle, or find pictures in a book. Let him develop his own skills, and praise him for it. You will be working on this always, but like so many other things, there is a continuum. This is not a time to leave the television running—in fact, there never is such a time. Beware of that "boob tube"—know that it entertains, but it does so passively. Use television sparingly and recognize its limits. It might teach your toddler his ABCs, but I can assure you he will learn them eventually anyway—and it will have no bearing on his college placement. (See "Television," Chapter 14.) TV time should not be greater than parent time. Time comes around only once—don't waste it.

DEVELOPMENTAL ISSUES

Language and motor skills are the big developmental issues for the toddler. As you look at your own child, know that children develop at different rates and work at many tasks all at the same time. Likewise, development along both motor and verbal pathways is complicated, with progress on both constant but variable. Some children are more physical—destined for Olympic competition. Others are more cerebral and verbally expressive. But some kids are awkward or lack coordination, and others just don't talk a lot. That's in their genetic programming. That's the way they are made.

Your job, as a parent, is to monitor your child's progress—to make sure he is developing appropriately for him.

Pay attention to your toddler. Make sure you are providing the right kind of environment for optimal development. That, of course, takes time and work. You provide this environment when you read to your child, go to the library, take him to the playground, build towers of blocks, and spend time together with unstructured play.

With language development, words should be coming, with pairing and phrases, by two years. It's still early for whole sentences and complicated thought processes, although the advanced (or chatty) toddler may pleasantly surprise you. The important thing to know is that new words should be coming (there should be a progression), the words should be fairly clear, and someone other than yourself should be able to understand about half of them. Your toddler should understand you completely, and there should be no need for special speech on your part. Your enunciation should be clear, but not purposefully slowed. Speak as you do to everyone, including adults. Treat your child with respect— speak to him as you speak to adults. Don't ever talk down to a child. Baby talk from an adult is not cute—rather, it is confusing to a child. Don't mimic your child's fuzzy diction, either. Your child learns to speak correctly by imitating your adult speech.

When speaking with your child—and I hope you do lots of this—leave time for your child's response. Don't push him— rather, wait. Language is crucial to communication; make it easy and comfortable for your child to express himself. Help him with some of his thoughts, but give him plenty of time to say what he can. Be polite to him—say please and thank you—and teach him to do the same in response. (See "Manners," Chapter 8.) Watch to see that he is, in fact, making progress, and he will probably do fine. Dialogue should take place, and it should be a two-way street, with two players—you and your child. If it is not, don't ignore it. Share any concerns you have with your child's doctor, and schedule an appointment for an evaluation if you have any worries or doubts. (See "Developmental Issues," Chapter 4.) You don't want to miss even a minor speech problem or delay. It can have enormous impact upon your child's social and intellectual development. You don't want to wish you had done something earlier. As a parent, you must respond to any concern you may have about your child's development, in any area.

In motor development, your toddler should be walking by eighteen months. He should be using his arms and legs—both right and left—with equal dexterity. He should be climbing and venturing around simple playground equipment. His control of both large and small motor groups should be improving with time. If not, speak to your doctor.

If your child is slow to use his body, were you, his biological parents, the same? Was your child's birth process (pregnancy, labor, and delivery) unusual for any reason? Make sure your toddler is toddling well. If not, ask questions of your doctor and schedule an evaluation. As with speech, you don't want to lose time here, either.

Your toddler is developing his social skills—although at times he may appear to be more antisocial than social. His play with peers will be more parallel play than real sharing. And sometimes, there will be biting and hitting—not really malicious, but a kind of sorting out, if you will. Toddlers (both girls and boys) seem to sense who in a group is more vulnerable. They may behave perfectly well in many situations, but somehow "have it in" for a particular child when in a group setting. They may try to assert dominance over one another, establishing a "pecking order," just like puppies and other young do in the animal world.

Many of my patients will ask what to do if their child bites or hits. I advise them to talk to their child: tell him that biting, hitting, pushing, and hurting other people are unacceptable. Work to avoid a setup in the future; learn to read your child and remove him from a situation that has the potential for trouble. Observe the situation closely—watch for sparks, although there may be none. You can use your strongest "No!" but do not bite your child back. Change the scene—move your child. Recognize your child's feelings as valid, but not the action. If your child bites, you are not alone. Many children do for a time. However, that does not justify the behavior but only recognizes it as fairly common. It, too, will pass.

As your child's language improves, have him make an apology to the child he has hurt. A simple "I'm sorry" will do. It's never too soon.

MEALS

Meals should be offered at regular hours, three times a day. Your child should be seated in his routine place at a table or high chair. He or she should not be allowed to roam or watch TV, and you should not provide a sideshow. Your toddler should feed himself with a little assistance from you. But he should require no entertainment from you or from any other source.

Your child does, however, need your company! You (or your loving and reliable substitute) need to be part of his meal taking. Whether this is family time or just the two of you will depend on your family size and schedule. But whatever the structure, sit down with your child—be there! Respect your child's need for companionship. Meals need to be quiet, calm, and relaxed—not rushed. Again, make sure you allow enough time. Mealtime should be a priority—a time of togetherness, not hurried, not ignored. You should offer your toddler age-appropriate foods—and something that he likes.

In addition to meals, you can offer your toddler snacks during the day. In fact, two to three snacks a day are appropriate, given a toddler's caloric needs. Remember, your toddler is in constant motion, and he is still growing at a fast pace. He needs calories for both—to maintain that activity and to grow—and that's a lot. So do feed him.

But what if your child won't eat? First, know that many toddlers, despite their energy and growth requirements, seem to do just fine grazing and picking, with only one "good" meal every two to three days. I just always hoped with my own child that the meal consumed was a nutritious, balanced meal—but you have to take your chances on that one. Toddlers are like cars—pulling into a gas station when on empty, gassing up, then driving off on a full tank, to return when empty again. But don't worry. Somehow most toddlers seem to know what their bodies need and are able to self-select balanced foods. Basic nutrition—some protein, iron, and vitamin C—does not require that three "square meals" be consumed daily. If some sprinkling of the necessary nutrients, minerals, and vitamins occurs on a regular basis, such as weekly, probably your child is fine. Don't worry about getting your child to eat fruits *and* vegetables; rather, get him to eat fruits *or* vegetables. Some children (including one of mine) hate green, so give them orange or apple juice and/or fruits. Protein can be dairy or meats or beans—just don't overdo the dairy sources. Probably sixteen to twenty ounces of milk and/or milk products is more than sufficient for a daily amount.

Iron comes in dark foods—red meats, dark green veggies—and if concerned, you can monitor your child's iron levels with simple blood tests. In fact, some routine screening of your toddler should be done to rule out iron-deficiency anemia. Anemia can be treated but, if left unrecognized, can lead to subtle problems, even difficulty with learning.

Do not allow your toddler to drink too much milk, filling up on dairy products and sacrificing other food sources. Remember, milk (and it should be whole milk until age two years) has no iron. Unlike the iron-fortified formula and/or breast milk offered to your infant, homogenized milk is iron-free. Too much milk is not a balanced meal and can contribute to milk-induced anemia. Also limit the amount of juice your toddler drinks. If your child always fills up on juice, he may not get enough of the other nutrients his body needs. Check with your doctor if you are not sure how much juice or milk to give your child.

If your toddler is still bottle-fed—and worse, sipping all day long on that bottle—it may sabotage all solid intake. It is a real invitation to cavities, as well! Perhaps it is time to say good-bye to the bottle. Does your child really *need* a bottle every time you go out—for every car ride, every trip to the grocery store, every nap and bedtime? Of course not! Who is in charge? Rethink the bottle and wean your toddler—certainly by fifteen to eighteen months.

In terms of what and when to feed—again, the meals need to be balanced. Often a variety of color will provide that balance. Give your child something white, something brown, and something orange or green. Snacks should be reasonable, with crackers or fruit, maybe some protein (cheese, yogurt, peanut butter)—even some sweets, just not all sweets. It is all right for children to have some sugar—it's a good high-energy food—just not all sugar.

Avoid bedtime meals, though maybe provide a tiny snack if dinner was very early. Do not chase your kids to bed with a full dinner to make up for uneaten meals and/or provide the "minimum daily requirement"—whatever that really is. (Only the child really knows.) After all, who is in charge? If your child knows you will feed him every night in the comfort of his bedroom—why bother with regular meals? He's gotcha!

The bottom line is, let your toddler eat pretty much what he wants at the appropriate times—just moniter the quantity of milk and juice drinking and sweets.

In the end, you cannot force your child to eat anything. You cannot force him to swallow, just as you cannot force him to fall asleep or use the toilet. Swallowing is under his control—so don't force it. If he looks like he's going to throw up, he probably will. Some kids have an easy gag and vomit at the slightest provocation. You have to respect that. If your toddler or preschooler tells you he will vomit if you force that last glass of milk on him, believe him. You should respect that. If he does vomit, who is to blame? After all, he did warn you. (It happened to me.)

Conduct weight checks only at the doctor's office, if you or Grandmother are concerned. Try not to compare your child with the child next door or even with a sibling. Don't rely on your own scale. Adult scales are often inaccurate at lower weights. Remember, children come in all kinds of shapes and sizes, with very different genetic makeup. Some are tall, some are short, and some are supposed to be skinny. It's not so much the absolute weight of your child that is important, but the trend of weight gain, i.e., the growth curve. Your doctor will carefully follow this over time and advise you as needed. Height is also important, just like weight, and it, too, will be followed closely by your pediatrician.

Once in a while special tests and special doctors need to be consulted if weight gain is truly a concern. Certainly, weight loss—in the face of no obvious source (such as recent illness)—needs to be addressed. To improve weight gain, your doctor may recommend offering calorie-rich food items to provide more calories to a child who doesn't eat much. This can sometimes give a toddler a "jump start" to catch up on growth. But it can also artificially fatten small and/or skinny kids, so try it only after consulting your doctor.

Just remember, when it comes to meals, who's in charge? Who has whom wrapped around his little finger if you're chasing your toddler around the house with food? Providing open platters for constant grazing is not sanitary and gives your child a wrong message—I can eat whenever and whatever I want all day. Meals should be happy and calm. Do not tolerate screaming or throwing of food. If this happens, remove your child from the scene—your child will *not* starve. Wait for a regular interval before offering more food, and then offer an appropriate snack. You can fix special treats for your child at times or even follow your child's diet requests or preferences (kids often don't like our adult choices)—but try not to offer multiple choices. Keep meals and snacks simple and pleasant, and participate. Eating is supposed to be a social event!

Bedtime

Bedtime is another biggie in family life. How many families disintegrate at the bedtime hour? Everyone is tired—especially if you all have had a very long day. With many dual-career families, mixing lots of activities and responsibilities, the end of the day can be exhausting. Is bedtime a battle or a pleasant time together? Arrange your schedule so that bedtime is truly quality time—not just marking time. Again, who is in charge? You or your life! (See "Schedules," Chapter 10.)

Bedtime is supposed to be a happy time together—not a fight or an afterthought. The end of the day is as important as the beginning and the middle. Your child may wish he could stay up, but with your firm, loving support (remember, no waffling), bedtime is a given, a constant. When it is time for bed, it is time! It's perfectly fair to warn your child that bedtime is approaching, especially as the child gets older, but hold to the time. Don't give your child mixed signals—"It is, but not really, bedtime." Either it is or it isn't, plain and simple. Otherwise, your child will push for more time awake, and discipline and expectations are a muddle.

Bedtime needs a reasonable ritual and a sufficient amount of time to accomplish your goal. Somewhere in the neighborhood of about thirty to forty-five minutes should provide enough time for bath (as needed, two to three times a week), changing into bed clothes, and a story or two or three. If you need more time, or want more, plan on it. Just don't make bedtime a "hurry up, we're late" situation. Rather, be relaxed.

Make sure you do spend time with books or telling stories. It is so important. It is a time for togetherness, for sharing—a time for learning, exploring, imagining. It's a lovely way to end the day and then nod off to sleep. Exposure and reexposure to books should be a priority. (See "Reading Together," Chapter 8.) How well I remember one single Mom who said she had no time to read to her toddler at night. She had a busy daily schedule, and reading at night was not a priority. We talked a little bit about rearranging her nighttime schedule—talked about the benefits of a story time. I'm not sure about the outcome, but hopefully, her child got a story.

With story reading or telling, think about what you want to do. Often, the challenge is striking the balance, i.e., determining what is enough, but not too much. Pick a limit, an endpoint, and stick with it. Limit your stories to a certain number—probably five or under, but not twenty. Be consistent with your story time so your child will know and trust your limit. If wrapping up is a problem, use a timer or a stopwatch. It can provide a very objective and clear limit—it rings! Set the timer for the time you want—even start with extra time and work backwards. Then honor it.

Don't play the "one more" game—one more story, one more drink of water, one more kiss. This is it! You might have to let your child cry a little—remember, he will try to get more, if you let him. But be consistent about your endpoint, and the crying will stop. Often, the crying is more painful for the adult than for the child. Just remember, you are the one in charge. If the crying is excessive and/or you are having trouble dealing with it, consult your pediatrician or family doctor.

Where to have your toddler sleep, just like for the newborn, is a family decision. The bed—where and what—depends upon you. But wherever your toddler sleeps, make sure he is safe and knows where you are. The family bed is a cultural or personal issue. If you so choose, make sure you as parents really want it for *yourselves* as well as for your child. Make sure you are getting your own sleep and have time as a couple to be together alone—otherwise, who are you kidding? Is the child ruling the bedroom, and do you or your partner resent it? Be careful. If you have trouble separating from your toddler, lie down with him for a short while, but leave his room *before* he falls asleep. If this is difficult, then wean yourself from your child's bed by spending nights resting on the floor, then by the doorway, and, eventually, away. It can work. Finally, if bedtime is not working out, talk to your doctor about what you might do.

One brief word about naps. I am a big believer in midday/early afternoon naps—really, for everyone—forever, if we could. Especially for the toddler—make sure there is a regular nap or quiet time for him *and* his care provider. Keep it early so it doesn't sabotage bedtime, and keep it short, forty-five to sixty minutes, if bedtime is early. It is very important that your child have a chance to renew his energy—and after lunch is a physiological downtime. Use it. Do not be in any hurry to give up naps—it only makes the dinner hour worse. Later, with your preschooler and school-aged child, you can modify nap time to quiet time. Make it a habit and take time out yourself. We all need it. Use it to read, to relax, to slow down.

POTTY TRAINING

Toddlers are very proud of their bodies and proud of anything that comes from their bodies. Little toddler boys will discover their penis; little toddler girls will begin to look around. This is all natural! For toddlers, urine and stool are not dirty, but natural phenomena. Only we, as adults, contaminate them. Poop and pee have a proper function and place. We will show our children how and where, and we should do so naturally. But don't get hung up on training—even if Grandma is pressuring you. After all, it is the child who will become trained, not you. Allow your child the space to decide when and how he will train—in a natural fashion, with no rush and no pressure. Your toddler may toilet train at two years, or not until three or four. Don't rush it and cause all kinds of other problems, like chronic constipation from withholding stool. Urine training is easier than stool training— make allowances. Some children have a very difficult time with evacuation, and this is probably physiological—i.e., it's not their fault! Keep the child's diet fiber rich so the stool doesn't become hard. A large, firm stool hurts to poop out. That child will resist the potty, I can promise you. Diet manipulation with prunes and/or a stool softener, on a regular basis, is all right. Just consult with your doctor.

Toddlers are also very curious about everyone else's body functions. Your toddler will watch with fascination as you use the bathroom. This is normal behavior and is laying the groundwork for successful functioning as an adult—even his own sexuality. The bathroom is just another room in the house. Be careful not to make it a secret place. Let your toddler see urine and stool so it won't frighten him. Let him do the flushing on your poop and his. And by all means, congratulate him if he does perform successfully—but don't overwhelm him with praise. What happens if next time he is less successful? Setting up basic acceptance of body function now, in a relaxed atmosphere with no pressure, will help to make your child successful. Expect "accidents"—treat them as no big deal.

. . .

It is possible to not only survive, but delight in your child's toddlerhood. Look at the world through your child's eyes, and see how exciting life can be. Wonder and marvel at him and with him. Watch your toddler always. Teach him to care about the place and the people where you live—teach and show him respect for people and property. Be nice to him and to everyone, and he will do the same. On occasion, treat your toddler like a guest— plan special outings and treats. Remember to say please and thank you. Remain calm, and he will feel it. Don't be frenzied and anxious, or he will feel that. Love your child and make your family the biggest priority in your life. Set this limit now and always!

Remember SECRET: Don't forget about your *own* needs, remember *calm*, *respect* your toddler's emerging self, and put in the *time*. SECRET won't let you down.

4

The Preschooler

The preschooler, your young child aged three to five years, is really coming into her own. It's almost magical as you watch her intellectual, physical, and social development take off. All cylinders are on "go" as she makes enormous progress on all fronts. The groundwork you've laid in the infant and toddler periods— the time and love, the consistency—will begin to pay dividends, as you watch this little person emerge. The pieces are beginning to come together. There will still be periods of frustration—there will always be! Your preschooler will still have unsatisfied wants, immediate demands that you cannot meet, but she should manifest some self-control. Dialogue is now more adult and play more complicated, as you begin to share and reason together. The threshold for tantrums should be higher as the ability to wait and understand why develops. These should be fun years!

SECRET

In terms of setting limits, our basic guidelines can still provide a foundation for rules and codes of behavior. Just as in the infant and toddler periods, SECRET can help set the stage for maintaining control. Let's review.

Self

Just as before, you, as the parent, need to take care of your own needs, continually. Don't forget about your own health requirements. Keep up with your own fitness and health maintenance—schedule your own appointments, as well as your child's. Eat, rest, and exercise. Feel good yourself, in order to model appropriate behavior. Take time to play.

Remember, how can you demonstrate kindness and caring if you're stressed and overtired? How can you be patient and forgiving if you're stretched too far? Your preschooler is really watching—absorbing—all the time. It's important for you to continue to be your very best self so your child can learn to do the same.

Then, as before, figure out what "rules" are appropriate for you and your household, and then honor them. Don't forget to *do* as well as *say*! Your preschooler will be very quick to pick up on your breaking the rules. Being a good role model is key.

Calm

Keep a lid on yourself. Even if your preschooler is more demanding than most, still maintain your composure. Speak slowly, breathe evenly, stop and sit down. Know that regardless of how tough today may be, tomorrow always comes. Your preschooler is looking to you for guidance—show her with *calm*.

Be humble, don't get flustered, and listen to your own heartbeat. Even when you make mistakes or start off on the wrong foot (and we all do), maintain your sense of humor. Right yourself without losing your cool. Remember, your preschooler is observing you. It's only human to err; a little humility goes a long, long way in fixing the problem.

Respect

Respect your preschooler's increased awareness and improved developmental skills. Talk to your child and play with her *lots*. Enter into and share in her world of make-believe.

Let your preschooler share in decisions, even simple ones. Just as you did with the toddler, let your preschooler pick out the story for your bedtime reading and choose the color of her socks. Let her help pack her lunch and/or help plan a Saturday outing. Let your child share in a few responsibilities—picking up the toys, collecting her laundry, hanging up her coat, putting away her boots. The "pie" image of shared control will surface more as you involve your child in planning and doing things together.

Be buddies, just not best friends. Remember, you are the parent. Respect each other for your individuality, as well as your assigned roles of parent and child.

Time

Just like before, make time for your child; give time. Spend time together every day, every weekend. Give of yourself through time!

Make your time together special. Keep it almost holy. Forbid distraction or interruption. Take no phone calls while reading a story—do no office homework while working on a puzzle or playing at the park. Leave the cellular phone at home. (What's so urgent?)

Make a real commitment to your child. She needs and wants *you*. Then, keeping in mind the preceding guidelines, you can begin to set age-specific limits while continuing to build for the future. So let's look at preschool issues—developmental, behavioral, social, and cultural.

DEVELOPMENTAL ISSUES

Intellectual Development

Intellectually, your preschooler takes on a new dimension as her thinking and language take a quantum leap. Your child will be like a little Einstein. Her mind is recording and remembering everything—just as in the toddler years, but now more than ever. She will not only be concrete in her thinking, but move on to new levels and begin to make all kinds of connections. Your preschooler will relate more and more to you and to the world around you. Associations—be it colors and shapes or words or people—will be automatic. You will be amazed! Your child will be brilliant! By now, if it hasn't happened already, your child's verbal expression will have a logarithmic explosion. Those long-awaited words will come—nonstop. Now your preschooler can tell you all about "it"—what she sees, what she's thinking or feeling—and she will.

The brain with its many circuits seems to be in overdrive when it comes to language. The verbal expression pathway is working overtime. Listen to the preschooler speak. The words just come. Subject matter changes by the millisecond as the mind switches gears—polyphasic thinking, as we know it, is now polyphasic expression. A child at this age speaks her every thought. If you listen closely, you will be amazed by the dribble of speech. What is so exciting is that this child feels free to speak and can do it. You or your surrogate is there to encourage just that kind of uninhibited expression. Dialogue may be more one-sided or child-driven, but nevertheless, dialogue is there. The fact that dialogue is occurring at all is reassuring to you, the parent, as you "hear" your child's thinking. You know that, if she can speak, she can hear, she can process, and she can put subject with verb. Then as her speech becomes more elaborate, your child will "color" her speech using adjectives and description, and you can delight in her even more. Your preschooler will listen more closely to you as you help impart more and more information into her magnificent brain. As a parent, your job is to help develop your child's speech with time spent (and lots of it) listening, answering, explaining, and then, as always, allowing time for your child to respond in kind. Respect your child's growing capacity for language, and allow time for it to develop. This is not a five- or ten-minute exercise, but rather an ongoing dialogue.

Your play—be it unstructured conversation, putting together puzzles, or taking a walk—will take on newer dimensions as you can talk about it. In terms of limit setting, there are no limits when it comes to developing your child's language. Quite the opposite! In fact, you will want to work hard to eliminate any boundaries that interfere with this wonderful task. Conscious effort to establish dialogue will do a great deal to develop your

child's mind and to lay the groundwork for establishing and maintaining lines of communication that you will always appreciate.
Build those lines and keep them open always. This you will hear
again and again. Remember, this adorable preschooler will be a
teenager someday!

As a parent you will want to work purposefully to allow plenty
of time for dialogue and expression—and to make it relaxed and
fun. Go places, do things, and now talk about it. Go to the park,
the library, the zoo—or just on a bike ride—but do things. Read
books; listen to music. Sing songs—lots of them. Expand your
child's world and share your thoughts with one another. Time
together needs to be more than time spent in the car, driving from
one errand to another or from home to day care. Not that time
in the car cannot be valuable, but your time with your child needs
to be more than that.

Be careful about rushing through any activity—take your
child at *her* speed, not yours. Remember to keep the time special. Allow for extra time, just as you did for the toddler. (See
"Time with Your Toddler," Chapter 3.) Delight in your projects
and outings together, and your child will do the same. If going
to the park is fun for you, the same will hold for your child. But
if you approach an outing as a task-oriented project that you are
doing only to be a "good" parent, but not necessarily for fun, your
child will sense your ambivalence. She will know intuitively that
your heart isn't in it. Well, what kind of message are you giving
then?

Find what works for you—the *self* in SECRET—and your child
will be happy, too. The truth is that your child will love to do
anything, as long as you are happy. Fun is what you make of any
activity—not just the exercise. And then, the more you do
together, the more fun you will have. You can even learn to make
a good time out of a bad! Again, know that the *process*, as much
as the goal, is always important. Going to the park can be as
much fun as the park itself. Walking and holding hands can be
very intimate.

As your child's thinking and vocabulary expand, if it hasn't
happened already, the world of make-believe will open up. The
world of pretend is there for your picking, without limits or

boundaries—a wonderful opportunity for imaginative play. Together, you and your child can expand upon our concrete world by entertaining each other with worlds of fairy princesses, kings and queens, and dinosaurs and monsters of all shapes and sizes. The world of pretend is limitless—and one in which we all can play. Your child can help construct an imaginary play world, probably much more easily than you or I. For some reason (and it may be as simple as the world hasn't had time to put its stamp on this kind of thinking), your preschooler isn't inhibited and can freely imagine. Your child will amaze you with her sense of complexity and order, as well as detail. Let her know that you notice. "Wow!"—say it! Show your child your respect! Try to play in that pretend world yourself. Don't feel that grown-ups can't do it. Why not? We spend so much of our time dealing with reality, why not a little dreamworld, too? Show her that it's OK to play games— she'll learn soon enough (if she hasn't already) what's real and what's not.

Imaginary play allows for dialogue about good and bad, as you and your child can reward the good and punish the bad. Aggressive behavior can be imparted and deflected to the soldiers or to the wild monsters. They can be the instruments and outlets for unacceptable actions as you play together. I'm sure you've seen little boys (and they are usually boys) who can make a gun or weapon out of anything, even in a household where no weapons or acts of violence are present. Somehow these little human beings are born with a tendency to be physical and aggressive. How better to allow release of this naturally driven behavior than in a play setting, where guidance and understanding are available. Know that this behavior is probably genetically programmed and even protective, in terms of survival needs. Remember, early humans had to hunt for food, fight against wild beasts, and even fight or kill each other to ensure their own survival. Their world was a very different place where survival skills demanded superb physical fitness and the ability to protect. So, it's OK for your child to play hard—even OK to have aggressive "pretend." It's just not OK to be violent in the real world. The distinction will be yours to make—again, those limits. Teach your child the difference between what is acceptable in a play setting and what is tolerated in the real world. This attempt to be realistic will help direct your child's energies appropriately. Show her that no real hitting, swearing, stealing, cheating, or lying are allowed.

As your child's thinking (cognition) achieves new levels, her understanding and acceptance of your explanations will expand. In the toddler years, your child may have had little capacity for words like "maybe" or "later" or "let's talk about it." The toddler was more focused on the immediate, with less capacity for the future. But now, your preschooler can begin to think beyond the moment. Your preschooler can begin to wait as she begins to understand the waiting concept. Teach your child by providing appropriate opportunities. Delay gratifications and rewards, even if just a little bit. Make her wait—an hour for a special ice cream cone or a day for a trip to her favorite toy store or museum. Put off special treats, ever so slightly. "After you do this, we can go . . . " "Because you've been so helpful, I'd like to take you to the zoo tomorrow." Keep the delays very specific and simple— only minutes, hours, maybe a day. Remember, your preschooler is just beginning to deal with waiting, and you will want to guide her gently. Then be sure to follow through with whatever has been discussed—honor it just like a promise. Make sure you deliver! Remember, it's the patterns you are setting that are important. Also, you will want to honor your child (respect her) by honoring the reward. Compliment your child on good waiting—let her know that you notice. Reinforce good behaviors—and, of course, role model them yourself. You can provide minirewards for a job well done—a sticker, a new story, a piece of chocolate cake.

As you dialogue and share time together, you may discover that your child has a wonderful sense of humor. This is a delightful experience as you laugh together. Nothing—except maybe love itself—is more real or true than laughter, or as ageless. You can always laugh together—have a good, jolly one. And you can't fake it. The happiness or silliness you share is pure and honest. Furthermore, I think humor is a sign of intelligence. How else would your child know that something is funny? Do laugh together. Entertain each other—show those genuine feelings of enjoyment. Let your child be a star and dance or parade or dress up. Let her be at ease with you and any world that you make. This, of course, does take time, as humor is often spontaneous. You will want to leave time for spontaneity.

With her increased awareness, improved communication skills, and capacity to think, your child is becoming a more complex individual. That's good. But what used to satisfy her curiosity and answer her questions will no longer do. What used to be more simple needs and requests are now more complicated. Patience and time will be required from you as you attempt to satisfy your child's drive to know. The toddler was more physically curious and required your ever-watchful eye. The preschooler is now more intellectually curious—wanting to know everything.

The preschooler will begin to ask "Why?" and "When?" and "Can I . . . ?" The questions can be endless. The preschooler is often a cross between Socrates and the district attorney—challenging, asking. She has so much to learn. That's her job. Ours is to answer appropriately—to support questions and sound reasoning. We need to respect the child's eagerness to learn.

However, there will be times when the question-and-answer session becomes too lengthy and has to be terminated. Sometimes these preschoolers get on a real roll, and there is no end in sight. This is delicate—to encourage, but not to discourage. A three-year-old can ask twenty questions in about as many seconds. Whereas a thirty-year-old has to know where to draw the line, to set the limit, when enough is enough. It's OK to delay an answer ("Let's get back to that later—at dinnertime—after shopping"), even to acknowledge imperfect knowledge (we don't know everything), but be kind when it's time to move on. Do come back to the postponed conversation. Don't forget.

Once in a while, answers like "Because," even "Because I said so"—used judiciously—must do. Not to be autocratic, but you shouldn't lose sight of the fact that you are, indeed, the parent—the one in control. And it's as much *how* you say "because" or "enough" as it is the words.

Sometimes conversations will become quite serious, even deep. Everything from personal requests to moral judgments—birth, death, God—it's all up for grabs. Remember, your preschooler is, indeed, curious. But the reality is that she is not ready for lengthy explanations. Keep them short and simple. Use only a few words, and wait for the next question if more information is needed. Your child's capacity to reason is expanding, but it still has a long way to go.

Now, what about the preschooler whose language appears not to be developing, in whom a delay may be present? First, it is important to know that all children develop at different paces— be it in verbal/cognitive areas or with physical skills. And all children are working on both kinds of tasks at the same time, with a huge spectrum of "normal" in each. Some children appear to develop faster in one area versus another—the very physical, coordinated child may be less verbal and vice versa. Also, children, like adults, have different personalities—some quiet, some chatty. But even allowing for normal differences, some children are behind in their speech development. Or at least, some children appear to be lagging.

These children *must* be evaluated (see "Developmental Issues," Chapter 3). Know that not all laggers are, in fact, behind. Not all are truly developmentally delayed. Some are just storing and about to have an explosion of language, but some have pathology that needs evaluation and treatment. The bottom line is—and this is the parent's responsibility (as well as the doctor's)—if there is a question of speech delay, at the very least, it demands attention. A hearing test (not just a screening) with a good pediatric audiologist and an evaluation with a speech pathologist should be arranged, and you as a parent can and should request them. I've never met an audiologist or a speech pathologist who would discourage any kind of testing in a child with a question of impaired development. That's what they do!

Furthermore, if there is a speech processing and/or expressive problem, there is treatment available to help your child. The worst thing to do is to ignore the problem. If there is a problem with speech and/or hearing, it won't automatically go away. It might improve on its own, but it won't just disappear. And it might get worse. As a parent, you must acknowledge any suspicions you may have. After all, if your child really is speech delayed, it can impact on both her language and social development. If your child cannot speak clearly, she will have a hard time being understood. Communication outside the home, and particularly at school, will be very hard, even frustrating. The child may be teased or stigmatized by her peers. She might get called "stupid" or "dull." Baby talk or babble that persists is not cute. In addition, some of these children become frustrated by their inability to communicate and then act out. Some become violent, which is then very inappropriately mislabeled as a behavior problem. Violent outbursts may be nothing more than a reaction to the frustration of poor speech and not being understood. This is not fair. Don't let your child fall through the cracks—get her evaluated. Take time to follow your intuition, and respect your child's need for testing and help. And know that a preschool child with speech or hearing problems may be eligible for therapy or preschool through the local school system at no cost to the parents.

Physical Development and Safety

Finally, as your child's mind and cognitive skills are expanding, your preschooler is also becoming more physically adept. As with every developmental stage, there is growth in the body, as well as in the mind. Your child should be running with alternating steps—no more "toddling." She will learn to climb—even climb very high. She can balance, hang from monkey bars, climb a rope, pump the swing—she can be a real circus act. Provide her with the opportunity for both small and large motor play. Let her be indoors and outdoors and use that body! Watch for progress.

But with her increased coordination, there is increased risk as the boundaries expand, as she climbs higher and dares to do more. The risks of heights and speed become real. Tricycles, bicycles with or without training wheels, more balls and bats, harder toys, smaller toys, smaller pieces, and even skates and skis—there is suddenly a lot more that can cause injury to your child. What is your role?

Just as before, you are supposed to keep the environment safe. Obviously, playing or riding on a busy street is forbidden, but what about a "quiet" street that may not always be so quiet. What about safety issues—helmets, knee pads, appropriate clothing. More than ever, you are the parent who must insist upon the right equipment. Take the time to protect your child. Helmets go with bikes. Play belongs in the yard. There is no play (summer or winter) around water without adult supervision. Skating on a pond in winter demands as much attention to safety as does swimming in the summer. Chasing toys (mostly balls) or animals outside the yard into the street or going off on one's own—these are absolute nos. Crossing a street alone is also a no. Make that clear. Make sure your preschooler is always supervised, just like the toddler, especially when outdoors. After all, she is still too young to assume responsibility for herself, although she may try. Make sure any other caregivers or baby-sitters don't get lulled into giving your preschooler more responsibility than she should have. Safety is still a priority. Just as with the toddler, accidents are often the result of poor supervision—and that's where your parental care must follow through. Just because your child is more able doesn't mean she is more responsible. Quite the contrary! The fact is, because she is more able, she may be at greater risk. If your child is in the yard and the phone rings, either let it ring and remain unanswered, or take your child inside and then answer the phone. Don't leave her alone. If inside, even for a minute, keep your eyes on the outside—always.

Just like the toddler, the preschooler has an inclination to explore. You must watch her all the time. Respect her physical mobility—by being there! Check out your windows—use guards, open them from the top. Put up some fencing in your yard. Put all matches and other incendiaries away. Recheck medications and cleaning materials; lock up the caustics and poisons. Make sure your syrup of ipecac is not expired. Have emergency numbers on all phones: police, fire department, poison control, your doctors, and neighbors. Keep extra batteries on hand for your smoke detectors so they're always in working order. Use car seats and seat belts—both you and your children.

BEHAVIOR

Behavioral issues will become both easier and harder in the preschool years—easier because you can talk, harder as the issues become more complex. If you have been successful in laying the groundwork that certain behaviors are acceptable, others not, then the preschool years should be calm. If your child aims to please (and most preschoolers do) and is an agreeable sort, these years with your dominating presence (not yet school or peers) should be very pleasant. Nevertheless, there will be times when your child misbehaves—refuses to come with you, is inappropriately physical or noisy, or uses foul language. There will be times when she forgets her manners, hits someone, or breaks something on purpose. She might steal (even if something trivial), lie, or simply test you. Your child is looking for space—and limits. Remember once again, your child is an individual, unique and different from you. You and she will not always agree. You're not supposed to. (So true, from infancy through adulthood.) But you are still the parent, who with maturity and experience sets the expectations for good behavior. Remember to be calm—model kindness, forgiveness, and acceptance. Give your preschooler time to act appropriately—try to avoid rushing. Remember, just as in the toddler years, don't schedule too tightly. Leave room for some flexibility.

But if (and when) your child does do something "bad," then there has to be an appropriate response from you—not corporal punishment, but *something*. Bad behavior cannot go unnoticed— or what kind of pattern might you be setting? Try to think out ahead of time, if possible, what kind of response is right for you. Back to *self*—what works for you and your family? Consider time out (one minute per year of age), deferral of a treat, change of scene, removal of a toy, or denial of a privilege.

When your preschooler crosses the line, there has to be some consequence—just as in the toddler period. Discussion alone may do, but at the very least, there has to be a firm acknowledgment of unacceptable behavior—with calm—and maybe a penalty. You cannot let your preschooler (or toddler or adolescent) get away with unacceptable behavior, ever. Otherwise, you set a very bad precedent for later on, and you risk giving a mixed signal. How can you expect your child to behave consistently if you are inconsistent with your own response? What kind of a message is that? You don't have to be mean, but you must be fair. So respond as you should, with purpose, commitment, and love. If you say no, it's no—the first time and the twentieth time. Otherwise, your no becomes a yes.

Often the "in between" behavior—the not really unacceptable but rather more bothersome behavior—becomes a challenge. What to do? Again, think about where you want to draw the line. Figure out how much of this behavior is tolerable, and then set the limit. I have one patient, a three-year-old, who loves to roar like a lion. He really can roar. The first time it's kind of cute; the tenth time it's truly noisy. I suggested to his mother that she decide how many roars are tolerable, and then draw the line there—maybe five or eight? After that, distract your child—move on to something else. If he continues to roar, what are you prepared to do? Always follow through on the limit you have set.

What about the child who wants the cupcake with pink frosting but has already bitten into the one with chocolate? Well—what do you want to do? It seems to me it would be appropriate to say no to the new cupcake. A choice has already been made. But beware—a simple cupcake incident can quickly escalate into warfare with screaming and yelling—but stick to your guns. If you said no, then it's no forever. Otherwise, you might as well give your child the whole package. Then who is in charge?

If maintaining order is really difficult, you can consider the following method (compliments of one of my parents): Keep a calendar visible, and divide the days into mornings and afternoons. Use stars and Xs to mark unusually good or bad behavior. So many stars earns the child a special reward. So many Xs takes away a privilege—no movie, no videotape, no candy bar. Be inclined to emphasize the good, and reward more than punish. Everyone likes to be stroked!

And then, make very sure that your own behavior serves as a good model—that you are the kind of person your child would want to emulate. Do you scream, lose control, and forget your own manners? If so, think and take time to regroup, even consider some professional guidance for yourself. Remember, we are all working hard to be the best role model we can. Are we doing a good job? Remember those elements of parenting we talked about earlier; remember SECRET—take care of yourself, be calm, show your child respect, and give her time.

Although the preschool years are usually a time of calm, for some this period can be a bit stormy—particularly for the four-year-old. Sometimes the four-year-old can be like a miniadolescent with occasional abrupt mood swings. What happens at four? Your formerly adorable three-year-old may try to pit herself against you on everything. She may demonstrate new but unpleasant behavior never seen before. Why?

First of all, I'm not exactly sure why. Certainly, there is a developmental component, because it occurs with some regularity. Probably there are some hormonal or body changes that we have not fully recognized. Some of these children (and they're usually girls) act almost premenstrual—with fits of crying, even a tantrum, brought on by the slightest provocation. A formerly even-tempered kid may now fool you.

I think in terms of setting limits it is important to stand firm and not bribe or pacify your child away from unacceptable or even unpredictable behavior. (Just like before and always.) Those tantrums of the toddler years may resurface. If so, just as before, let the tantrums come and go. Let your child scream, but afterward reassure her that you love her. If she screams and makes a scene in public or private, let her. She simply cannot have her own way all the time. Your child may ask for and receive an occasional treat or a small item. This is fine. But make it clear, with consistency and love, what the limit is. Your child cannot have every cookie, every cereal box, every toy she desires—the answer is just no! If she explodes and you have to remove her from a particular scene—do so. You still have physical control—pick her up, if you must. When quiet is finally resumed, you have the advantage of talking about what happened. Both you and your child can reflect upon the behavior, just like before. Expect some hurdles. But remember, you are still in charge, even in the most volatile situation. Don't let your child intimidate you. Don't fall into the "I want more" trap, because "more" is never enough. After all, who is the parent?

If the frequency of explosions is increasing, speak to your child's doctor. If you ever feel *you* are losing control, think about getting some professional help. If you find yourself in a rage, take that as a warning. If you're provoked to hit, or almost, talk to someone. Again, don't hit! Watch yourself, as well as your child.

Being a parent is not easy, and some days will push us beyond our *own* limits. Sometimes one parent seems to get provoked more than the other. It's not too soon for that mother/daughter or father/son thing, with unspoken competition for Daddy's or Mommy's attention. Children (both sons and daughters) will often select one parent to please and one to pester. It's all part of growing up, testing us for those limits. (Recall the "Mommy versus Daddy" show described in the section "Consensus" in Chapter 3.) Know that we are all human, and some days we are more stable than on others. This is true for everyone, I promise you. The bottom line: you must know your own limits, your *self*. Watch that you're not beyond those limits. If you are close, get help and/or relief before something happens.

Age four will pass, and there is calm around the corner at age five. Recognize that some of this explosive behavior is a rite of passage. If your child is too volatile, take a break. Get away from each other. Try nursery school or time at a baby-sitter's so *both* of you can have some time off to cool down and regroup. It is important (and OK) to recognize the need for space—be it for the child and/or the adult—and then to allow for it. You can love your child enormously, but sometimes you may clash. Then make sure that your time together is really quality time, not just marking time.

SOCIAL SKILLS

Play time with your preschooler will become more fun for you and your child as she develops better skills for integrated, sharing play—not just parallel play. The toddler may be starting to branch out, but the preschooler is really ready for playing together. It is a time to learn and practice courtesy with one another—a time for taking turns and teaching respect. It is a time for really developing manners such as saying please and thank you. (See "Manners," Chapter 8.) It is a time to enjoy, as your child becomes a more social creature and, with your lead, a socially acceptable one. Respect for one another begins in the home, as each parent shows love and respect for the other and then the same for the children. It is the theme of mutual respect that is transmitted and that sets the stage for your child's doing the same.

Play can take all kinds of shapes, from spontaneous get-togethers to planned parties. Just make sure that the emphasis is always on play, with fun for everyone. Play groups need to be low-key, allowing space, time, calm, and respect (SECRET) for your emerging child. Keep the groups small and maintain consistent adult supervision. Birthday parties for the preschooler tend to get out of control. Keep them simple. Whatever happened to those small gatherings of family with a few friends, celebrated with cake and only a few presents? (For further discussion, see "Birthday Parties," Chapter 11.)

Meals

Meals, in general, will be more social, as your preschooler is becoming more social herself. You can talk to each other and share in conversation. Keep meals fun and interesting. And just as before, be there! You know your child's likes and dislikes, so keep her happy. You don't have to go overboard and fix a completely separate meal, but you can give her peanut butter and jelly when you're serving calf's liver. Don't force broccoli if she really can't stand it. At the same time, don't offer multiple substitutes, only one. Just give her some leftovers—not the entire supermarket or refrigerator. And don't go crazy over a perfectly balanced meal. Over time, your preschooler will naturally select a balance—although it may not be obvious. If you are concerned about nutrition, talk to your doctor.

Let your child participate in meal planning and setting the table. Your preschooler can begin to share in the family chores (see "Household Chores," Chapter 8). Just make it fun. Work with your child, and praise her for a job well done. Give her some very small responsibilities—share some of the decision "pie" with her.

As hard as you may have worked in the prior years to establish a calm and relaxed atmosphere for meals, you will still have to spend time reinforcing those moods—really, always. Planning and serving meals takes time and effort. It is an art. It takes continued commitment on your part. But if you are consistent, it should become easier, just by habit. The secret here is to recognize that meals are important family time—to be honored. They are a very real opportunity for social and intellectual development, with time for listening, sharing, and speaking. Who is in charge? It should be you.

BEDTIME

At bedtime, just like mealtime, the preschool-aged child can participate even more in the routine. For bedtime, your preschooler certainly can choose the stories and/or the format for that time together. Let her decide how to divide the time between structure and free-flowing talk. Let her choose what books to read and how many make-believe stories she wants to share. Let your preschooler even have a surprise or special story of her own. Recite some nursery rhymes, and let her fill in the blanks. She will know every word in the familiar books and stories. If you skip a word or phrase, she will correct you. Her memory will outdo yours—be prepared. Let your child show off a little, and marvel at her. Spend a moment of quiet together, and never forget to tell your child that you love her.

Bedtime good nights for the preschooler should be calm and something you both look forward to. But because of her growing mind and imagination, fear of burglars, the bogeyman, or monsters may spoil the quiet. If so, reassure your child that she is safe. Let her keep a light on, play some music, or keep a flashlight handy for spot checks. Just as before, stay close by, on the same floor level. Let her know that you are near—no abandonment to the downstairs or to the basement. Teach and remind her, just as before, to fall asleep on her own. Praise her for success—even give a minimal reward such as stickers if she's struggling. And if instead of getting easier, the bedtime ritual is getting harder and separation is very difficult, go back to the beginning.

Work together to set limits—use a timer to objectively signal the end of story time, and wean yourself from your child's room. Seek help if you are unsuccessful.

Sometimes stress in the household manifests itself by unsettling bedtimes. Is there a lot of yelling and screaming in your house? Is there a real concern over health or finances? Your preschooler is very sensitive to your feelings—all children are—don't hide the obvious. Are you worried about something? Talk about and correct what you can, and reassure the rest. Yes, there are some things we cannot fix, but we always have each other. And that, no one can take away. Reaffirm each other—reinforce the basic foundations of love, caring, and support. Take time to work through the family's stress. The secret to bedtime is a calm, happy household, where routines are established and honored and where time is taken for closure to the day. Chaos, confusion, bitterness, and stress do not set the stage for a relaxed, easy bedtime hour.

THE BATHROOM

With regard to bathroom function, the preschooler should be attaining a certain level of competence. Hopefully, by age three or four years, and certainly by five, daytime control with urine and stool has been mastered. Nighttime control usually takes another year, but there is no hurry, even now. The worst thing we can do is to pressure a child into performing too early or enforce any artificial deadline we may have for daytime or nighttime control. If we do, when we have to face an "accident" it becomes a measure of failure. Do not set your child up for failure in this way.

Some kids are simply not ready for control at age two or three, especially at night. So let them wear pull-ups—it's low-key and takes a minimum of effort. No mess, no big deal. Everyone's happy. Don't be in any hurry for any training. It will come—at age three or age four (or even later), when your child's body is ready. If you're concerned, talk to your child's doctor. It never hurts to make that phone call. The limit here is, no diapers in kindergarten. Poop—eventually—belongs in the toilet bowl.

Respect your child's need to control her own elimination. Be there to support her gently.

When it comes to bathing, the preschooler still needs to be supervised—*all the time*! Bathing is still dangerous. You still have to watch your child. Even five-year-olds can slip and fall, and even drown, in the bathtub. Water is still a threat, even if your preschooler can swim. She has no business being alone in or around any source of water, ever. If you're rushed and cannot supervise the bath, then skip it. Take no shortcuts here. Rather let your child be dirty than endanger her.

GETTING DRESSED

The preschooler can help dress herself in the morning, as well as undress herself at night. She can become more involved with clothing selection—even make simple decisions about weather-appropriate attire. But you still want to limit the choices to a few; don't give her the whole closet for random selection, but guide her choices and help her choose. The problem comes with how much you are willing to let her do. (See "Choice," Chapter 3.)

What happens in the morning if you have only allotted a very specific amount of time to get dressed and your preschooler wants to dress herself completely—and you *have* to be out of the house by 7:30? Is dressing in the morning a stressful task? Is it a battle to dress your preschooler?

First, look at the clothing design. Keep it simple: no buttons, zippers, bows; instead, elastic waistbands and Velcro. Clothes should be easy to pull on and off. Keep socks and tights loose— no tie shoes (you can worry about learning to tie shoes next year). Provide pullovers (shirts and sweaters) with loose necks; don't make it a struggle to get dressed. Choose your child's clothes the night before and stick to that choice. If there is protest, remind your child there's another choice to be made tomorrow. You may have a few tears, but they will pass and a workable pattern should develop. Make sure you are not cramming too much into the early-morning routine—don't hurry up and rush to get out. Mornings shouldn't be stressful. If they are, how come? What happened to that "calm" home front? Who or what controls the morning hour? Have you considered your preschooler's needs, as well as your own? Try to respect your child's need for time for entry into a busy day. Not all of us are quick starters—figure out where you all fall.

Know that some kids (just like adults) are slow—they don't hit the deck running. If you have one of those, start earlier—or plan on being a little late. If your alarm already goes off at 6:30, how about 6:00? And then make sure there is time for a nutritious, relaxed breakfast—some protein and carbohydrates—even a special treat. Mornings—just like bedtimes—are important. Work hard to start the day with the right mood, and then perpetuate it. This is not easy—it definitely takes time and effort. You will want to welcome a new day with composure.

PRESCHOOL

School—when and how much—is already an important concern at this age. But I think it is important to recognize that this "preschool" period is called that for good reason. It is truly *pre*school, i.e., before formal schooling begins. Perhaps there is a message there—maybe school is not absolutely necessary yet.

Despite pressure from friends and family (sometimes even pushing for prenatal enrollments!) to get your child into the "right" school, even at age three—preschool is *not* a must. Don't be in a hurry to sign your child up, "just because," especially if you're doing it because everyone else is. If your child is happy at home and you're happy being with her, then postpone preschool. Your child will gain so much from her time with you. It's not as if you live in a vacuum where your child never sees other people. She sees plenty, I'm sure—at home, at Grandma's, at the park, at the zoo, at the grocery store, at church or temple. Just because your child does not go to nursery school, she is not a stranger to other folks. Better yet, she is probably very comfortable in her more simple world.

By the same token, if you would like to arrange some social time for your child with age-related peers—great! Or if you would like or need some time off yourself, then go for it. Just make sure that your child is happy in whatever setting you choose. Make sure that the teacher or parent in charge is a "warm and fuzzy" kind of person who exudes love, understanding, and flexibility—someone who mimics your attitudes and ideals. Then you've found a good spot—the right "match."

With regard to time off for you, remember that you, as the parent, *are* part of the equation when it comes to deciding on preschool. It is important to recognize that you (both the mother and father) have valid needs. Time off from parenting for whatever you choose—to provide balance in your day and to ensure your own happiness—means happiness for the whole family. Remember *self*—it is important. Just as the body has many parts working together, the family, too, has many persons working as a corporate whole. If all the parts—which include you—are well (and feeling well), chances for success are better. It's OK to address your own needs as well as those of your child. Do you want or need to place your child in a preschool setting to give *you* some time off? If you feel the need for a break and you've found a group that satisfies the above criteria (happy child, good teacher)—go with it. Just don't overdo it! The take-home message is that time off, as well as time on, is valid—not frivolous, but legitimate for recharging. (We've said this before in Chapter 3.) It's OK to put your child in a good preschool to give *you* time away. Just make sure that you do use that time for yourself.

Also, there is rarely only one option for preschool, only one setting right for your child. It truly depends! Preschool, play groups, cooperative arrangements, formal or informal, requiring tuition or not—there are a number of alternatives out there, all potentially worthwhile. The real question is what is the best match (if any) for you and your child. Approach choosing a school with the same sense of purpose and calm that you maintain at home. Don't forget SECRET—respect your child's need for play and space; look for a loving, relaxed environment; figure out what works for you and your family; and don't rush into a less-than-satisfactory situation.

• • •

The preschool years are so special. They are a time of fast-paced growth—with the opportunity for wonderful times together. Don't let them fly by so quickly that you miss them. You will never get them back. Don't postpone this time together and then lose it. Enjoy your preschooler, always! There's nothing cuter than a curious, active, verbal preschooler. The world is still her oyster— so be a part of it. Share her joy and excitement. Continue to make your child a high priority, and let her know it. Practice SECRET.

5

The Early School-Aged Child

(ages six to nine)

The young school-aged child is spreading his wings—entering the community in which you live and learning to become a responsible citizen. His world is expanding, as school and neighborhood become major parts of his life. How well have you prepared him?

Make sure your child knows that his place at home is secure, providing a firm launching pad for school and life outside. Let him know that you love and value him for himself, alone. Remind him that he is special.

Have you parented well—spent the time, given the love and support—and enabled your child to carry on by himself? Because now, there will be new things affecting your lives. There will be new twists and turns to the old concerns. Safety, growth, and development are still primary issues, but the how tos and wheres and with whoms can make even seemingly simple plans complicated. School, neighborhood, community, and church or temple will all begin to claim time and energy. Fitting in family time—

or even free time—will become a challenge. The early school-aged child is brimming with potential; it is our job as parents to appropriately channel that potential, not abuse or overdrive it.

SECRET

Remember SECRET—it still has applications, just as before. But as always, there is room for ramifications consistent with the increased capabilities and expanding needs of your child. Let's review.

Self

If you haven't already, it's time to give your*self* some credit for being a good parent. Is your child happy? Does he feel good about himself? If so, then pat yourself on the back. Good job!

Don't forget: Continue to maintain your own fitness for both physical and emotional well-being. Take care of yourself and recognize your own needs as well as your child's. Let your child see that, in addition to his activities, there are yours. The real issue is balance.

In determining what works for you, more than ever, you need to draw and maintain your own family limits. Your codes of behavior are yours—do stick to your guns. Outside pressure from school and peers will come into play. What is appropriate for you and your child? Don't fall into the trap of doing something just because "everyone" else is doing it. Parents are not sheep.

Think independently and fairly. Set good examples. Be true to yourself.

Calm

Monitor the mood in your household. As the pressures from outside mount, as the demands for your time and your child's time increase, watch out for composure. Who is in charge? Who determines what is being done? I hope *not* the outside world. I hope the answer is you! Continue to maintain calm—it is something your child can count on.

Remember kind words and actions. Say please and thank you. Listen to each other.

Respect

The need for respect is constant. Continue to respect your child for himself. Over and above love, respect demands affirmation of your child's individuality. It means you truly value your child for himself. As your child enters the world of school, he needs to know he is valued at home. He needs to know he is special somewhere. How better to prepare your child for school and the outside community than a firm grounding at home! He needs to know you care.

As you respect him, respect his choice of friends and activities. Remember, he is doing the choosing, not you, the parent.

Respect all people yourself. Be a role model for that respect. Listen to what you say about controversial issues, because your child is listening. Choose your words carefully. Race, religion, violence, issues of sexuality—your child wants to know what you think. Remember, you are molding his thinking as well!

Time

Time will begin to get squeezed more and more. Don't let it! Monitor time—keep some free for unpressured fun!

Still, as before and forever more, spend *time* with your child. Not just a quick fix, but real time together—relaxed, open-ended. Not just shuffling from one event to another, but time doing. Take some afternoons off for outings, not necessarily fancy events, but time together. Keep your priorities in line—make and preserve time for your child!

Remember, parenting is a real job. As your child enters school, make your presence known there. Take time to become a part of his school activities. Be a chaperone for a special outing or a room parent. Join the PTO. Let your child see you there—committing to working for him and the community; do this for him, as well as for the greater good.

Take time to serve your child a few more pieces of the decision "pie." Let him make more and more choices—but still keep them focused and simple. Empower your child; whether it be decisions on after-school activities or family outings, allow him the opportunity to choose. And, of course, support him in his choices.

So then, how can we weave all of this into the very real issues of day-to-day living with your school-aged child? How can we practice SECRET, maintain control, and yet leave room for our children to grow and change?

Behavior

By age six, your child should know exactly what you expect and where the line (your line!) is drawn. Honesty, kindness, respect and consideration for others, cleanliness, and timeliness—your school-aged child can understand these concepts and begin to honor and practice them. Make your expectations clear. The responsibility for communication is yours. Make sure you continue to "practice what you preach"; the modeling you provide by setting an example will speak louder and better than your words. You must continue to maintain the calm we've talked about. And time—good, undistracted quality time spent with your child—remains a persistent priority. You can't just pay lip service to the "to dos"—you have to live them, as well.

The school-aged child is still at a very impressionable stage—meaning you can still impress upon him your standards of behavior. But he is also observing others, particularly those at school and in the community. He'll see children—and adults—who don't play by the same rules, who don't answer to the same honor code—people who are not fair, who cheat, who bully, who hit—even if it's only a little. Integrity is a sacred word, but it is not always upheld.

Your child will begin to question, as he compares your limits against others: Why don't you hit? Mary's mother and father hit her. Why can't I swear? Joey says the "F word." Someone stole my pencil—someone tore my paper.

Your child will be checking on and testing you (that's his job—just like before and always)—really stretching you and your limits. Hold your ground! Be calm, be firm, and be consistent. Your child will discern your division of right from wrong and begin to understand the reasons why. And then with time, he will develop his own code of ethics.

But don't be fooled. At some point your school-aged child,

although perfectly aware of your expectations, will cross your line. He will push too far—just like that toddler (and adolescent). So what are the repercussions for bad behavior? What if your child hurts another, steals, cheats, or lies? What if he goes where forbidden, is mean, or is impatient? Children are not perfect—just as we parents are far from perfect. So what happens?

As always, it is very important to recognize and react to unacceptable behavior. If your child hits—it's time out. If he steals, have *him* return the merchandise. If he "borrows" what he covets, he must return that, too. If he spits or swears, he must apologize. If he does it again, deny him a privilege or treat, as well—no McDonald's, no trip to the park, no movie, or no friends over. Hitting, stealing, swearing, lying, whining, and being mean are all, without a doubt, unacceptable. Appropriate responses from the parent include recognition of the misdeed and then payback—suspension of a privilege, apologies to any injured party, replacement of damaged or stolen property.

Chastise or criticize with calm the behavior, not the child. Remember, it is the action that is bad or unacceptable—not the person (see "Behavior," Chapter 3). Give fair warning, and then follow up on any misconduct.

Remember, don't ever hit your child, and don't punish him unreasonably. Even think about helping him work through the payback process. He needs your support from beginning to end.

Consider the options: a phone call or hand-delivered note to his friend whom he punched, then a talk about anger and how one can direct those intense feelings. Feelings are real, but the action may be wrong. (Punch a punching bag, not your friend.) You cannot tolerate stealing—not ever—candy, gum, toys, or whatever. How about having your child earn money (rake leaves, collect newspapers, return bottles) to pay even a small part of the cost of the stolen item, even after it has been returned? How about earning and then making a contribution to a children's charity as recognition of good behavior compensating for bad? If your child swears, do not put soap in his mouth, but respond with stern and frank talk. Make sure you, as the parent, watch your own tongue, as well as those of any other care providers and/or children. Supervise the television and the movie theater. Children don't make up bad words—so double-check for any source of foul language. Children mimic, and they will say what they hear.

Establishing codes of conduct, the rules of the household, takes years of hard, steady work. There is no time off, especially with a child at this age, because he is measuring you against the world. There is a risk of becoming too rigid in your thinking, leaving no room for dialogue or flexibility, no way to approach a problem or behavioral issue with an open mind. Do listen to your child—reason *with* him, not at him—but don't be persuaded against your better judgment. You are still the parent!

The young school-aged child is becoming more socially adept and increasingly aware of others. His social skills—sharing and caring, learning to be sensitive to others—are improving. He's becoming less impulsive, more considerate, more able to listen. He is learning how and trying to be patient, and hopefully, he is less needy. He is working hard not to interrupt. Your job as a parent is to encourage him in all of these tasks and to praise him for success. Guide him along, and make sure you're sensitive to his place and needs. If he is having trouble, help and encourage your child wherever he is. Make him wait a little now and then—teach him to be patient. Acknowledge him when he asks a question or makes a request, but sometimes delay your full response, tactfully and with kindness: "I cannot answer you—or get to that—right now. Please give me a few minutes." You can put him off just a little—without frustration—and then give him your full attention when the few minutes (and make it only a few) are up.

Remember, your child is still young—don't expect perfection. Your child will meet with partial success, and that's normal—in fact, good. Help him redirect his behavior when he gets off track, but with gentle reminders, not negative slashing. Be kind and calm yourself (SECRET!). Don't scream at him, "Can't you *ever* wait? Can't you see that I'm busy?" What kind of message is that? Watch your tongue, especially if you're having a bad day. Verbal abuse can be as hurtful as hitting. Know that there will be times when your child just *can't* wait! (The same is true for adults, too.) Try to recognize when that may be, and help to avoid or intercept those situations. For the child who is continuously impulsive, watch. Maybe this is a warning signal for something else (such as an attention disorder), and you should consult with your child's doctor.

The school-aged child can begin to participate even more as a working member of the family. Tasks can be assigned not only at school, but at home as well. He can take on age-appropriate chores—preferably jobs he will enjoy. Let him take part in running a smooth household. Begin to hold him accountable for easy jobs (the newspaper, the dog, setting the table), and do so with a gentle hand. Again, you are in a position to teach and lead, and he's old enough to respond. Let him share in the household duties, even if just a bit. (See "Household Chores," Chapter 8.) Praise your child for a job well done—let him know that you notice. Help him to be successful. However, if he really seems unable to follow through with any assignment, really unable to focus, keep the tasks very simple and specific, with no distractions—and follow up. If this is a pattern, again, it may speak to a larger problem (either an attention or processing disorder), and you should (as above) speak with your pediatrician or family doctor.

Teach your child how to earn a few things and/or how to wait for that special gift or toy, be it a major or minor purchase or present. Give him an allowance—a regular amount of money for participating in the household duties. This kind of "paycheck," if you will, is entirely reasonable. Let him both spend and save. (See "Vacations," Chapter 11.) Help him use his money wisely. Postpone major gifts until birthdays or special holidays. There is no harm in waiting.

The early school-aged child should be pretty stable. He has his home, his school, and his friends. His life is clearly defined and rather predictable. This age is often the calm before the storm of preadolescent and adolescent years. Your child is still yours, although the world is beginning to move in.

Have fun with your school-aged child. Do things with him. Capture these moments and establish a routine of being together, something you can fall back on in later years. There are lots of things you can do together—enjoy a show, learn sports, go fishing, take a bike ride or a walk. Grab the opportunity to be together before peers assume a position of prominence—before parents are not "cool." You only get your children once; don't miss out on this perfectly delightful stage.

Work to reinforce all the rules and limits you have previously established. Help your child to be honest and forthright about feelings and actions. Be kind to one another; even help the less fortunate. Explain why you do what and when. But allow your child the room to question your position of authority in a healthy way.

Let him see (and he will) that, on occasion, you are not perfect—that you make mistakes not only in action (I should have done . . .), but also in judgment (I should have known better). Let him see that you are human, and that you accept and deal responsibly with your own humanness. If you admit your mistakes, then your child will realize it's OK for him to make mistakes once in a while, as well. He will become much more comfortable with accepting (and your accepting) his own errors. Perfection is not human—try to let your child know this. Dealing with the lack of perfection and correcting and/or accepting one's faults—that's life!

Despite the calm of these years, there may be a few battles at home. Well, these battles are normal—and no surprise. Where else but in the home do people live in close quarters, eating and sleeping under one roof? Where else do people feel and vent whatever emotional baggage they may carry? My only caution is to watch that your battles do not become wars; make sure you can regroup and talk about any blowups. You want to be able to come back to neutral ground, where everyone is respected and has space and voice. It's not so much the disruptions that are a challenge, but how you handle them.

Make sure that any upset isn't reflecting a persistent unhappiness in the home. Is your child acting out because he needs and wants more of your attention? Are you really hearing and seeing your child, and does he know that? Perhaps something else is wrong.

Each child is unique and special and will need something unique and special from you. Some children are more needy. Ask!

Talk to your child. Remember to be *calm*—be composed. Are you neglecting him—not necessarily on purpose, but perhaps unwittingly?

Are you so busy in your own world, especially if you have outside commitments, that your child is starving, not for food or clothes, but for *you*? Does he just need some of your time? Set aside unhurried, uninterrupted, one-on-one time with your child—*his* time. Pick an activity where you will be together, and let your child share in the choosing. Take a Saturday morning or a midweek afternoon, even take time away from a career obligation. Go to a children's museum or eat at a restaurant, but do something that is interactive and that he enjoys. If you go to a movie, go someplace afterward so you can talk—about anything. Make sure you feel you have touched base with your child, and he will, too. Plan on another special event in the near future. Make this a "regular," and it will pay benefits in your relationship with your child.

If you have more than one child, then you must be fair, even though the needs of the individual children will differ. Arrange special outings with each of them to touch base. Each parent can take each child now and then. I promise you these will be very special and memorable moments.

If you are prominent in your community, know that your visibility can be a liability to your children, especially as they enter the community through school and extracurricular activities. If you are a leader or star in your town, make sure your child still has room to be a kid—that he has your permission not to be perfect, but to make mistakes. If you, the parent, are well known in your community, then that community will be watching your child. Now that he is off to school and performing on his own, his behavior will be noted—and may even reflect upon your position. What a burden this can be for both you and your child! It may be more than either can bear.

Make sure your child is not feeling too pressured to "measure up." Work hard to sustain his spontaneity and free spirit. Don't let him be intimidated just because he is being watched. Make sure he can still "breathe." If, in fact, you're under the community's scrutiny, then talk about it as a family. Don't ignore the obvious, because your child may resent you and your position for what it is doing to his life. He may blame you for any misfortune, and his behavior may swing to the opposite pole from yours. Your child knows what standards of behavior are expected. He knows he is not supposed to lie, cheat, steal, injure, or malign—but remember, he is only a kid! Make sure there is a little room for straying. And if and when he strays, remind him of the rules—but don't lay a total guilt trip on him, especially if there is talk about him at the office.

Consider the local preacher's son or the local doctor's daughter. Both are high-visibility children, and both families are professionally linked to their towns, really dependent upon their communities. How can a preacher or a doctor advise others if his or her child is making mistakes? Truthfully, perhaps he or she can advise all the better having had a little trouble at home. Nobody's perfect. And a little humility goes a long way.

School

When your school-aged child (especially a first grader) enters his school building, more than ever before, you as a parent relinquish control. Your child's teacher and school environment will now set standards and measure your child's progress relative to established norms. The teacher will structure a curriculum and set goals for your child. Your child will have very definite responsibilities. He must, simply stated, behave himself, follow directions, conform socially, and do the work required.

A first grader is supposed to learn to read and to complete his assignments. He is also supposed to become a part of the group. All of a sudden, there is a very real evaluation system in place, a grading scale—maybe not actual grades, but some kind of report card on a regular basis. Academic performance, effort, and social adaptability—all will be monitored and rated. The child must answer to his teacher and the demands of the system. The school has rules and regulations of its own that must be obeyed in order to survive. Children must act in an orderly fashion, respect each other, and follow the teacher's cues. The work may be hard and not always fun, but that's life! Work is a reality, and it has to be done.

Now, how better can we prepare our children for school than if, at home, rules, regulations, and expectations have been clear! It will appear only natural to the child who lives with appropriate limit setting to continue with consistent rules at school. Contrariwise, what about the child who has never been disciplined—who knows no boundaries and presumes he can do what he wants, when and where? How does this child function in the school environment? Ask the teacher.

The child who has lived in a calm environment with good parental role models, where all people respect each other—this child should be fine. Remember, the school should be more of an extension of the home—a safe, warm place where children can develop and mature. Hopefully, parents and teacher are giving the same messages and upholding the same standards. Consistency not only at home, but carried over to the school, allows for a constructive environment where your child can grow and learn to trust. Home is still your child's anchor and will remain so through adolescence, if not forever. But school is now a major influence, as well.

With regard to your child's success, ask, is he happy? To quote a friend of mine, "Does your child leave home with a smile and then come back with one?" Likewise, do parents and teacher see the same child in their respective settings? Be it a quiet or active soul, a gregarious or more private personality, if the home and school environments are happy and supportive, your child should feel free to be himself wherever he is. The adults in charge should see consistency in personality and behavior. If not, something's wrong.

Beware of the child who appears very different at school than at home. Take this as a warning that something is not all right. Find out why this is and which environment is unsettling or wrong. Is home unhappy and your child is acting out at school because of it? Or is school too restrictive or not restrictive enough? Make sure your child isn't bored or having trouble focusing. Perhaps he is confused with the expectations or the assignments. Maybe your child is being teased—for whatever reason—by his peers or even by his teacher or by you. Did something happen? Is he having trouble learning? Or is he acting out because no one has ever said no to him?

Listen to yourselves as parents, listen to the teachers, and watch your children. What do you and they observe? Try to figure out why there is a disparity. Then, your job is to fix it as best you can. This can be a very unsettling experience—even a heartbreaking, awful time. The "fault" may or may not be with your child. It may be you, asking too much or too little. It may be the system or a teacher or administration that has not recognized his needs. Psychologically, your child may have a hard time separating from home and difficulty adjusting. There are many, many possibilities.

But fix it you must, to ensure success in the long run. If your child is misbehaving or is unhappy for whatever reason, you cannot ignore the problem and wait until next year comes. Work with your child *and* the school *now* to make things better and happier. School teachers have vast experience and don't miss much. Know that all of you (teachers and parents) have your child's best interest at heart. After all, their goal and yours is the same—to teach your child skills in preparation for a happy, successful life. Work together to bring about success. Seek professional help, if necessary, and work to do the best you can for your child. This will take time and patience, but the rewards are enormous.

Remember that our schools are just that—schools—places for learning reading, writing, and arithmetic. Our schools are not supposed to take the place of parents. The school's objective is to educate. Its mission is not to introduce limit setting, not to instill morals, and not to provide health care and basic nutrition, but rather to support the family unit in these basic goals. The backbone for discipline, moral integrity, health care, and nutrition should come from the home—from the parents. The school is part of the team, in that it should supplement the home but not replace it.

Unfortunately, given disruption at home (including poverty, which exists all too much in America), our schools are having to assume more of the primary parental responsibilities—at the sacrifice of time for education. Of course, without discipline, without respect for others, without good health care and sound nutrition, how can any child learn? How can a teacher teach if a child is hungry—or worse, threatened by violence? Weapons and threats of injury have no place in the school—instead, it should be a place for lunch boxes and completed homework assignments. But until our home environments can provide the foundation children need, I'm afraid the schools are caught in between. Until we can, as a society, establish across-the-board standards and discipline, our schools will pay a price. Ultimately, it is the child (and society) who pays. Work with your child, your school, and your local government to effect change. Make your school a safe place where your child can learn comfortably and thrive.

AFTER SCHOOL

The early school years are very busy—maybe the busiest years of childhood. There are so many opportunities and choices for you and your child. Probably too many! Parents are often surprised, even overwhelmed, by the complex demands placed upon them as they schedule and arrange their school-aged children's lives. In fact, many parents, with good reason, leave the outside workforce at this time because their children now need a full-time, at-home parent. Being a parent takes on a new dimension as you add more assignments to your role, including that of a highly skilled social coordinator and chauffeur.

Your school-aged child may want to do everything—and developmentally, he is ready to try. He can read, he can ride a bicycle, he can throw and kick. He loves being with people. The earlier years were simpler, with life spent at home and/or in day care. Now, as your child is so much more willing and able, the choices for play and study are numerous. And the logistics and planning for these activities get very complicated.

The basics of who, what, when, and where lead to lots of concerns and questions. Ask, as always, is everything safe? Make no assumptions—just like with the toddler. Make sure you know who is supervising. Who provides the transportation, if needed?

Check it out. Is there a cost, and who will pay? Make sure you can afford an added expense. What are your child's buddies doing, and is that a relevant factor?

Life for your school-aged child is not just home and baby-sitter (or child-care)-based but rather community-centered, with lots of changing of places. Parents are often caught unawares as their children's days require a different kind of supervision and organization. As you enter the world of after-school activities, it is often time to reassess your role and make sure that you're still able to do it well. Are you really able to control your life and that of your child—to take advantage of some fun and worthwhile opportunities, yet maintain order and calm? Or, instead, are you and your child stretching too much, trying to squeeze in more—for what?

As parenting becomes more complicated, are you still in charge? Are you really controlling those after-school hours and not letting them control you? Reexamine who or what is driving the household.

The trick is to plan your child's after-school program very carefully—to select activities that are fun and stimulating and that allow growth in a relaxed setting. Choose carefully. Make sure—and here's the real trick—that you still leave some time for unstructured play, for spontaneity. Don't fill every moment or every afternoon with scheduled classes and events. Don't overload your kids. Your child doesn't have to do and take everything—dance, gymnastics, music, sports, and scouts—all at the same time. It's not possible. Seek balance. Make choices. Pace both yourself and your child. More is not better—quality does not come from quantity. You can always try one thing this year, another next year.

Watch for that crowd thing! Try very hard not to fall into the trap of following along just because everyone else is doing something or going somewhere. Even though everyone else is doing Monday afternoon ballet or Saturday morning baseball, it might not be a good activity for your child. Or the idea may be OK but poorly executed. Is the instructor or the coach doing a good job?

As a parent, you must stand on your own two feet and make

your decisions independently. This is a very important message to pass on early. You must do what is best for you and your child. The "crowd" pressure will be constant, especially in later years. But don't be fooled! Don't feel forced into an activity or an event you and/or your child didn't want to do just because it is the more popular course—just because "everyone else" is doing it. Maybe no one else has taken the time (and this happens!) to really assess what is going on, and they were buffaloed, too. If it doesn't seem or feel right to you, don't do it. Remember, parenting is not a popularity contest. Your child may not be happy with you, may not like what you have decided, may not even like *you*. Well, welcome to parenting.

Know that your child will learn to respect your decisions if you are consistent and fair. Take time to explain your position—the whys and why nots. But be prepared for lack of acceptance. Remember, your child may feel differently—and those feelings are always legitimate. He will want to do what everyone else is doing and certainly doesn't want to be the odd man out. (Perish the thought!) He won't like you for making him that.

We've said it before—you're not always your child's best friend. In fact, if provoked enough, your child might verbalize some pretty strong negative feelings about you. So be it—accept the feelings, but hold firm. Work through the process. Do try to remain fair, and you will begin to establish a foundation of rules and expectations that will stand you in very good stead. Have dialogue, but stay in charge. Allow no name calling and no foul language but maybe a few sparks.

After-school time and activities should be fun. As stated previously, make sure you're not overdoing and overdosing, pushing too much to squeeze everything in. Keep competition less than serious. Know that your seven-year-old has many years ahead to focus on more serious sports, music, or dance. Keep the after-school activities easy, not stressful.

You must limit your child's life and thereby keep it under control. Keep constant vigil, or it can run away from you. Spend time calmly sorting out your priorities and options. Respect your child's need and desire for both variety and rest. Recognize that you, too, can only provide so much—be it time, money, or even transportation.

Now, to switch gears a little bit, what about a free afternoon—a play time with a friend? How about a spontaneous gathering? How do you go about arranging it? The answer: carefully! Remember, safety first—always. Buckle those seat belts, wear helmets, learn how to swim, don't talk to strangers, never wander off alone; and most important, make sure a competent parent or adult is supervising constantly.

But how can you guarantee appropriate supervision at another home? You might have to be a little pushy or forward, perhaps a bit of a detective. What if you don't know the other child's family? Remember, you are your child's advocate. Your job is to ensure his safety.

When your child wants to visit a friend, scout out where you're sending or bringing your child ahead of time, if you can. Maybe you and the other child's parent have another friend in common who can give you some information. Or you can go with your child and *stay*—invited or not—if you or your child is unsure about an unfamiliar home setting. Explain to your host or hostess politely that your child requires your presence for a while, anyway. If your host or hostess is sensitive, maybe you'll be offered a cup of tea. If not—if things appear disorganized and you get bad vibrations—take your child home. Don't leave him! Be selective and smart.

Build a relationship with friends and neighbors with whom you and your child are comfortable—do it slowly—and then send your child off to their homes with confidence. Talk about safety issues with the other parents. Don't neglect, out of a misplaced sense of politeness, to ask about where the children play, who's at home, access to emergency care, and whether they know how to reach you—real basics. Ask! One more time, who is in charge? Make sure your child knows how to find you or a backup neighbor if he needs you—for whatever reason. That will give you both a sense of comfort.

Invite your child's friend's family to *your* house, and play hostess or host to both parent and child. Recognize that they probably have similar concerns about you and wonder about safety and kindness in your home. That's good—you have a soul mate.

MEALS

Meals by now should not be an issue, if the groundwork has been laid. But if not, it is never too soon to make mealtime a priority. Meals—meaning breakfast, lunch, and dinner, as well as after-school snacks—should be prepared and served, just as before, at a predictable, regular hour. Your child needs food on a regular basis to grow and concentrate. Make sure you offer the right kind of foods, and then let your child self-select what he wants and therefore needs. Offer essentially the same kind of menu each day—a protein source, a vegetable and/or fruit, a starch, an iron source, then maybe a dessert. Look for balance in color, and you'll probably have balance in nutrients. Don't insist upon a "clean plate," only reasonable choices and behavior. Don't worry about vitamins. Resist buying multivitamin tablets; they're expensive and rarely necessary. If you're concerned about nutrition, ask your doctor for advice. Don't fall victim to someone's marketing efforts for extra anything.

Mealtime should be timely, and food served promptly. The evening meal should take place by 6:30 or earlier, depending on the afternoon snack and/or bedtime. Children should not be made to wait to eat—they need regular calories, and lots of them. Kids should not be allowed to become cranky and headachy from hunger. Whose fault is it if they misbehave for this reason?

Make mealtime a happy time, as with any age group. Use it as a time for sharing, a time of caring and praising. "You did that—that's wonderful!" Let your child share with you what he learned at school. As you talk about your day, give him equal (or extra) time to describe his. Don't make mealtime just an eating event. Make it a social time—casual or formal, but a time together. Remember *time*. It should be relaxed, not stressful, a time of grounding, a time for calm. Even if all family members—both parents or either parent—cannot be there, make sure you or your care provider *sits down* with your child when he is eating.

Mealtime is not a time for the television; it is a time to be with people.

What about the child who resists mealtime? Just as for the younger child, remove all other distractions—no TV, no games, and, certainly, no noisy interference. Warn your child about dinner's impending hour so a favorite activity can be drawn to a close. No surprises! Do sit with your child, if not to eat yourself (you may be waiting for your spouse), at least to share the time. Don't be rushed—be relaxed and happy. Exercise calm and composure. If you have more than one child, have them all eat together. The elements of SECRET can fit very nicely into mealtime: prepare yourself, make peace, be kind and respectful, and give time.

If a meal is refused, or if behavior at table is unacceptable (throwing food, acting out, bad language, or teasing), let your child be excused and go a little bit hungry until the next regularly scheduled meal. I promise you he will not starve. Do not allow your child to eat that meal later at 9:00 P.M. at his convenience or whenever he wants. Now really, who is in charge? Who does the scheduling, the cooking, and the cleaning? The kitchen should close every night. It should reopen in the morning, when everyone may be in a better mood—not at midnight!

Of course, you do want your child to eat properly. If nighttime meals are a constant source of battle, this needs to be discussed with your family and maybe your child's doctor. Mealtime should be happy, a time of gathering together and talking about the day's activities, not a time of bickering and complaining. It should be a time to nourish both the body and the soul.

Bedtime

Just as with the toddler and preschooler, it is nice and comforting for the early school-aged child to have a routine at bedtime—a slowing down, a quiet time, especially one shared with one or both parents. This presupposes that at least one parent is home and available for the nighttime ritual, which is just not always possible. But do the best you can, and make sure it is a parent *most* of the time. In your absence, your surrogate—a grandparent, a baby-sitter, whoever is with your child—can follow the same routine. But keep a routine in place, and keep it simple.

I would aim at thirty minutes for settling down and in—to include bath (as needed), putting away toys and clothes, thinking about the morning, and, finally, the story time. Pack up your child's school papers and lay out the morning clothes; do as much as you can at night to make the mornings easier. Try as parents to make bedtime stories a sacred, protected time. This is time together and also a time of learning—a time to imagine, explore, and talk, just as in earlier years. Let your child do some of the reading as his own skills are developing; praise him and help him. Respect him. Know that the stories do not always have to be read. You can make up your own or play make-believe and share in the pretending. "Once upon a time there was a . . . [and your child can participate]." Maybe even play or sing some music. What the bedtime hour (or half hour) should *not* include is busy, active, excited play. Nothing scary or stressful. Remember, you are preparing your child for sleep.

For the child who has a difficult time with bedtime, make sure this is the child's difficulty and not the parent's. Make sure you as the parent are able to separate from your child and are not giving mixed signals. Then, as earlier, pick a very specific time for that last kiss or good night and hold to it. Use a timer, leave on some music, or whatever, but be out of your child's bedroom at your appointed hour and before your child falls asleep. Help him to settle himself (just as in the early newborn period). If your child has scary thoughts about monsters or burglars, stay close by on the same floor. Make sure he knows you are within hearing range. Let him keep on a low-level light or night-light. Let him have his own flashlight, as well as a cuddly blanket or stuffed animal. Reassure him that he is not the only child with scary thoughts—perhaps you did the same when you were young. Check under beds and in closets before the last good night. Consider putting star and moon glow-in-the-dark stickers on the ceiling for special attention—to watch over your child while he sleeps. Depending upon your faith path, prayers and trust in God can be reassuring. Assure your child that he is never really alone.

Still, your child may resist. He may not want to miss out on any activity going on with the awake members of the family. He may be a real night owl and require little sleep. Or he may be generally unhappy, and that unhappiness surfaces at night. Whatever the reason, try to bring any busyness in the family to a conclusion before your child goes to bed. Try to wrap it up for everyone—which probably makes sense, anyway. It may be time for everyone to gear down.

If some fun or activity does persist after your child goes to bed, don't make it a big deal. Involve him before bedtime, and warn him about the hour as bedtime approaches. Make sure he gets his due—his turn—before having to leave. You don't want to purposely exclude your child from ongoing fun, but you don't want to penalize everyone else, either. Just because Mary, who is seven, has to go to bed, that doesn't mean that Johnny, who is twelve, has to stop everything. At the same time, Johnny can be taught to be tactful and kind to Mary. Johnny probably has homework to do, anyway. And what's wrong with his reading a book?

If your child is resisting bedtime because of unhappiness during the day, or because he really needs more of your time, explore that. Discuss your child's feelings. Take time to sort out any difficulties or upsets. And finally, as the goal of a successful bedtime is achieved, reward your child. Give stickers, an ice cream cone, a special card ("I am proud of you"), but don't overdo. If your child regresses, you don't want to breed more anxiety and feelings of failure. Instead, say, "Whoops, we can do this," and go back to the beginning.

The Bathroom

Personal habits like washing, cleaning, and toileting are usually mastered tasks by age six or seven, but not always. In particular, bathroom function—with attention toward bladder control and regular stooling—may not be fully attained. As a pediatrician, I can tell you that many, many normal school-aged girls and boys have episodes of bedwetting and soiling. Many school-aged children are not able to hold their urine overnight, and many have problems with evacuation. Enuresis—the involuntary release of urine, or "wetting"—is seen in many school-aged children, especially at night. You will often find a strong family history of bed-wetting—usually a parent or someone else in the family had the same experience. It is important to know that it is no one's fault and probably has a physiological basis. The problem develops when we see "wetting" as a problem and blame the child for his lack of control. The child goes to sleep, probably sleeps very soundly, and does not waken to the signal of a full bladder. Whether he is missing a hormone signaling urine retention (which may be the case) or not, this child will wet. His days are probably dry, and his internal anatomy (kidney and bladder) is probably normal, but he still wets. I can only counsel you to make this not a problem. Time and patience will take care of it. Use plastic liners on the bed or use disposable pads; make no big deal about washing sheets. Disposable pull-ups are also available in older children's sizes. Do not stigmatize your child. Talk to your child's doctor. Know that bedwetting is not uncommon, and your child needs your support, not criticism. Bedwetting alarms are available, but there's no quick fix. Restricting fluids or waking your child before you go to bed may work, but probably not. Special prescription medications, even nose sprays, are now available but are usually reserved for the older child whose life is adversely affected by restrictions on sleep overs, overnight camp, or sleeping in a bed other than his own. The important points: do not punish your child, and seek professional help as needed. Respect the fact that this is involuntary.

With regard to stooling, leaking of stool, chronic constipation, or difficulty with evacuation may surface in the school-aged child. Prior suspicion or evidence of a potential problem may have been there, but signs are often subtle and noted better in retrospect. The soiling seven-year-old may have been a constipated baby. Know that the school-aged child with stooling problems is not to be taken lightly—nor blamed, nor scolded. But the problem does need your full attention. And it needs his doctor's involvement as well, for a careful evaluation of your child. This includes a thorough physical exam as well as evaluation of his diet, activity, and bathroom habits. Sometimes a laboratory test or two may be performed—a sample of urine and one of stool for culture—but not a whole battery of tests. The diagnosis is usually not hard to make, but the treatment can be difficult.

The important question to answer is, how did your child get "stuck"? Does your child hold stool—and has he always—and why? Is he afraid to poop because it hurts? Maybe he once had an accident and was teased. Examine his diet—see if it's rich in binders (dairy foods and starch) and weak in grains or fiber. If so, change it. Check the caliber of your child's stool—soft or hard? Make sure your child takes time to poop—sits on the commode twice a day to encourage stooling. If he's a "couch potato" type of kid whose body (and gut) is rather immobile, increase his activity level. Look for leaking around impacted stool that has probably been there forever. Perhaps the gut innervation is abnormal. Your doctor will have to determine this.

These are all questions and concerns that need to be addressed with your doctor, with or without the consultation of a specialist. Attention has to be focused on these very real issues. Bowel function can have a very negative effect upon your child's overall development and happiness. Self-esteem is affected. You cannot ignore this issue! Children who leak smell. Their schoolmates will notice and then tease and/or exclude them. It can be a very vicious cycle.

The limit you must set is on yourself—to work through this problem, to allow patience, to make this a priority. Be on your child's side. Take lots of time to work it out, and get help.

• • •

You should enjoy the company of your young school-aged child. Watch and relish the person you are helping to mold. But realize that he is still his own person with questions and observations of his own. Keep home life calm—simple, secure, and predictable. Be there for him, now and forever. Monitor his school behavior, mood, and performance. Maintain respect for his individuality, and give him time. Allow for his world to expand—but with control. As always, remember SECRET.

6

The Late School-Aged Child

(ages ten to twelve)

The older school-aged child is reaching a new plateau. She will and can function *almost* like an adult. This child can reason, can check her emotions, can take care of her own personal needs. She can assume greater responsibility for herself and help more within the family. She is less dependent upon you for her day-to-day needs. However, she still needs you—but in different ways. The hitch is that your child is only "almost" grown up.

Your ten- to twelve-year-old is not ready to assume adult behavior. Believe it or not, she is still in basic training—just no longer a new recruit. She still requires supervision and must answer to that code of rules and ethics that you have defined. Your child still needs you to show her the way and to check her behavior. Just like the teen years that follow, these preadolescent years are marked by change and increasing peer identity and pressure. Your child will challenge you, the parent, more—as well as the "system." And in that setting, it is time for you to allow for some letting go, while still holding the line. This is a preview of the teen years, when the very same issues and concerns begin to expand. For now, it is vitally important that you continue to make time for your child, continue to exercise calm, and, more than ever, demonstrate, demand, and then reinforce acceptable behavior. Remember, it is a building process. We start early with the very young child and build through each and every developmental stage. The foundation for rules and regulations should be set early, preferably in the toddler and preschool years. But if you're a little bit behind, better to do some catch-up work *now*. Don't forget to say no—gently but firmly. And expect a few blowups.

SECRET

So let's review SECRET for the late school-aged child. Remember those key guidelines: SE for *self*, C for *calm*, RE for *respect*, and T for *time*.

Self

Just as before, you really must be comfortable with your own self. Know thyself—respect yourself. Know that your child will be watching you more than ever and comparing you to other adult figures—teachers, coaches, scout leaders, and other parents. What does she see from you? We must recognize that our behavior patterns will set a very real example for our children. We, as parents, need to stay in charge of our own words, actions, and behaviors, or our children will learn more about hypocrisy than consistency. Your child needs you for a very real constant—a dependable anchor—especially now, with adolescence right around the bend.

Reexamine your own demands and codes of behavior; even discuss them with your child. Do some moral game playing ("What if . . .") and talk about honesty and integrity. Be open to challenge from your child, but with the understanding that you are ethically sure, in mind and action, about yourself. You are, hopefully, in control.

Calm

Don't forget about calm. Remember, your child may be developing some labile, unpredictable behavior. After all, this is preadolescence. This is the warm-up! So it is important that you keep yourself in check. Think "peace," "calm," "composure." Don't be in a hurry to rush anything—breathe evenly. Be the very best role model you can.

Watch that your child is relaxed, feeling good about herself, and at peace—not moving at a frenetic pace. Make sure pressures from home, school, and community are not overwhelming. Maintain control by checking for calm.

Respect

The respect you have always had for your child will be challenged as you must give her more room to spread her wings. Do you trust your child? Do you honor her by allowing her to make decisions? Think about the image of the control "pie"—more and more pieces being shared with your child, as she takes on more and more responsibility for her own behavior.

Respect your child's choices (just as before), her friends, and her activities. Respect her ability to achieve—but also support her *effort* when achievement may fall short. After all, what is "short"? Make expectations for school and extracurricular activities realistic. Respect your child! Help her as best you can. Provide structure, limit her commitments.

Time

As always, you have to be available for your preteen. Don't be an absentee parent, spending more time at the office, on the tennis court, out of town, on committee work, or on the phone! Don't cause your child to say, "My Mom's never home anyway!" or "My Dad doesn't have a clue."

The patterns are set early and then reinforced over time. Set the stage for your developing child. If you have been sincere in making time for your child, your child will recognize your caring. You may not agree—but at least you care. Your child needs to know that. There is no better way to be a constant in your child's life than by giving of your time. Your presence counts. And as you're looking ahead toward the teen years, the more you can do to lay a firm foundation and keep the lines of communication open *now*, the better success you will have in guiding your child through the morass of the teens. That all takes time.

As always, spend time, make time, and don't cheat time. Be there for your child—not as a slave, but as a nurturing, committed parent.

Now the specifics. Let's look at a few age-specific issues as we apply the principles of SECRET.

Behavior

The ten-year-old child should, by now, be a working member of the family, with her own accountability. Just as parents have their own jobs and responsibilities—providing income and maintaining a home, being available—your preteen is now old enough to participate more and more in the daily functioning of the household. This means taking on new responsibilities—even jobs for her!

At home your preteen's role should be clearly defined as she becomes a less dependent member of the household and a more participatory one. This is a time when assigned chores can become more complex and even physically taxing, especially as your child grows in size and strength. But chores still need to be fun and fair—not onerous. They don't have to dominate the household, nor take all of a Saturday or holiday, but there's nothing wrong with an hour or two committed to sharing the load. Everyone needs to share in the delegation and execution of those chores. Mom, Dad, sister, and brother all should play a part.

Some eleven- and twelve-year-olds are really big—even bigger than their parents. Working both indoors and out, they can help with some serious heavy-duty snow shoveling and/or yard cleanup, even help move furniture, hang curtains, or clean windows. Daily jobs like the dog or the garbage or the newspaper or the dishes, as well as weekly responsibilities (the lawn or parts of the house) need to be hers, at least in part. Recognize that the intent is not to abuse, not to burden, but rather to teach "there is no free ride." It's OK and proper to get help for ourselves from our children and to prepare them for the running of their own households. Respect the fact that your child is capable—take pride in her effort, her contribution. Let her know that you notice and that you care.

The bedroom is often an area of confrontation and conflict. Whose bedroom is it, after all? Whose house? You may not agree, but I feel strongly that a child's bedroom should be kept tidy, but not necessarily spotless. It doesn't have to be perfect, but how about generally in good order? Remember, it may be her room, but it is still *your* house! You pay the rent or mortgage, and you set the standards. (Make sure your room is neat, too.) You might get some argument here, but I feel strongly about parents maintaining the last word. Your child should not live in a sty, unless you like it that way. At the same time, there should be no hysterics—just gentle direction from you. Don't forget about SECRET—calmly spend time with your child maintaining a safe and clean space for her.

At home, teach both sons and daughters how to cook—even the basics will come in handy eventually. Make sure all your children know how to use the dishwasher, washing machine, and dryer. Show them where the main water supply to the house is located—you never know when a pipe may burst. Let them become familiar with fuses or circuit breakers—they are old enough.

Try not to separate or delineate chores as boy and girl jobs. A job is a job—with no gender bias. Certainly, the job doesn't care. The only limitation would be strength. (See "Household Chores," Chapter 8.)

The preteen can even do some child care—preferably with you close by. By twelve years of age, your child can be left alone with a younger sibling or other young child for short periods of time. She can become a full-fledged baby-sitter, as you ease her into that position of responsibility. Teach her to develop and use common sense, what to do in emergencies, and whom to call when frightened or injured. Teach her some basic first aid—even CPR. You will be amazed at the capacity of this preteen child to take on responsibility, if you let her. Always leave backup—yourself or an available neighbor—and watch your child grow and succeed. Acknowledge her success. Give her the opportunity to demonstrate her developing skills.

By ten years of age, your child can take complete responsibility for herself in the morning. Be it her waking up, getting ready for school (dressing, eating), and/or arriving at school (or the bus stop) on time, she's old enough to do it herself. Her personal habits should not require supervision—from bathing to toileting. No longer should she need you, the parent, to supervise her every move. (Nor does the six-year-old, for that matter.) The ten- to twelve-year-old should be able to find what she needs and in the time allotted. If not, help *her* work on the solution. You can help; you can suggest workable options—but resist taking over. If your child is late rising or slow in getting organized, give her an alarm clock. Set it thirty minutes ahead of her usual waking time. Place it across the room, not next to her bed—make her get out of bed to turn it off. Have her pick out her school clothes the night before. Leave enough time for breakfast, and have breakfast ready for her. Make it nutritious, with lots of carbohydrates and protein for your growing child. Greet her nicely—remember calm—and be relaxed yourself! Be there for support, but not to nag. And then see what happens. I know that mornings can be very complicated. Our job, as parents, is to keep them simple. After all, it is the start of a new day.

Packing for school may need a little checking, but you shouldn't have to pack her bag for her. If your child tends to lack organization, try to anticipate her needs the night before and guide her properly.

If your preteen is late or forgets something, you can cover for her once in a while, but don't always bail her out. If she wants or needs something, let her figure out the solution. Don't let her ruin *your* day just because she couldn't get ready for school on time. It's not your fault. Don't *you* go running up and down flights of stairs and go into a complete panic on her behalf because she cannot find her sneakers for gym class or because she forgot an assignment. Remember, you are not your child's slave—not her cover. You're her parent. It's time she takes responsibility for herself. She might have to miss gym and/or take that detention. If she forgot to complete an assignment for school, she must deal with that. Help her to prevent its happening again, but with her input, not just yours. It's time she learn the consequences of not planning her time well. Help her, but don't shelter her.

If, despite your very best efforts, mornings are a bust for you and your ten- to twelve-year-old, look deeper. Is there a reason why? Is your child unhappy at school, and the mere thought of going off in the morning paralyzes her? Look for the cause. And then work to figure out what you can do about it. Certainly do some conferencing with her teachers and/or counselors. And finally, if appropriate, try a different morning routine. But just make sure you're not playing into your child's hands. You are supposed to be in charge!

Don't forget, you are your child's parent—the one to guide and mold, not serve from dawn to dusk without question. You love your child, but your job is not to fulfill her every need or whim; rather it is to enable her to achieve her own goals. Just as there are limits to behavior, there are limits to your parenting role. Don't wait on your child hand and foot—don't foster dependence upon yourself. Rather, allow your child the time and space to take care of herself. Let her make mistakes. Your child has a mind and has legs. She can think out solutions and run her own errands. Remember *respect*—it's time to respect your child's own ability.

Do remember the word *no*—it still has a place. Use it judiciously, but use it, nevertheless. "Mom, will you get me my homework assignment—it's upstairs?" The answer—unless your child is physically impaired—is no. Remember, your child can motor upstairs even more easily than you. She can also clean up her own room—clean up her own mess, wherever it is.

And finally, don't let your child order you around, *ever*—just as you would never order her. The fact is, no one should order anyone in the household. How can that show respect? Bossing, fresh talk, and swearing should not be tolerated. Sit your children down, be straight with them, and make it very clear where your boundaries lie. If she doesn't get the message, ground her. Deny her something—take away a weekend activity or cut off the phone privileges, but do something.

During the preteen years, it is now time to begin including your child on the adult side of the fence. She is no longer a baby or young child whose needs are primarily physical, but rather an emerging adult who has lots to offer. Take advantage (if you haven't already) of your child's developing maturity, her clear mind, her energy, and her capacity for fun. Include her in your "adult" conversations—ask her for her opinion. Listen to her. Talk with her about current events—recent sporting or entertainment items. Seek out her input. Extend an open invitation to her to join in on almost everything. Let her know that you enjoy and value her company, always. Welcome her, as well as her buddies.

Plan lots of outings and plan them together. (Don't forget *time*.) Let your preteen share in the delegation of responsibilities. If you're going camping, let her help plan where. Together, look at what needs to come along—who will bring and do what. Who can and should carry the food? Who will pitch the tent? Who will read the map? Your child knows. By sharing these responsibilities, you show respect for her and build on her ability to make decisions. You honor her.

As we are all working so hard to build within our children a sense of responsibility and independence, remember that there are limits to what we should ask. Test the waters—make sure your child is happy in her expanding role as a more grown-up member of the household. She doesn't have to be smiley faced all the time, but make sure you don't push too much. Praise her for a job well done, and help constructively where she may have fallen short. Always assume your child is trying, and work positively with her to be successful. Try not to criticize, but rather discuss situations constructively. And finally, know that this growing child can provide you with enormous fun and companionship as you include her in more activities and expect more in return. Keep the door open to her always.

Some of these young girls and boys are learning hobbies like hunting, fishing, or sewing or are concentrating on music or sports with serious plans for the future. Their studies at school are becoming increasingly important, as achievement will have an impact on future learning and career choices. It is a time for us, as adults, to support growth but keep a lid on our child's activities. Remember, your child must still have some time to play— to be spontaneous. She still needs to have a "life"! Watch that you and she are not overdoing it. Watch and prevent burnout—that is your role. Just as with the younger school-aged child, don't overcrowd her schedule—don't overburden her day. If necessary, you may have to step in and restrict activity—set limits—for the well-being of your child. (See "Schedules," Chapter 10.) Don't worry about your popularity; rather, worry about your child.

The late school-aged child is often into collecting—be it stamps, coins, postcards, baseball cards, dolls, insects, shells, or whatever. It certainly is appropriate to encourage some kind of collecting and cataloging. A lifetime collection of anything is worth having and can be a vehicle for learning, as well. It can be a shared activity, bringing parent and child together, as long as the child is truly interested.

Likewise, a hobby—photography, fishing, boating, sailing—can be seriously pursued at this age. Children are naturally curious and can begin to develop lifelong skills now. Just always make sure that, whatever your child is doing, safety is provided. You, as the parent, *must* still ask questions, always, about water safety, adult supervision, and injury prevention—take *nothing* for granted. Make sure someone is watching—anticipating accidents so they can be avoided. Just as before, you only get your children once; assume nothing.

Weapons—be they firearms or knives—have a certain appeal to preteens. I can only implore parents to discourage exposure to weapons—have no guns in the house! But if hunting is a way of life for you, and your child will be handling a gun, then teach your child how and when to use a firearm—but under the strictest control and supervision. Never leave a loaded weapon at home. Unload and lock up both guns and ammunition. Know that kids *do* find those weapons—not necessarily to use or to be malicious, but out of a sense of curiosity or through some "macho" drive. Look at the statistics, and see the number of injuries and deaths caused by children "playing" with guns. These accidents are not true accidents—they should have been prevented. This is not a "right to bear arms" argument, but a safety issue—innocent victims are being killed.

Some kids love to whittle, and I think a ten-year-old can be allowed to do this. Again, you are the parent who has the final say on this matter. Under controlled circumstances, with clear respect for the knife, whittling can be fun. But the knife must be used safely.

As always, success at home will depend upon your ability to run a smooth household. A calm environment, with conscious time for your children (do you have an eye on your watch or your child?) and respect for each member of your family will provide the best foundation for your preteen. As always, the mood or tone is key. Remember SECRET. Provide, as best you can, a comfortable environment for your child—let her feel at ease.

School and Homework

School life for your preteen should now be an established routine. School should be a happy and stable environment (see Chapter 5), with predictability. If not, you must investigate—find out why. Just as before, you have a responsibility to ensure your child's success.

What's new for preteens is the homework! As your child advances through school, homework becomes more and more important, demanding more time and effort from both you and your child. But remember—your child's homework is hers, not yours. It is important that you not do it for her. Rather, you can help your preteen design an appropriate plan, a study time and place that will work for *her* to complete the tasks assigned. Help your child follow through, by supporting with a firm but gentle hand. If the plan fails, then regroup and talk about it. Spend time trying to figure out why it isn't working. Are your expectations too great for your child? Does she really need a little more help from you in setting a schedule and then keeping to it? Eliminate distractions when it is supposed to be homework time. Don't let your house become Grand Central Station in the late afternoon and early evening with people and noise constantly present. Is your child used to being part of the activity and very reluctant to pull away for homework? Is she too tired?

Make homework a priority—set boundaries. Find a quiet place, make it neat, set a time, and allow no interruptions such as phone calls or snacks, and then see if your child isn't doing better.

Know that sometimes an unacceptable or substandard performance with homework can be an indicator of general poor performance at school. Maybe school is really not going well and is a real problem (identified or not) for your child. Maybe your child is having similar difficulty with her assignments at school—either with the understanding or the completion of assigned tasks. Perhaps your child is unhappy or unfocused—confused or bored—in her classroom. If your child is not successful with homework, you must be in touch with her teacher to ask and investigate. Don't wait for a scheduled parent-teacher conference. If you suspect or think a problem may exist, you are obligated to investigate. After all, you are your child's advocate wherever she may be. Your responsibility is to optimize your child's environment so that she can succeed. You must ask appropriate questions of her and of her teacher. It's OK to be concerned and involved—you are supposed to do that.

EXTRACURRICULAR ACTIVITIES

The older school-aged child often has many interests. Sometimes channeling and/or sustaining those interests is a real challenge. Clearly, a ten-year-old has the ability to participate in choosing what sports and activities to pursue. The challenge for the parent (just as before; see Chapter 5) is to keep the choices limited—to have balance, not to overload, and now, to see that there is some kind of consistent follow-through. If your ten-year-old plays on a soccer team, that means practices and games are a definite commitment. Are you both (child and family) able to honor that commitment? Or is there a conflict? Choices may have to be made. Is there room for compromise? As before, don't fall into the "more is better" trap. It's not!

If your twelve-year-old is taking music lessons—is the practicing being done? And if practicing is resisted, why? Is practice time a real battle? For sure, any practice is better than none, but the mood has to be right. Can a compromise be made?

Beware of stopping as well as starting. Once begun, don't hurry into giving up on the piano or flute—or any instrument or sport—because of frustration. How much is your child complaining, and why? Know that once formal lessons or sessions have stopped, one rarely goes back. Progress usually comes to an immediate halt. Know that it is really for you, the parent, to decide when your child should stop anything. You can make compromises, even ease up on an already crowded schedule. Make sure the teacher or coach is competent but not too pushy. Stretch out the lesson schedule to one every other week. The delicate part is trying to figure out how much to push or not. (See "The Very Gifted Child," Chapter 9.)

Try to figure out what is best for your child—for now and the long run. Will your child ultimately regret stopping? If she is under too much pressure to perform and measure up, and what used to be fun is no longer that, it may be time to slow down, even stop. Try to answer these concerns as best as you can. Spend some time on this issue. Your child's schedule is very important and will influence her greatly. Remember SECRET—find what works for all of you, discuss the issues or options with calm, respect your child's wishes, and take time to work through the process.

As your child spreads her wings, remember to be a part of your child's world. Be available to attend her games and/or performances. *Be there*—even on the periphery—visible but not intrusive. Maintain a presence without being overbearing. The boundaries—where you stand and sit, what you say and don't say (i.e., commend but not necessarily coach)—are a little blurred when it comes to your child's efforts. But mostly, I think it is important to be around, to show your child that you care. And finally, compliment your child on a job well done. Praise whatever performance your child has given. Whatever the outcome, win or lose, just as with household chores, you can be sure your child is trying. She wants to do her best, too. Remember to commend your child often.

Peers

By age ten, eleven, and twelve, friends—i.e., peers—take on an increasingly significant role in your child's life. Life outside the home becomes more and more important. Peer group pressure becomes a growing force, exerting its own set of demands and controls, only to peak in the teen years. Peer issues become complicated. "Popularity" can be a major thing. Tears get shed (by everybody, I promise you!) as popularity shifts take place every day. Preteens may feel, "No one likes me." We all have those days.

So be prepared. Remember, as always, it is important for you to honor your child's ability to choose friends, as well as activities. If you have been successful in teaching and modeling the appropriate rules of behavior, your child should have little trouble choosing her own friends and actions—hopefully with like-minded standards. She should know what codes of behavior are acceptable and expected—kindness, honesty, respect for others—and then develop a peer group with the same attitudes and ethics. But even if there is conflict or, rather, some rebellion, you must give your child the freedom to choose and, eventually, to demonstrate her own competence. Remember, your child's friends are *hers*, not necessarily yours. You cannot choose them, anyway. She has her own needs and preferences, so support her in her choices. Respect goes both ways—she for you, and you for her. Show it, and hang loose. Be there.

Invite your preteen's friends to your home, and be there to welcome them. Let them feel the warmth and comfort of your home so they know they are truly welcome. Let your child see that you honor, and hopefully approve, her selection of buddies. Be "cool," just not too cool. Listen to yourself and monitor your own tone of voice when speaking to your preteen about her friends. Make sure you're sincere—don't fake it!

Watch out and monitor parties. Who's home and who's supervising? What kind of gathering is it, anyway? Know that there is no need to rush into the boy/girl thing yet. Coed parties can escalate into trouble already. Kissing, petting, smoking, drinking—even intercourse—they happen even in junior high school! Say no to these gatherings and spare your child!

Remain a part of your child's life as she expands her world. The teenage years are right around the corner—this is your last chance to bond before peers really take over. Let your child see that you take notice of her, and that you care. You want to build a strong alliance—almost a partnership as well as a support role—which will serve you very well in later years.

CHANGE

Physical and emotional changes are important in your preteen's life as she or he begins to approach maturity. The late school-aged child is preadolescent, and now, new feelings may become very powerful as the child's body begins to change. Hormones, particularly in the preadolescent female (later for boys), can produce mood swings—a new experience for every child and parent. Body changes may not be welcomed, especially if your child begins to mature early. This can be hard. Your child may not be emotionally ready for change, but you cannot slow down the course of nature. You and your child may be very comfortable in your roles at age nine, but watch out for years ten through twelve. Physical change is inevitable—and does take place. Breasts bud, hips start to round out; male genitals begin to enlarge. Hormones flow.

A great resource for open discussion about body changes is your doctor—but also tap into the schools (sex education courses) and the local library and/or bookstore (get books with lots of pictures). Leave books and articles in your child's room. Sprinkle her or him with information.

As a parent, be available for questions, and answer them as well as you can. Educate your son and daughter about changes in both sexes. Tell your child about menstruation and wet dreams, so there will be no surprises or frights. Explain about sex and how babies are made. Try not to be embarrassed about delicate issues, particularly about intercourse and passions.

If you are uncomfortable about these discussions, tell your preteen just that. After all, he or she will sense it anyway. Just be open about your discomfort being the problem and not the subject material. Becoming informed is only right and fair for your child.

Recognize that if you are able to have open and relatively comfortable conversation now, it will be easier to follow up in later years with the real nitty-gritty. How can you have a successful discussion about sex—pregnancy, sexually transmitted diseases—in the teen years if you've never approached the subject before? You can, but it will be more difficult. It's always better to lay a little groundwork now—that is your job. It takes time and compassion, as well as commitment.

MEALS

The preadolescent is hungry! She or he is growing and needs to eat—lots! So stock the pantry with extra bread, cereal, peanut butter, and fruit. Make sure food is nutritious and abundant, as a child at this age is nibbling all the time. Snacks will be mini-meals, and meals should provide lots of calories, protein, and vitamins. Your child needs lots of everything and will count on you to provide.

Mealtime should be smooth and peaceful and remain a time of sharing. Just as before, take pride in serving nutritious, attractive meals, where you welcome the time together. As schedules get busier, and dinnertime more complicated, save time for dinner as a family. Remember, nothing makes home a nicer place than lots of good food and a relaxed atmosphere. Not only will your child look forward to coming home, but her friends will join in, too, as word gets around.

BEDTIME

Bedtime should be an appropriate hour (8:00 to 10:30 P.M.) determined by you the parent and adhered to by the child. Hopefully, by age ten, a bedtime routine of shower or bath and time to unwind (with story, reading, or music) has been well established, so there shouldn't be any surprises. Your child should know the rules. Lights definitely go off at the appointed hour—and stay off. Your child should be able to settle herself, but a good-night kiss and hug with a special moment of sharing with you is still a good idea. Remember, you are still the parent. A time together is still a cherished moment. Tell your child you love her, and tuck her in. Grab these special moments together always.

Make sure that your child falls asleep easily. If not, ask why. Is her sleep fretful and uneven or quiet and steady? How easily does she arise in the morning? Do pay attention to her sleeping habits, especially if there is tension at home or at school. They can be very telling.

• • •

The late school-aged child understands a lot about fairness and justice, but she or he may be rather perplexed by some of the unfairness and injustice in our world. Certainly, we as adults have a hard time with this as well. The truth is that life is often painful, hard as that may sound. People get sick and sometimes die; adults lose their jobs, even though they may have worked faithfully and competently. War, poverty, violence, and strife exist. Without being a conveyor of doom, you can begin to let your child know that we don't have answers and explanations for everything. And like it or not, we cannot control external circumstances. We do the best we can, and sometimes that has to suffice. Life is hard and not perfect, and there are no guarantees.

How do you softly pass this message on to your child? First, what is most important in life? The answer is each other—the love and support we give. For what are riches and wealth worth if we cannot be happy with one another? There is an old saying: success is measured not by your bank account, but by the measure of love, peace, and happiness in your life. If we are successful as parents in establishing a warm environment with clearly defined rules and boundaries, then maybe this kind of success will be not only ours, but our children's. Then they can bring happiness and love into their world and maybe right some wrongs.

The preteen years mark the end of early and middle childhood. The groundwork you have worked so hard to lay—working and being together as a family, learning to trust, beginning to be independent, setting limits on your behavior, as well as your child's—should now pay its benefits. Your efforts to maintain SECRET will show. The fruit of your labor will be collected very soon—in adolescence!

7

The
Teenager/
Adolescent

The teenage years, at long last! This is what we have been waiting for. If ever there is a time when you, as the parent, have to figure out what works for you and your family and what doesn't, it's now. If ever there is a time when you must exercise calm and control, respect your child as an individual, be available, and leave time for him, it is *right now*. Adolescence brings its own set of challenges.

Looking back, reflect upon your own pilgrimage as a parent. At some time there was probably an ominous cloud hovering on your horizon, a black cloud filled with mystery and conflict. It was called the cloud of adolescence. Well, here you are.

"Wait until he is a teenager!" How many times did you hear that? How often were you reminded that your little darling toddler would one day turn thirteen? Once upon a time, you had an adorable, innocent child. Now you have an adolescent!

Certainly things do happen in adolescence that are unique to the teen years—just as with every other developmental stage. But there is no reason to fear this period. If you as parents have done your work, then these years with an almost-adult should be rewarding, not necessarily turbulent. If you have spent true quality time with your child, worked hard to be fair and honest, and taught and demonstrated the principles of kindness and respect, you can cash in on your efforts. If you have set appropriate limits and talked openly, you can expect consistent behavior.

If, however, you have not done such a good job—if you've been capricious, unpredictable, unfair, and self-centered—you can bet that your teen will be looking to stretch beyond your limits and even his.

Adolescence is a time of risk taking: sex, drugs, alcohol, cigarettes, weapons, car rides—do you know where your child is? That is perhaps why it is so dangerous and feared. The threats—of violence, venereal disease, AIDS, pregnancy—are real. The risks are enormous, involving high stakes—lives!

The risks are not only those taken actively by your child, but those that by chance will cross his path. He has achieved adult stature and physical maturity, but with the inexperience of his youth, he lacks the wisdom of an adult. He feels he is beyond reproach, untouchable, in control of himself and his environment. Right? No, wrong!

SECRET

Let's look one last time at those elements of SECRET as they apply to the teenager.

Self

Remember again that you, as well as your child, are an individual, with your own code of ethics—your own standards of behavior. By now, your child should know very well what your expectations of him are and where the line is drawn for acceptable behavior. You've spent thirteen years drawing those lines—figuring out what works for you, what matters. Now it's time to stand firm, to hold to what you believe is right and appropriate. Believe in yourself—trust yourself as a parent. Follow your instincts.

Know how much leeway you are willing to give your teen.

Where is your "comfort zone"? Where is his? Talk to each other—to your child, to your spouse. Be very concrete about the household rules and expectations and your various roles in the community.

Feel good about the limits you are setting. Feel good about yourself.

Calm

Just as before, it is vital that you maintain your composure. Teen years can be explosive. Remember, it only adds to any confusion if you are out of control. It never helps if *you're* exploding. You may not like some of the things your teen does, nor approve of his behavior or friends or dress, but nevertheless, you must maintain your own calm and composure in dealing with any issue. Your adolescent is looking to you for stability—you may be the only stable element in his changing and challenging world. If he can't depend upon you, then what? It behooves us as parents to remain in control of ourselves, despite what gets thrown our way.

Let your teen know that, no matter what happens, you are there to help or support him through anything. You are a constant. Reassure with calm; demonstrate patience. You are his family, with unconditional love and support for him. Let your teen know that there is always a home to come home to—a place to restore and renew.

Respect

Respect your teen's capacity for making decisions in matters from schoolwork to dating. Do set appropriate standards: curfews, household responsibilities, and school and community objectives. Involve your teen in these discussions. Respect his ability to make choices and to make friends—and as always, support him as he finds his way.

Remember the "pie" representing control, with slices divided between you, the parents, and your child? Let your teen have the whole pie—serve it up—but you keep the pie plate. You keep the pieces together. You can be the stable force.

More than ever, respect your child as an individual. Make space for him. Don't crowd him. Know that he is not you.

Time

Time—your time, your teen's time—don't forget that your adolescent needs *you*. He needs to know you will make time for him—not just to see him off to school or drive him to an activity, but to talk and to share ideas.

The problem with the teen years is that you really never know when your teen might need or want you. Let's say, it might be 50 percent of the time—but *which* 50 percent? Your 50 percent or his? So be available, or at least reachable, *all* the time. Let him know that. Always take his phone calls whenever and wherever he calls. Don't let time be a pressure in your relationship with your teen. Don't give the impression that you don't have time for him. Quite the contrary.

Check in with your adolescent—show him that you care. Leave messages, send a card, or purchase little gifts (a magazine, a set of batteries). Take time to plan activities together—lunch, shopping, or a sporting event. Know that peers might take precedence—but not always. And that should be OK.

Think about SECRET—it can help set the right tone in your home. Think about what your teen sees in you, his parent. Try to be objective about your home and family. Welcome your teen and his friends with a calm presence. Now, let's consider specific adolescent issues.

Behavior

The adolescent years are a time of testing and experimentation, more than ever. It is a time of enormous temptation and independent choice. It is a time when you must give more and more space to your child to make his own decisions and then deal with the consequences.

School, friends—your child is now empowered to determine his choices in each arena. But you, as his parent, are not quite ready to give him total free rein. In fact, it is too soon to say, "You're completely on your own." But the truth is that your teen is *almost* on his own. By now he should know what you expect and why. He should have developed his own code of behavior—

his own morals. But—and here's the catch—they may or may not coincide with yours. Well, you have to choose your battles.

Perhaps the hardest thing a parent has to do is give space to that kid who just doesn't fit the mold—be it your mold or the school's. Beware: ask, are we, as parents, imposing our values and goals on a child who wants to go a different, but not necessarily wrong or contrary, path?

Does your child march to a different drummer? Does the saying "you can't fit a square peg into a round hole" apply? If your teen is different, for whatever reason, it is best to recognize that. Your child is his own person—and this will become very clear in the adolescent years. For the child who just doesn't fit your expectations, remember, those are *your* expectations, not his. Just like that newborn baby or preteen, your teen is unique—one of a kind. Let him follow his destiny. It's never a matter of fault—rather, of fact. But that doesn't make it easy.

Despite valiant efforts on your and his part, your teen may not choose or want to do what you advise or practice. You wear your hair short and neat—his is long and straggly. You spend time and money on your appearance—your adolescent goes out of his way to look disheveled and unkempt. He loves the army surplus clothes—the more holes, the better. You may be a jock—he's an artist. You say please and thank you—he blows you off. You were successful at school—he hates it and flat refuses to go. And at times he even likes being contrary. Where do you draw the line?

This is the child feared in the teenage years. What did you do wrong to deserve this child? Quite frankly, nothing. Give yourself credit. This is the way your child was made—his God-given (if you will) nature. There is nothing "wrong" with him. And now, like it or not, you must give him space to be himself, assuming (and this is important) his life is not endangered. And even then—as with the drug scene—protecting him can be difficult. Respect him for himself—not for you, not for the grandparents, not for anyone else. Let him be himself. (Don't forget SECRET.)

Adolescence is often a time for protest and challenge—be it reasonable or not. It is a time to be assertive. It is a time to establish one's identity—a time to separate. So what do you do?

As a parent, you must be open about feelings—yours and your child's. Let your child know where your approval and/or disapproval lie. But also let him respond in kind. Let him talk with you, even disagree. If nothing else, the lines of communication have to stay open. Listen and acknowledge each other. You may not like what your teen represents on the surface, but you still love him. Remember that unconditional love—it is there and is even probably mutual. Keep it grounded! Be honest with each other, and allow for that expression of honesty. You cannot dictate to this teen, or you will lose him. He will walk out the door. And then not only do you have no control, but you don't even know where he is. Hopefully, your child has the stamina and courage to do what is ultimately right—to stay out of real trouble involving mainline drugs, weapons, disease, pregnancy, or the law. Just don't you yield to bad or unacceptable behavior, and don't sweep it under the carpet. Rather, discuss problems like adults— with control—and try to work out acceptable options.

Being a parent of a teenager can wrap you up in knots—even make you physically ill—as you try to work through a difficult time. But remember, you are never alone. If you need help, call! There are plenty of resources for you and your child—be it family, friends, school counselors, doctors, or others. Do seek professional help for you and the family if you're in trouble. Don't regret not doing all you can to salvage an "impossible" child— because no child is really that.

We've talked about disagreements, even battles, on the home front. Probably no time is more volatile than these teen years. More than ever your child is now seeking to establish his own identity, both at home and at school. He, almost by nature, should be in conflict with you, as he is separating and branching off. So allow space for friction. Allow time to sort things out, but without hysteria. Don't forget about *calm*. Allow for sincere dialogue, with respect for each other. You may have difficulty coming to agreement. But ultimately, you are the parent. At the very least, you both should understand where you are coming from. Allow for some give-and-take. If you have fireworks, wait for a cooling off. If tension is severe, again, seek professional help. It's OK to get angry, but don't fly off the handle. Where else but in a family setting can you have such honest disagreement?

Hopefully, if you have been successful in passing on some of your values, your teen is prepared to meet the challenges of the fast-paced adolescent years. He has a solid foundation that will enable him to deal with the unpredictable with maturity and responsibility. Life is unpredictable by nature, and no time is more so than the adolescent years. Rowdy parties—unsupervised, unchaperoned events—may happen, despite your best efforts and those of your child. Your daughter may be caught in compromising circumstances—you cannot control everything. Guys will be after her body! Your son may end up in the wrong place at the wrong time. Violence happens—drugs and booze and guns are all too present. Speeding in cars is almost a rite of passage. Things happen that are not necessarily anyone's fault. Even chaperoned parties are not always as advertised. The lights go down, the parents go to bed, and sometimes the teens do, as well. Parents collect car keys so drinkers cannot drive, but the teens are savvy and carry an extra pair!

I suppose it's amazing that as many teens survive as do—but nevertheless, there are too many accidents related to uncontrolled speed with or without the influence of alcohol. There are far too many pregnancies and much too much drug overdosing. The innocent as well as the guilty (but what does that mean?) are victims, and then we all suffer. So how can you as a parent maintain some control? How can you work to help bring about a positive outcome?

COMMUNICATION

First, you can promote open discussion—those lines of communication mentioned previously. Be open with your child about the world out there. It does no good to be an ostrich with your head in the sand and pretend your child is protected against any harm. Things happen. Talk about the obvious risks and what you might be able to anticipate. Talk to both girls and boys not only about the risks of sex, but also the rush of hormones and uncontrolled feelings that may drive one's passions—either your child's or those of his or her date. Feelings are real—sex and intercourse are not unnatural. Teach your child not to get *into* a situation that is likely to get out of control. Know that date rape occurs—talk about it *now* with both son and daughter. What might be ways of avoiding an attempted rape? How could your teen escape? Talk about the risk of being alone in an empty house or a secluded area or out late at night. Teach your children to respect their dates and that it is wrong to try to pressure, manipulate, or even force their dates into anything.

Have a bail out! Have a formal agreement with your teen that, if he is *ever* in an uncomfortable or "wrong" situation, you will come to get him in *any* place at *any* time—with no questions asked and no repercussions, period. All your child has to do is call. Even have a backup person—a neighbor or relative who will do the same if you are not available. You have to trust your child's judgment and give him the leeway to make decisions as well as the credit for identifying a bad situation.

Let your teen use you as the scapegoat. "My parents would *kill* me!" "I am *not* allowed . . . " Your child can use you as the fall-back. Being the "bad" guy—the old stick in the mud—might just give your child the "out" he needs in a difficult situation.

Let your teen know when you are pleased and proud of him, but don't overload him with such praise that there is no room to fall. Even the superstars have their moments of trouble—they, too, falter. They are human and will have their day, just like everybody else. Maybe your teen does know the rules and expectations you have established. And he may adhere to them most of the time. But, maybe—once in a while—his curiosity gets the better of him. The temptations are too great, and he must taste the fruit of the vine—be it cigarettes, alcohol, drugs, or even sex. He wants to know what the big deal is. The risks increase as you expand the temptations, and hopefully, your teen is mature enough to know that. Certainly a can of beer is less risky than crack cocaine. But one beer or one joint—or one sexual experience—can lead to more. Vodka or gin in a water bottle—that's an old trick! Watch out.

Some parents choose to introduce their older teens to alcohol in the home. Certainly, under controlled circumstances this can be accomplished successfully, as you teach and demonstrate respect and control of alcohol yourself. But be very careful about giving a mixed message. Do you abuse alcohol? If so, how can you expect something else from your child? Do you think it's cute when your child drinks? This is not a good or safe message. A sip of wine with a special dinner in the home can be instructive and allow your curious teen an opportunity to make his own conclusions—hopefully, the right ones. Talk about alcohol and its limits, and listen to your teen.

Make sure liquor bottles are not too available in your home. It doesn't take much for even unprovoked teens to raid your liquor cabinet. (The same goes for the medicine cabinet—especially prescription drugs.) Teens know how to water down the booze so you'd never know if they siphoned some off. (Do a taste test.) Remove the liquor, or at the very least, lock it up. Clean out the liquor cabinet. Throw away the nearly empty bottles. You can tell your teen you trust him but that sometimes situations (such as controlling his friends) get beyond his control. The lock is to protect him—and ultimately, you as well. Serving teens alcohol in your home is illegal—don't do it.

Let your teen know when you are disappointed with his behavior—it's like a wake-up call. It helps to remind him that you are still the parent and you are still watching. It says that you care. Basic rules still need to be observed—like courtesy and respect for one another, honesty, and trust, the last being the hardest. When you speak to your teen, be sure to be on his level. Give him time to respond, and do listen. Ask open-ended questions, and affirm his response. Make sure you are both speaking the same language—speaking *with*, not just *at*, one another. Those lines of communication must stay open.

Remember to maintain calm. Continue to work as hard as ever in maintaining your calm. No longer an infant or a toddler, but a full-fledged teen, your child will now demand extra control on your part as you "stick to your guns." Work hard, as always, at being nice to each other—showing love and respect, even affection. Don't forget about hugs and kisses. Even laugh together—laughter is very therapeutic.

Be consistent in your expectations. The rules of the household have not changed just because you have a teen. You still expect help with chores and courtesy with each family member. No screaming, no yelling, no cheating or lying—rather, respect and peace. Be there! Yes, your teen can take care of himself, but he actually needs your presence. He still depends upon you for his stability. Anyone, young or old, likes to know he's special. A warm welcome from Mom or Dad is appreciated even in the teen years. So be there when your teen gets home from school. Fix a nice meal—even bake a special cake. Don't forget to treat your child like a guest, at least once in a while.

Remember the *time* principle of SECRET. Do take time to be with and appreciate your adolescent. Go places—do things. Take in a movie at the theater. Go out for Chinese food. Go skiing, whitewater rafting, or hiking. Do a walkathon, and get pledges together. Tell him you love him. Tell him you're proud and know he's going through a lot of change and growth that can be very difficult. Tell him you are available always, and prove it. Don't *you* drop out, or your child might.

Just as in the preteen years, maintaining your presence is an art—no butting in, no intrusions, but a sense of support. Let your message be "I'm here for you—now and always." As before, your child needs you maybe 50 percent of the time—but which 50 percent? Be available so you don't miss it. You still control the reins—you are the driver—but hold them loosely!

Rules and Limits

A curious thing often happens as your child comes to adolescence. All of a sudden you, as the parent, don't know anything. It's true that parents are not perfect, and hopefully, this is no surprise in the teen years. But you, the parent of a teen, are neither stupid nor incompetent. Experience and wisdom do count for something. But there will be times when your child feels, "You don't know anything!" The pendulum of your child's estimation of you has swung to your being totally out of the know. How does one meet this challenge? Again, by maintaining calm—with frequent, open, neutral dialogue. But remember, just as in other stages, as your teen is testing and challenging the limits, he is also *looking* for them and needs them.

You the parent are not an imbecile. You've been around the block a few times. You were even a teen, way back when. Your teenager and emerging adult may ascribe to you little credibility, but hang in there. Don't give up. More than ever, your child is looking for direction from you. He just may not know it! He needs your limit setting—and you must be firm. And what are those limits?

Teens may not stay out late—certainly not until the wee hours of the morning. They have to come home. They need to communicate where they are, where they are going, and with whom. They need a weekend curfew—probably around 11 P.M. or 12:30, depending upon their age. Weeknights should be spent at home. They can drive or be driven by friends, but there should be certain restrictions. Is the driver newly licensed? If so, beware. Why not wait six months or at least six weeks before becoming your friend's passenger? Teens should not drive recklessly—fast or with poor judgment. A dent in the car or a speeding ticket is time to withhold driving privileges. A car is a powerful, potentially deadly machine, not a toy. Teens *cannot* drink alcohol at their own parties, and it is illegal for adults to serve it to them as minors. The law is very clear about this. Confront your child. Ground him if there is drinking. Deny him an important privilege. Stick to your guns!

Talk about issues of safety and decency. Talk about healthy bodies and keeping them that way. Require seat belts for everyone. Make drugs and cigarettes off-limits, and discuss why. Involve your teen in these discussions. Ask him for his opinion, even though you have the final say.

School performance needs to be monitored. What kind of grades does your teen maintain? Are they appropriate for your child? Have they dropped? If so, why? Is your teen sacrificing his education? If so, for what? Is his homework getting done? Make your teen accountable. You must let him know you're watching, and talk about it. In the end, he determines his grades. But let him know you care. Apply "soft" pressure.

Remember to say no—just as with the toddler or preschooler—when appropriate. And when you use that word, hold to it. Don't be capricious or unpredictable. Don't be afraid of your teen. It's no to drinking, no to unchaperoned or improperly chaperoned gatherings, no to all-nighters, and no to bad driving. You might be the only parent saying no—well, good for you! Your popularity with your teen may suffer, but that is not the point. Don't forget you are still the parent. (Who's in charge?)

Your teen should be able to anticipate your response to any request, because the groundwork already has been laid. The family expectations and honor code are givens. He knows what you're thinking because you have talked about it before. He knows the rules—the limits. If the answer to a request is no, then say it. Don't hesitate. "No" is a very good word—teach your child to use it, as well. Use it with love and conviction. Make "no" mean something.

Know that it is a little late to make demands and assumptions of a teenager if none have been made until this time. Trust and space don't come quickly or automatically at age sixteen unless the groundwork has been firmly laid. At the same time, if you have not been successful, work harder at it now. It's just not going to be easy.

As with all children at all ages, some teens are easier than others. We, as parents, know that. (Some adults are easier than others, too.) Some teens are having a more difficult time growing up. If so—why? Is it inborn, genetic—or does it reflect an unhappy home, even school? Do you need professional help? Be honest with your answers. Let your teen participate in exploring any problems.

And then, as always, when considering behavioral issues and standards, continue to look at yourself. Make sure you are a good role model. What kind of integrity do you reflect—at home, at play, at business? I promise you, your teen is watching you. Your actions do, in fact, speak louder than your words. Are you considerate to your family, friends, and fellow drivers on the road? Do you drink, swear, speed, or cheat—even a little? Don't run the yellow light—don't cut off your fellow driver.

Your adolescent needs to know that he can count on you. We're talking not about perfection, but rather consistency. "The apple doesn't fall far from the tree," if you know what I mean. Check on yourself. Certainly you can't expect more from your teenager than you deliver.

FLEXIBILITY

As you work hard to parent and to support your teen, it is very important that you maintain a certain flexibility. This may sound contradictory, but in fact it is not. Rather, it is crucial.

As you build a firm foundation of limits and expectations, let your child know that on occasion, given good reason, exceptions can be made. This is not inconsistency but rather justifiable privileges. If you have established codes of behavior and rules of the household, allowing for slight variability in the context of a special event or reward will earn you many points with your teenager.

You don't want to be rigid. Life is not that way. Rather, you want to be in charge—for your child's guidance and protection, but not for your ego. Your teen needs to know that. It's true—it's a very fine line between being in charge versus being inflexible. Once in a while "Because I'm your parent" or "Because I said so" will work, but only as a rare last gasp. You can't be absolutely rigid in your rules and regulations. Life itself demands a certain flexibility. Know when to give a little. Know when you can extend a curfew or offer an unusual privilege such as driving Dad's new car. Recognize when a little bending here or there is appropriate. In the context of established norms, an exception to the rule will be recognized as such and appreciated. It shows trust and affirms maturity as you loosen those reins.

Teenage behavior has its ups and downs but also some smooth sailing. If you're successful with limit setting, in setting the right tone and being available for your son or daughter, then these adolescent years need not be awful. Indeed, they can be some of the best.

LIFE ON THE OUTSIDE

It is one thing to work hard to establish peace and stability at home. It is entirely another thing when it comes to the "outside." As your child's world expands, the pressures from external forces including peers, school, and the community increase. How can you help?

First, it is very important to try to raise happy children—individuals who feel good about themselves, who are loved for themselves and know it, who don't have to look elsewhere for approval, and who are grounded at home. Love is supposed to be unconditional (we've said this before), and your children should begin to recognize that by now. Your teenager hopefully knows that you love him regardless of circumstances.

A supportive, nurturing home environment will begin to prepare your teen best for the outside world. But, even when successful at home, we cannot guarantee anything at school or with friends. We cannot guarantee academic or social success—not for any child. It's just not that simple. We wish that we could!

Life circumstances are not always favorable—and often, they are beyond our control. The world is not always a friendly place, despite our efforts to guide and steer our children toward favorable environments. In fact, the outside world can be downright vicious and mean. Remember the toddler who zeroed in on the vulnerable playmate and bit him or the school-aged child who was teased because he smelled. Well, take a look at some of our teens who are merciless with their peers. Even a rare teacher or coach can do real damage to your child.

Some kids are dealt a more difficult hand than others. Some teens fit in, but others don't. Some are cute, coordinated, smart, and at ease with people. But others are not—they're obese or slow mentally or physically or clumsy—or just lack "style." They may be miserable at school, where they're the constant butt of classroom jokes. It's not a question of fairness, because it's totally unfair. These kids *can* do well, but they may have a rougher road than the gorgeous, gregarious, "popular" athlete. Some kids grow up with a silver spoon—everything is easy. But some have to work very hard for everything they achieve. Your adolescent may be struggling. Be there for him.

Your bubbly, spontaneous, happy toddler may be less so as his world of peers and peer pressure takes over. Once uninhibited, he may now be inhibited. The world is watching and exercising its influence. For the teenager, you can only be on the sidelines looking on the field of play. As with the preteen, you cannot call the plays, nor act out the calls. You cannot do your child's work, nor take his tests. You cannot try out for the school play or music group or soccer team for him; you cannot build his circle of friends. He has to do these things for himself—and accept the results.

Your adolescent child is really on his own in many ways. His identity—social, intellectual, physical, emotional—is being shaped. Once self-centered as a toddler, then less so as a school-aged child, he is now back to the "me" and "my" stage—measuring himself against others. His peer interaction will affect his self-esteem, his self-worth. Does he have friends—or is he a loner? (I worry very much about the latter.) Does someone like him for himself, outside the family? Watch. Does the phone ring for him?

Who is in control? That is very complicated. The truth is, parent and child share in that assignment. But the balance has shifted, as we advise and watch and our children act. The outside world makes its demands. Our children have to stand on their own feet. The control "pie" is truly theirs—and that can be a good thing or bad. We can hold the plate, but the pieces are theirs. We can intervene if things get really bad—and intervene we should, but only in the extreme.

So—and it's worth restating—it is important that parents be available for their adolescents, for whenever they need you. As a parent, you can offer guidance and lots of support. The message has to be loud and clear—call *anytime*. Nothing—not our "other" jobs, not an important conference, presentation, or tournament match—*nothing* should take priority over that call from your teen. Let him know that!

School

Most teens look forward to going to school. They love the peer contact—the social scene. Many are intellectually curious and even enjoy learning and studying. But every so often there is a mismatch. Just as that square peg does not go into a round hole, for whatever reason, your child may not fit society's expectations or yours.

Some teens do not succeed in traditional school settings—not because they're stupid or unmotivated but sometimes on a different wavelength. Some are truly unhappy in a regular high school environment. The traditional classroom and curriculum are not their bag. But why? For some perhaps unclear reason, there is a certain incompatibility. Maybe it's the forced structure— maybe not. Maybe your child has a slight learning disability or more right- versus left-sided brain preferences. Maybe he's more hip or artsy than traditional. He might be better with his hands than with the books.

Some teens need a more nontraditional, free-floating environment to thrive. And others do better in a vocational setting. Of course, adolescents do have to go to school and accomplish certain basic learning—and most want to. They need to learn, expand their minds, and develop skills—but sometimes where and how is not always clear. If your teen is not making it at school, you must seek help. Talk to professionals (teachers, advisers, counselors, doctors), and find out what your options are. See if your teen is in the right place for him. If not, do *your* homework. Take time to respect his needs, and find the best possible match you can. Do some testing. Let your teen know that you are doing your best for him. Even making the effort can help. Let your teen participate in the gathering of and reacting to the collected information. Ask questions, be his advocate, and together you can only make things better. If placement elsewhere is advised, do the very best you can to carry out that placement. It can truly make all the difference in bringing your teen to success instead of failure.

Know that if your child is having trouble anywhere, it can be a real source of anxiety, even friction, within the family. This can be major. If you had expectations of Ivy League and your child wants none of it—only wants to paint or work with wood—you will be disappointed. But it's not your child's fault, nor yours. It's really not a matter of fault at all. Again, remember—he is who he is. Don't forget to respect him for himself.

How you handle the situation can make a huge difference. Are you still calm? Don't get angry—don't place any blame. Rather, support your child wherever he may be. Don't forget about SECRET.

SEX

While we counsel against sex in the teen years, we cannot be blind to the fact that some teens are doing it. The teen pregnancy rates are sky high. Why? There are lots of reasons: availability of sex, blind naïveté, curiosity, peer pressure, unpreparedness, and even the desire for social attention and recognition.

Pregnancy? Teens may think, "It will never happen to me." Wrong! How about status—teens may feel, "It's cool to be pregnant." Well, pregnancy might call attention to oneself, but it's definitely not "cool." Unrealistic expectations? "My baby will be mine—will love me unconditionally—will never cry—will be perfect." Wrong! "My baby will give me credibility." Maybe!

What sexual relations do is put your child very much at risk for pregnancy and sexually transmitted diseases (STDs). Talk to your teen about disease and babies. Know the statistics. Disease can be permanent. It's real. As for AIDS—your child "sleeps" with *all* his or her partner's previous partners (as well as *their* previous partners). Make no mistake! Talk to your teen as a mature person—these are the facts.

As for the newborn parenting—do some reality testing. Have your teenage daughter spend time talking to and seeing a newborn's parents. Let her help care for or baby-sit newborns and older babies. Talk about the responsibility that comes with being a parent—there is no free ride. Talk about the realities of pregnancy—weight gain, stretch marks, nausea, fatigue, swollen ankles. A teen's baby is just like anyone else's—he will cry, be up at night, get sick, and need constant supervision and nurturing. Being a parent has a glorified image, not only to teens, but to many of us. The constant hard work of parenting—the round-the-clock demands, the reality of being a parent—these concerns do not occur to the teen who dreams of a perfect world with her baby. Educate your child!

If your teen is going to be sexually active, then by all means he or she must take responsibility for himself or herself. Talk about and be informed about condoms, birth control pills, and barrier methods. If you cannot talk with your child about these issues, get your doctor involved—that's his or her job. Don't be fooled—every act of intercourse has risks of pregnancy or STDs, no matter if the partners swear on their virginity and/or protection. It only takes one previous exposure to unprotected sex to pass on the AIDS virus or other sexually transmitted diseases such as chlamydia, gonorrhea, or herpes. These can lead to silent sterility, chronic infection, and, of course, death.

It only takes a drop of semen for a girl to get pregnant. And the protective measures are *not* 100 percent protective. Using a condom means little if it isn't used the right way and at the right moment. Taking birth control pills on an erratic basis does not prevent ovulation. It's true, we are caught in a double standard as we advise, "Wait for sex, but if you don't wait, protect yourself." But the realities are that many teenagers do have sex. So try to talk openly with your child, and then leave him or her the freedom to make an intelligent, informed decision.

If your teen becomes pregnant or impregnates a partner, know that whatever the outcome of any conception—a term pregnancy, complicated preterm delivery, miscarriage, or termination—all of your lives will be forever changed, and perhaps haunted, by this event. Work hard to prevent pregnancy. Recognize that abortion is a complicated issue and has serious consequences. It is not a means of birth control and not an easy out. Adoption and raising a child also carry their own complications.

I think one of the best lines used to counsel teens against sexual intercourse is that there is no benefit to teenage sex. Why the hurry? Practice does not make perfect—you have a lifetime of adult years to become expert in sexual relations. And the risks are far greater with teens than with adults. Multiple partners mean multiple risks. That's fact! Teach your daughter (or son) how to respond to the line, "If you really love me, you will do it." You call that love? Or how about "Trust me." Forget it!

Do let your child know that if trouble, pregnancy, or disease does ever develop, he or she can still come home. This is not a license to be loose, but rather a reminder that you love your child unconditionally, and that you are always there for him or her. Desperate teens who seek abortions (especially those outside a clinic) die! Embarrassed teens with obvious signs of infection are reluctant to seek medical care and then pay a high price (like sterility) as well as spread more disease. This is true, I promise you. Treatment is often very simple. So do remind your teen that if he or she makes a mistake—as serious as it may be—not to compound it. Come home!

And finally, with regard to sex and sexual relationships, again, teens experiment—and might do so with both sexes. The question of sexual orientation may be unclear to your teen, as signals come in from all directions. Help your teen through this period. Be available. (For further discussion, please refer to "The Gay Child," Chapter 9.)

THE SUCCESSFUL TEEN

If you have a "successful" teen—one with excellent grades, nice friends, and lots to do—make sure you, the parent, are watching. He may seem fit on the surface but, in fact, may be suffering more than he lets on. Some teens have a daily schedule that would choke a corporate executive! A heavy academic load, multiple extracurriculars, responsibilities at home, and an outside job—the list can be too long. How can we let this happen? Teens are human, just like us adults. There is a limit to what even they can reasonably accomplish in a twenty-four-hour period—and this *must* include time for sleep. The adolescent who is succeeding often adds more and more to his daily routine. Where is the endpoint?

Clearly, we as parents must not relinquish our responsibilities yet. Here is a very clear example of where we can and must get involved. Is your teenager too committed to everything? Is he too pushed or driven? Is he able to go to bed at night at a reasonable time (certainly by eleven o'clock or midnight) and sleep soundly until morning, with time for catch-up sleep over the weekend? How is his temperament—even or erratic? Is there ever free time to do the unexpected—even "veg out" once in a while in front of the TV (as much as I resist the television)? Is your child too driven, for whatever reason—does he have too, too much on his plate? If so, you must put on the breaks and restrict his commitments. The outside job, one extracurricular, one course, or one household responsibility—something has to go. If your child is overextended, cut something. You can give your child the option to choose; if he or she is unable, it's your turn. Here you will not be very popular, but your child's survival, not popularity, is what it's all about. Talk to your child's counselor or teachers, and share your concerns. Our children can walk a very fine line as they strive to do their very best. Respect the fact that your teen is capable— but still human.

Examine what kinds of pressures you yourself exert on your teen—be it conscious or not. We sometimes lay a heavy trip on our children if we are successful and driven. Just because we were valedictorians, our children do not have to be. If everyone in the family has gone to Harvard, does this child have to also? Certainly not! But your teen may feel differently. He may see not getting into Harvard as failure—as being the "boob" of the family. So he's going to kill himself to get in. But maybe he would be better off somewhere else anyway—with no legacy to haunt him. Talk openly about these concerns. You can have some impact. It is important for your teen to leave room for some fun. If not, make changes!

The Job

Outside work—the job, a way to earn money—has become more common with teens. They're cheap labor—good hires for entry-level jobs. And a job can provide a means for developing independence. Because after all, it's his money, not yours.

One word of caution! Why do teens need so much money? Are they sacrificing school and/or the opportunity for sports, music, or club activities for the almighty buck? They have a lifetime for employment—but only a few years to gain valuable skills and experiences. Watch that the emphasis on work isn't misplaced. Why is your teen working outside the home? Do you know?

Some teens appear a bit lost for whatever reason—either a lack of fit at school or outright rebellion at home. For them, that outside job (or other activity) can provide grounding and stability. It comes back to that old basic—every person is unique with his own needs and strengths. For some, working after school and on the weekends puts order into a somewhat disordered life; it keeps your child out of trouble and adds in a positive way to his life. Instead of stretching too much, that outside job can provide needed structure. Teens do need to be busy—just not too busy. Too much free time—total lack of structure—does often lead to trouble with too much opportunity to experiment. Again, know where your child is and what he's up to. Also know and respect your child.

Beware of the teen on a beeper. Make sure he is not involved with drugs. What is so important that he needs to be available by beeper? Who is controlling his life? Is that beeper a leash?

FOOD AND REST

Adolescents are still growing. In fact, their bodies are changing in many ways. The boys are growing tall, and the girls are rounding out. This is natural! With this growth comes the requirement for many calories and lots of rest. There has to be time for both. Your teen needs to eat, and eat well; he needs to sleep, and not just grab naps. Why do you think your teen turns into Rip Van Winkle on the weekends? He needs sleep that he hasn't been getting. Let him catch up.

As far as calories go—your teenage son will eat you out of house and home. There will be a limitless pit in his stomach—which will always be on empty. He will have hollow bones! He will consume meals before the real meals and come back for more in two hours. Loaves (plural) of bread will evaporate; liquids (milk, soda) will be consumed by the gallon. As for their sisters, teenage girls eat less but need calories, too. The skinny figure of a twelve-year-old should be a rounded shape at sixteen. Your adolescent female is developing her mature body—and that needs calories. So make sure you have the pantry stocked. Serve meals—real dinners, not just frozen pot pies—and sit down together as a family. Make dinnertime, just as in earlier years, a family time—a time for sharing and touching base. Make it a priority, no matter how much homework your child has to do, no matter how busy you might be. Aim at a minimum of two family dinners a week—one on the weekend, one midweek—or more if your family schedules allow.

When discussing diet, we cannot ignore the issue of eating disorders. Many of our teens, in their striving for perfection, are sacrificing their bodies—even their lives. Girls more than boys are affected, but both sexes are vulnerable. Eating disorders—and I mean anorexia nervosa and bulimia, considered by many to be part of the same spectrum—are life-threatening disorders. Adolescents die! There is approximately a 10 percent mortality to this condition. It is very frightening.

As a parent, you have an absolute responsibility for monitoring your child here. Is he or she eating or just pushing food around the plate? Has your child had *any* weight loss—of any kind? Watch for early wakening and running of extra miles—cramming more physical activity into an already crowded day. What kind of example are you setting? Don't draw too much attention to a little bulge of subcutaneous fat. Try not to be fastidious about counting calories yourself and always dieting. What kind of message are you, as a parent, giving? Are you too achievement oriented—and that includes maintaining a size 2? When was the last time your teenage daughter had a period? Watch and monitor her menses—even check her pads.

Signs and symptoms of an eating disorder can be subtle. But even subtle warnings need to be heeded. If you see an overenthusiastic interest in food—a sudden desire to cook, but not to eat; an exaggerated, distorted concern with body fat and image; multiple exercise regimens a day, not just conditioning; or secret bingeing, then purging—take action! Be concerned about your ballet dancer, competitive runner, or wrestler. Are you or your child's instructor or coach placing too much emphasis on achievement and ignoring the cost?

If you suspect any of the above, you must solicit professional help—either your family physician and/or a counselor—*right away*. Treating eating disorders is very hard—our success rate is not great. But the sooner intervention begins, the greater likelihood of success. Don't deny the problem, but seek help. Be upfront. Don't sweep this one under the carpet; it's just too risky. Your child may look OK, but in fact, he or she may be disguising a shrinking body under bulky clothes. The inside of his or her body might be totally out of whack with chemical disturbances and electrolyte (salt) imbalances. Cardiac rhythms can become abnormal and even lead to death. Karen Carpenter was a statistic—don't let your child become one. Take time to monitor, to care, and to notice and respond.

ILLNESS

Teens are generally healthy, but once in a while they do get sick. Stress and fatigue can take their toll on anyone, and a growing adolescent is no exception. Your adolescent does need a healthy diet, a reasonable schedule, and time off to sleep and rest, to refuel. If not, he can get sick. He's just like anyone else.

Kids need to be paced. It is our job, as parents, to monitor them. An occasional day off from school for R&R is not a bad idea, especially if your child is reaching his limit and looking a little run down. Look and relook at that schedule. Watch to see if he's dragging, coughing or wheezing, even running a fever. Don't send your child to school if his temperature is over 100 degrees—put him to bed.

Probably the most common adolescent infection we are familiar with is mono, or mononucleosis. Mononucleosis is a virus transmitted by respiratory droplets and often, but not always, by some known close contact; it is the "kissing disease." It gives variable symptoms of fever, swollen glands, sore throat, and fatigue. Sometimes it involves the liver and spleen. It can lead to a very serious, even life-threatening illness, with the airway threatened (by swollen tonsils), the liver dysfunctional, and/or the spleen engorged. Usually, mono is a self-contained and self-limiting illness that resolves over time, without any adverse consequences, but not always. Obviously, medical attention with continued follow-up is essential.

The thing about mono is that it is incredibly boring! There is nothing fun nor exciting about feeling ill, being extremely fatigued, and having to sleep and rest. There is no medical cure—mono is viral, so antibiotics have no impact. You truly have to wait it out—and that can take months. Contact sports have to be postponed, and sometimes, school schedules greatly altered. Sometimes a semester or a year has to be dropped and then repeated. Everything else has to take a backseat to allow time for the body to heal. You, as the parent, must realize that limits on activity have to be very strict. Your physician can advise you—let him or her set those limits—and be patient. Respect the illness—set aside lots of time for recuperation. Be around for your teen. He will need you.

Some adolescents are more at risk for mono than others. The teen who is run down and often tired from overscheduling will be more susceptible to any infection. Mono is no exception. So, again, watch that your teen isn't overdoing it.

Sports

Sports take on a new dimension as your child enters his teen years. As skills improve and size and weight increase, the potential for excellence becomes a reality. Suddenly, a local star can be catapulted into more select competition, even with aspirations for national achievement. The soccer player, the ice skater, the tennis player, the skier—all of a sudden, competition can become very serious. Dreams for Olympic-caliber performance and college scholarships are within reach.

It is very important that you, the parent, not let these dreams or any dream stretch your teen too much. Remember, sport is just that—sport. There should still be a place for scholastics and people. There should still be time for fun and time to unwind.

Make sure that any push for excellence is coming from your child, not from an overbearing adult, be it parent or coach. Make sure the goal is one your child truly aspires to—not yours or the school's.

Watch that, with increased participation, overuse injuries do not take their toll. Knees, in particular, have a predilection for injury when the body is used too much. Joints can be damaged—including ankles and shoulders. Anterior cruciates in the knees and rotator cuffs in the shoulders are at risk. If injured, the healing or repair—even surgery—can be long and painful, sometimes with loss of function. Your child wants to enjoy sport for all of his life; don't let him ruin his chances now. Make sure there is adequate warming up and cooling down. Make sure trainers—and good ones—as well as ice are available for all practices and competition. See how fit the whole team is, and ask around. If your child is being pushed beyond his endurance (or yours), and/or if he is being injured, you must reexamine the demands that are being placed on his body. He may have to throttle back. Sometimes it is just too much. Don't let your child play through pain. Rather, pain means *stop!* Your job is to take time to observe carefully so injury can be avoided or at least minimized.

As with sport, all achievers—the musician, the actress, the debater—present special concerns. The very gifted child at any level brings on challenges of his or her own. (See "The Very Gifted Child," Chapter 9.)

MENTAL HEALTH

The subject of mental health is complicated, especially for the teen. With so much physical and emotional change going on and mixed messages of violence and hatred coming from the media, it almost seems like a healthy reaction if our teens are somewhat perplexed about the world out there. We are. Nothing is permanent—rather, change is the constant. Teens have questions about society in general and certainly have questions about themselves. Concerns about self-worth and identity are paramount in the teen years. Let it be known that the answers to many of these questions will be slow in coming. Let it be very clear that support through this period is available, not only with you, but with trained professionals if needed. School counselors, mental health workers, and other professional advisers are all available for teens. Sometimes just having a neutral person to talk to—to validate feelings—is enough. Make sure these doors are open.

Teenage mental illness—just as with an adult or a young child—demands recognition and treatment. The consequences are severe. It's a fact—teenage depression and suicide are on the rise, and I'm not sure why. Is it a way to bail out from too much pressure, unhappiness, no friends, no love? What a heartache and irreparable loss!

What can we do to make a difference and save some of these teens? Watch! Monitor for any change in behavior or personality or any impulsive acts. Watch to see if grades take a dive or the peer group changes. Be up-front and open about your concerns. Talk about it! Spend time with your teen, just as you did when he was younger. *Time* is important. Keep those lines of communication open. Be available! Find something that you can do together that your child truly enjoys. Show him that you care. Build on your relationship and be sensitive to his needs. Hopefully, that will help make a difference. And as always, involve professionals if any hint of trouble develops.

Behavior Beyond Home

As our teens grow—as we teach and set limits on all of our behaviors—we as parents must watch that the focus on self doesn't lead to greed and the "I want more" syndrome. We must watch *ourselves* as we climb the ladder of success. Are we victims of the "more is better" philosophy—accumulating, buying, storing more and more for another day? What kind of example are we setting?

As we teach love and respect, we need to pass on our corporate responsibility to give. We need to share, not only with each other, but with the less fortunate. Do give of your time—take on some worthwhile project and involve your child, if you haven't done so already. Give of your talents—don't waste them. Despite a very busy schedule, see if you and your teen can't come up with something, even a time-limited project. Serve a meal to the homeless, read to a shut-in, spend time with an inner-city youth, or volunteer at a hospital. Do it! Don't be in a hurry to take— rather, give. Share your family and your holidays. Your teen is old enough to participate in projects within the house, but also out- side. Don't deny him the opportunity to do so because there's "no time." Make time—even if it's only an afternoon a couple of times a year. Praise your child for the caring he demonstrates— it will carry him far.

. . .

As your teenager establishes his own identity, as he takes charge of his life—he must also take responsibility for his choices. We are not entirely responsible for the choices our children make. We *are*, however, responsible for allowing for choice and for enabling our children to make choices. We, as parents, share in the respon- sibility of our children's destiny, but our child shares in it, too. In the final analysis, teenagers cannot blame their parents for all of their misfortunes, mistakes, or unhappiness. At some point our grown children have to face the music themselves. We are still there to love and support, but the choices are theirs. We did the best job we could—we modeled good behavior, we set limits, and we gave them freedom to choose. Hopefully, with calm, time, and respect, a consistent pattern was set at home; by honoring SECRET, we were able to empower our children to carry on in a confident, responsible way.

The outcome may be less than desirable for us and/or our chil- dren. But we as parents cannot be recipients of total blame. We may be guilty of wrongdoings—who isn't? We may have been less-than-perfect parents. That's only human. But at some point your child, now an emerging adult, has to take charge of his own life. Who is in charge? You, as the parent, were. He, as a young adult, will be! You will always be family, working together, but the responsibilities will shift. You, as a parent, will always be there as emotional support, but now you've let go of the reins.

The choices we have made will determine the lives we lead. The same goes for our children. Hopefully, by observing SECRET—being true to our own selves, maintaining calm and composure, respecting our children as individuals, and ensuring time for them—we as parents have done the best job possible to lay a foundation for their success.

PART III

How to Set Limits

in specific situations

• • •

This section is slightly different from the previous chapters. Instead of looking at children by age and developmental groupings, here I've chosen to look at situations that have no age boundaries—circumstances that we as parents all may face, regardless of the age of our children. These are general topics, from the slightly trivial to the more serious—from carpools to grandparents to chronic illness. But regardless of their significance, they all have impact upon our lives. They all affect our ability to parent; they can enhance or interfere. In short, these issues are real, and some of us confront them daily.

You'll see that there will be some overlap between topics and cross references made to other sections. It's the nature of children and our own complexity to have some overlap. We cannot isolate any one stage or condition. We, as human beings, are not that simple; otherwise, life would be too predictable.

The tenets of SECRET can still be applied, particularly as we hit some bumps along the way. Don't forget to be true to yourself—figure out what works for you. Take control of your own life—be a role model of calm and composure. Respect your child for herself—make space for her. Allow your child to participate more and more in decisions. Spend time together—be available.

8

Family
Issues

As we address the challenges of parenting, especially as we focus on different developmental groups, it is very important that we not lose sight of the family. The family is that unit of structure in which we raise our children. It's where we do our parenting. It is the family that provides the foundation for our children—the source for their decision making and problem solving.

How that family functions will have enormous impact upon us and our children. Families that are secure and happy have a much better chance of supporting their members, wherever they are—of raising successful (meaning happy and independent) children. Families where love and acceptance prevail, where limits are established and honored, will survive—and so will their children. These are the good role models!

Likewise, families that lack organization—where rules and limits are always changing, where the unpredictable is the predictable—these families will tend to breed confusion. The children from these homes will have a more difficult time finding themselves because the limits have not been clear nor practiced.

If confusion has reigned, then more than likely, confusion will be perpetuated.

The components of SECRET—knowing your*self*, staying *calm*, *respecting* all persons, and spending *time* with your children and family—still hold. For the family to function well, these tenets provide a very workable framework. They provide a sense of order and stability—but, as always, require practice and commitment.

So let's look at family structure—both traditional and non-traditional—and then consider particular family issues: everything from sibling rivalry to grandparents and sharing household chores—even pets, baby-sitters, and manners—and then a few special topics. Realize that maintaining control and setting limits are real concerns with all of these issues.

FAMILY STRUCTURE

It is important to realize that each family is unique, with a complexity of its own. Small families of two and three, as well as large families with more, all have their share of concerns and problems. No family is isolated from the challenges of parenting. The challenges may differ from family to family, but they do exist.

The traditional family of a married heterosexual couple with its own biological children conceived "naturally" is still the tradition, still the norm. However, today, as singles and couples form families with nontraditional structures, children are being raised in a variety of household units. Be it a single parent—who may be single by choice or circumstances (separated, divorced, or widowed)—or a whole spectrum of less traditional arrangements (mixed marriages by race and/or religion, lesbian or gay couples, communes), children are growing up in different family structures. Also, as the technology of reproduction expands, the options for bearing or adopting children increase. In vitro fertilization, artificial insemination, surrogate childbearing, and adoptions (to couples or singles) are no longer uncommon. In fact, with each passing day there is more opportunity for variation not only in family structure, but in birth origin. So how does this affect our children?

Any family—traditional or not—has the potential for success or failure. Structure, by itself, does not guarantee a definite outcome. This is important to realize. The structure of a family is no ticket for success or failure. Rather, it is the love and nurturing within the home that will determine a child's foundation. Time together, open lines of communication, mutual respect, commitment to each other, and establishing calm—these are all equal opportunity conditions. When it comes to raising a healthy, happy child, a traditional family can fail miserably—just as a nontraditional family can succeed beautifully. Wherever we are, whatever we have, we all need to be sensitive to problems, to listen and to recognize both acceptable and unacceptable behavior. We all need to work together—and even seek help and/or change, as needed.

However, here's the catch—the nontraditional family will, without a doubt, face more scrutiny and questions from others; it will have to do more explaining. Like it or not, the child from a nontraditional family will be looked upon differently by some. This is not necessarily fair or right, but people who are less tolerant and less understanding may challenge you and your child if you vary from the norm. The child coming from a nontraditional home needs, more than ever, your love and support to meet the special challenges she will face at school, in town, and even at places of worship. Know that a strong foundation comes from a home where rules are clearly delineated—where good behavior and respect for each other are modeled and reinforced, more than ever—regardless of color, religion, relationships, or sexual orientation. Remember SECRET—recognize your needs (*self*); maintain your composure (*calm*); *respect* individuality and be tolerant of personal choices; and take *time* for your children.

The child of a single parent misses out on the teamwork a parent couple provides. Discussion may take place between parent and child, but not parent to parent. Parenting decisions become unilateral, with no give-and-take. The child of a single parent does not have the opportunity to watch his or her parents work things out, balance each other, and support each other. The back-and-forth dialogue that goes on in any partnership or relationship is not seen. The agreeing and disagreeing—lessons applicable to life in general—are not witnessed.

Maybe this child can have that experience secondhand—through an aunt or uncle or grandparents—or through another relationship of the single parent. Certainly, the most important thing is that the child's relationship be solid with the single parent. Truly, this mother or father will have to work all the harder to be available and to set limits—to be the equivalent of two parents in one. It can be done—and done well. But it will mean extra work. And then, sometimes the single parent can even devote *too much* time and attention to his or her child. Make sure that you, as a single parent, also have a life of your own—even if only in brief spurts.

The child of separated or divorced parents presents a distinct dilemma, because now there are at least two parents influencing this child's life—but parents who, for reasons of their own, are no longer living together. The fact is, they may not get along at all; they may not even like each other. Their task is quite clear—but often difficult to execute. They need to love and support their child together—although separate—without letting feelings of bitterness, guilt, or anger toward each other spill over on their child. These parents have to set very strict limits on themselves—and be nice to each other! Sometimes, they have to hold their tongues and check their emotions. Maybe this will be an easy task—maybe not.

Divorced parents should not malign nor attack each other but rather must support each other in the mutual raising of their child. Scars from parents' fighting can cut deeply. Be careful what you say about your ex-spouse—directly or not, even inferred through body language. Open your hearts and minds to accept each other so your child can have a rich relationship with both of you. Tread lightly. Let your child know that any differences you may have do not involve her—but show it, as well as say it. Don't forget to respect your child's other parent.

Stepparents enter into a different kind of relationship with their stepchildren. They are neither parent nor friend—neither sister, aunt, brother, nor uncle. But they *are* the grown-ups of the household and, by that claim alone, can assume a position of authority. It shouldn't be a matter of power, but of respect. If it's your home, then you can draw the line with *all* children who enter. Your stepchildren will test you again and again—not only because you occupy that adult position, but also because you compete with that child for your spouse's attention. Still, you can and should say no when appropriate—and as always, with calm and assurance. Over time you will gain respect, but it may take a long time for that to happen. Hopefully, you have the full support of your spouse as you all work together to establish the limits. There will be some rough moments—some storms—but don't give in.

The child from a biracial or gay marriage will definitely face questions from the outside world, although maybe not right away. She may be teased or even shamed. People are human and often pick on what may appear more vulnerable or what they don't understand. Some folks do not tolerate any variation from tradition and attack—especially if they feel threatened or uncomfortable with your situation. Again, that's not fair and not right, but it happens.

The child from a nontraditional family must be prepared for a few extra bumps—and that will also take extra work. Just as teenage years bring on rocky times, the child of a nontraditional family will encounter issues—even walls—that friends from traditional families will not have to face. Talk about appropriate responses to anticipated questions ahead of time. Prepare your child for the obvious questions—"Where did I come from?" "Why can't we celebrate Christmas and Hanukkah?" "How come I don't have a girl and boy Mom and Dad?" Be up-front with your child and community, and you will have an easier time supporting your child as she grows. Don't forget about SECRET—remind yourself about calm and respect. As always, reinforce your love, and, as in any family, affirm and reaffirm your child's place in your heart. The limits here are for you—make time, be calm, and be available to face the world. Seek help, as needed. You don't have to fight it alone. Make it clear to your child that she and you are people with a right to choose their lifestyle. And then, make sure you remain tolerant of others—just as you expect the same from them.

The child from any kind of family can tolerate, answer, and survive questions of a less understanding world given support and understanding at home. Families—whatever their structure—need to be solid, dependable, and a real springboard for their children. But it may not be easy.

For the families struggling with structure—going through difficult changes—acknowledge the difficulty but also the strengths. "This is a hard time right now, but we will get through. We still love you." With divorce, uncertain relationships, or changing of partners, extra stress comes into play. This is all the more reason to work on being calm.

Sibling Rivalry

Siblings do rival—and it's really a forever thing. They are not supposed to get along with each other *all* the time. That is just not human. Remember, siblings are individuals with very definite needs and attitudes. They will clash now and then, particularly as they are growing up—seeking their own identity and space. Siblings rival each other for your attention, for your praise, and for society's success and acclaim. Firstborn, second born, son or daughter—it doesn't really matter. It's the sorting out that is part of growing up. A pecking order (remember the biting toddler) will be established—but always open to challenge and change, just as any relationship is in flux with give-and-take. Getting along with each other is part of living together—it's part of life. Some say if you can survive siblings, you're ready for anything. It is for you, the parent, to make sure things don't get completely out of control—that your children do survive, not only physically, but emotionally. When siblings quarrel, don't intervene always; allow your children slack and freedom to settle most issues. But as head of the household, ultimately, you are still in charge. Jealousy is natural—and it is your job to diffuse it.

As a parent, your children will look to you to maintain order—and this you must do. You cannot allow physical abuse, just as you wouldn't ever hit anyone yourself. Wrestling between siblings is OK, as long as no one gets hurt and your older (or stronger) child is fair. You cannot allow for verbal torture either—just as you would not do this to your child or anyone's child. Allow no slander and no cutting, biting words. The themes of kindness and consideration often lose their meaning in a household—particularly with siblings. But words like "hate" and "kill" are not acceptable. Nor are swearwords. Remember, it is for you to show kindness and consideration to each family member (again, you are the role model) and then demand the same from your children. It is for you to show respect for each child—and then to expect the same from the children. It is hard to see those you love most at each other's throats—but this happens. It will hurt you to have to punish your children for unkindness toward one another. But just as with any other unacceptable behavior, there has to be an appropriate response from you. Take time to know when to act—be around, and observe with a keen eye.

What should you do when your children fight? First, separate your children if they cannot be kind to one another. One can go to one time-out spot, another to a second. Stop whatever activity precipitated the unkindness or unacceptable behavior, regardless of "fault." Try to focus on the behavior, not the child or children. Just as before, treat the action, not the child, as unacceptable. Do not label your children. A question of guilt or fault may be difficult to ascertain: "He did it." "No, she did." Remember it takes two to quarrel. If your children don't get along, chances are good that both are a little bit guilty. Do the best you can to keep your powers of observation sharp and objective. Watch your children interact. Spend time with them separately and together. Keep them busy and active. Idle time leads to poking and shoving, and then it just escalates. Pent-up energy gets misdirected. Don't allow for boredom! Life is too precious and exciting. And as your children become increasingly verbal, make sure you discuss with each sibling appropriate behavior.

When your children are very different sizes or endowed with very different talents, you have to make allowances for any disparity. A large older sibling cannot bully a younger one; a gifted, talented sib cannot torment another. The bigger and/or smarter sibling has to control herself, and not take unfair advantage of her strengths. She cannot lord it over another. You as a parent will be the referee. Be as consistent as you can—and open to fair discussion.

If punishment is necessary—taking away a toy or postponing or canceling an activity or privilege—just as with any reprimand, implement that punishment right away. Restrict your warnings, and follow through with your threats. Do not threaten unless you are prepared to take action. If your children are misbehaving and you warn them firmly to stop, yet they don't—you *must* act. "Sorry guys, it's no TV tonight—or no special treat." If they promise to stop, but it's too late, remind them that you warned them. Still—no treat! You can't go backward. They will have another chance next time.

Try to resist comparing your children one with the other. Remember, they are different. You'll only breed unhappy, even resentful, feelings if you expect the same exact performance from each child. Don't say, "Well, your *sister* never did that." Even identical twins are individuals who, more than ever, need separate recognition and expectations.

Be proud of your children—but make sure your praise is fair, if not always equal. Just as there is disparity at home in size and intellect, the same is true for school and outside activities. Some children will do better with their academics, at sports, and at making friends. Children are all different. Know your children. Expect more from the gifted one. A grade of B from a very smart child may require less effort than a C from a child with a learning disorder. So temper your pride and praise with the ability of each. This will require skill, diplomacy, and lots of time on your part. Let your children know that you care and, as always, that you are watching. Be open to talk if one feels slighted—and that's bound to happen now and then. Respect your children for both their strengths and their weaknesses.

When you are setting limits—laying down the law—you need to remain consistent from one child to the next. Don't vary your philosophy. The rules of the household are just that—for the whole household, not just a select few. Issues of safety and respect for one another apply to everyone. Kindness, manners, honesty, and listening to each other know no bounds. It's true that you can expect a better performance from an older or more gifted child than from a younger or more distracted sib. However, the overall expectations remain constant. Communicate with calm and firmness—with love.

Remember that one of the greatest gifts you can give a child is a sibling. Learning about give-and-take and developing social skills—these are real issues between siblings and will carry over to all relationships. As a parent, remember to let your children sort things out. Let them take turns being in the lead and following. Insist upon some sharing—but not all sharing. Team play—which is what a family is all about—with different persons, having different abilities and assigned tasks and responsibilities—that's a most valuable experience. If your family works—if you as a parent are successful with modeling appropriate behavior and setting limits and your children can rival for your attention appropriately—then they will be well prepared for the real world.

Don't despair over sibling rivalry. Instead, look upon it as a good thing. Acknowledge your children with pride. Let them "bump heads"—just allow no bodily harm. And pass on the elements of SECRET—it will stand them in good stead.

GRANDPARENTS

They say that alternate generations have a special bond. Grandparents can have a very special relationship with their grandchildren. Why this is, is not entirely clear. Maybe with the added years the elderly have a better perspective on life and can slow down enough to sit and enjoy their grandchildren purely for who they are. Grandparents are better able to admire those grandkids for themselves and not necessarily for what they have done or should do. The grandparents are not as invested in the grandbabes as the parents, and sometimes that distance can be an advantage— there is less pressure to perform and only time to be loved.

But sometimes the grandparent role expands, and grandparents become the primary parent. This can get sticky. For example, if Grandma is the daytime sitter and provides most of the child care—does she become the surrogate parent and make all the parenting decisions? Or if you have multiple generations living together under one roof and Grandpa pays the rent or mortgage—who makes all the household rules? Sometimes it is not clear who the parent really is. Sometimes it's hard making space for one another.

With your own children, wherever you may be—whatever the child care or living situation—you must try as diplomatically as you can to sort out the generational roles. Make it clear to your child who is in charge. Make it clear to yourself. Who should be calling the shots—be it behavioral expectations or rules for your household? Try to talk freely and maturely to each other; seek counseling, if necessary—whatever it takes. Know that families can become very intense; they are not always that calm haven we've talked about earlier. Yelling and screaming at each other shouldn't but does happen. And it is damaging to everyone—particularly your child. Large, multigenerational families can be (and often are) wonderful. All these people to love your baby—but not to fight over her. Just be sure it is clearly understood who is in charge. Otherwise, your child will play one adult against the other.

Sometimes it can be difficult deferring to the rightful parent, but ground rules need to be established. Grandparents should be working with you to support and reinforce you in your parenting efforts—not to undermine you. If the roles are blurred (if Grandma is, in fact, in charge) look for ways to work things out correctly. Talk about what is best for the child—and work hard to abide by that. Seek legal counsel if necessary.

Whatever you do, however, don't close the grandparents out. Do include them; just define the roles. Remember, grandparents do know a lot about children—they have raised a few themselves, maybe many. And they probably did a very good job. Consult them as advisers—as the rich resources they are. Take advantage of their experience. Ask for help and/or relief—but do not abdicate your own responsibility.

As our children grow, and as the grandparents become even older, there is often a role reversal. In time, the grandparent generation may become dependent upon us and our extended family for some form of nurturing and/or daily care. We often become the care providers for our elderly parents. This is as it should be.

What else are families for? As grandparents complete the cycle of life, we all need to be supportive and involved with their care. But there are still challenges and even limits to be set. How can we provide the time and care required without overwhelming ourselves? As much as we want to provide for our own parents, what are the realistic expectations? The challenge is to involve everyone, even our children, and still leave space for ourselves.

Make sure your children do spend time with Grandma and Grandpa—even if under a little duress. It shouldn't take a lot of time. Teens, in particular, may object, as they're busy with their own lives. It can be a delicate, artful process to balance everyone's needs. As always, it takes time and communication. But in the end, we are all really responsible for each other—and truly benefit from being together.

Families need each other—all generations. Life cycles from birth to death, from infancy to old age. That's nature! We need not, and should not, shelter our children from these experiences. They should be a part of their grandparents' lives—not only because the elder folks have so much to offer, but because our children can also give. There is a real richness in multigenerational families and events. Work hard to take advantage of them—but stay in charge. Respect the elders and take time to be with them.

BABY-SITTERS

Hiring a baby-sitter is probably one of the more daunting assignments we have as parents. Picking up the telephone and making the calls to find someone to care for our children while we are away is often a little intimidating—and a bit of a gamble. Whether planned well ahead of time or truly last-minute, whether it's for our newborn or school-aged child, we've all had occasion to have complete strangers come into our homes and care for our babies. This is quite an awesome thought, if you stop to think about it. How much we entrust to these presumably well-recommended strangers! The recommendation may have been third- or fourthhand, particularly if you had to run through a long list. But whatever the references say, you're always gambling a little when you leave your children with somebody else. So how can you be sure that things are really OK?

First of all, baby-sitters do provide a wonderful service—one never, ever to be discounted. They provide surrogate care for your child so that you can do other things and have balance in your life. They allow you time to go out for dinner or to a movie, time to exercise, time to rest, time to be with other adults.

Parenting is fun but stressful. We all need some time away from our children so we can come back refreshed and continue to be the kind of parent we want to be. It's important to have "away" time, to nurture *self*. It's also important for your child to know your time away is valuable, too—as long as it is not done to excess. So, knowing that, back to the question of the sitter.

I've mentioned references—do check on them. Ask specific questions about how well and how long the references have known your sitter and under what circumstances. Get a job history—long or short, it has to be available—especially if you are considering a long-term relationship yourself. If possible, have the sitter visit you before doing any formal sitting. See how your child responds. Check your own vibrations.

When using your sitter—and this is key—check in or back, and even come home early unexpectedly. See if your child is safe and happy and the house maintained satisfactorily. Recognize that a little bit of a mess might be a good thing—particularly if it means that everyone has been playing and having a good time. If the crayons are out and everyone (including the sitter) has been coloring—great! If the kitchen looks like a tornado came through it, but chocolate chip cookies are coming out of the oven—yums! Do make sure your child is clean and fed—basics that need attention. Make sure when you pop in that your sitter knows exactly where your child is—presumably with the sitter. But do a little snooping. Consider safety first, always.

Know that you can always telephone home if you are uneasy about anything. You can always ask to speak with your child—who may be verbal or not. Maybe you just want to hear your baby's cooing. Let your sitter know that you are a conscientious parent—that you value his or her role, but you will be checking up.

Just as you do with your child, set limits on your sitter. Here are a few suggestions: Allow no other visitors when you are not home—male or female—without your previous knowledge and consent. No other children (it sounds obvious, but you would be surprised). No smoking, no alcohol, and no drugs. How do you feel about your sitter driving your child—yes or no? Tell him or her. What about walks—and where would you suggest they go and *not* go? Think about what will make things easier for your sitter (and ultimately your child), and tell him or her. Be very concrete about your child's schedule—meals and naps, the usual routine. Make sure your sitter knows what to do in emergencies—ask about CPR training. Emergency phone numbers should be very prominent: 911, police, poison control. (Have syrup of ipecac available and tell your sitter.) Does your child have any special health problems, medications, or allergies? Have a written list so nothing has to be committed to memory. Write down a phone number where you can be reached, as well as backup numbers. Tape the list of phone numbers near the phone so it won't be blown away or thrown away by accident.

If your child is verbal, ask her how things went with the sitter. Listen to the words and watch your child's body language—make sure they agree. If your child is nonverbal, does she seem to be in the same spirits as when you left her? Is there a sense of calm, of control? SECRET can be applied to your sitter: she should feel good about herself, exercise calm, respect your child, and spend time with her.

Talk to your sitter about his or her own limits. Taking care of children is not always easy; there may be times when your sitter's patience is short. Talk about putting variety into every day with periods of activity and quiet. Set limits on your sitter's time alone: eight hours at most, not twelve. Make sure you, the parent, are always available for a "bail-out" if tensions rise. Communicate honestly with your sitter to ensure your child's safety.

Unfortunately, in this day and age, the question of abuse—be it physical, emotional, or sexual—is often raised. And yes, sometimes the baby-sitter is the culprit. (Sometimes it's the parent.) If you ever suspect any inappropriate touching or hitting, you need to confront your sitter, sort out the facts as best you can, even consult your physician. Do assure your child that anything that might have happened is not her fault. Seek help to work through any difficulty.

I hope that these tips help smooth the road for a successful baby-sitting experience. If you, as parent, remain vigilant but not neurotic, everyone can benefit. Use baby-sitters appropriately, and everyone wins. Respect and acknowledge your sitters—recognize their contribution to you and your family's well-being. Reward them. Make sure they know they are special.

Nannies are more long-term sitters who have some semipermanent status in your household. They can really be the glue that holds the household together—or the source of dysfunction, if not working out. They can make or break your home life. They may live with you or not.

Nannies take on a major responsibility in the caring for and raising of your child. Often they spend more time with your offspring than you do. So ask—what kind of training does your nanny have in early childhood development? Has he or she ever done this before? Why did he or she choose to become a nanny? Listen to the answers.

To your nanny you must relinquish some, if not many, of your parenting roles. Are you prepared to do this? If both parents are working outside the home, even part time, know that you cannot be full-time parents, too. You can be SuperMom or Super-Dad, but you cannot be SuperDuperParent. You cannot be there for everything—teach your child everything she knows, expect bonding only to you, *and* hold an outside job. You have to abdicate a little, if not a lot. But both you and the nanny must be very clear in knowing that you, the parent, are still in control. The same goes for day care, where you also hand over some of the parenting reins. Make sure you, the parent, are kept informed—the lines of communication must be wide open.

Sometimes patients come in to see me as a pediatrician with Mom (or Dad) and Nanny—and Nanny has become the spokesperson. Mom seems to be more of an observer. The child is upset and cries—Nanny provides comfort. When I ask for any details of the illness, Nanny fills in all the blanks. Nanny is in the driver's seat—the parent in the back. Now, what will happen when that sitter leaves? Just be careful that your roles as parents have not been displaced, even sabotaged by your Nanny. God bless Nanny—because we truly need her (or him)—but God bless the parents, too.

Grandparents often provide child care—be it an evening of baby-sitting or daily care for working parents. Make sure that this is a good thing and not coupled with unstated expectations or payback. As stated previously, check the balance of power. Make sure it is clear who is in charge. If not, talk about it. It won't just go away and may get worse. Eventually, your child will learn to play one against the other—and that can cause real fireworks. Again, who is in charge here?

However you use baby-sitters—wherever you place your child for child care—make sure that the person who cares for your child has your child's interests at heart, first and foremost. Make sure the child-care person takes note of your child and has something special to say about her. Child-care options are numerous—pick the right one for you and your child.

PETS

Pets are a wonderful part of a family—just like children and adults, another "significant other." The only difference is that you can lock them up. In all seriousness, pets—be they dogs or cats or snakes—are living things that require care, nurturing, and discipline, just like a child. A puppy dog requires hours and days and months of "parenting," just like a baby. You have to feed him and take him to the vet for routine shots. You have to teach him to sit, stay, and come. He will require hours of repetition to accomplish the simplest of tasks—just like your toddler. Don't be fooled. Pets need time, and lots of it. Know this up-front, before you make any mistakes.

Don't get a pet just to make your child happy—to make your family "complete"—unless you are truly prepared to make the sacrifices that a pet requires. (It is amazing how much pets and children have in common.) A gerbil or hamster requires less care than a cat—and much less than a puppy or a horse. Do a little, if not a lot, of research before adding to your family. Talk to your friends who have a feline—see how it is working. There is nothing cuter than a baby anything, but those babies grow into larger animals with larger needs. A dog remains a puppy for about three years—with the energy of a rambunctious toddler. He has to be exercised lots and constantly trained. Who is going to do all of that? You—or your child?

Pets are supposed to add to the family—not divide. Make sure everyone (age appropriate) shares in the pet's care so everyone is competent in the animal's management. Make it fun. If your child promises—even swears—she will do the morning walks, hold her to it. Whose dog is it, anyway?

Know that you can establish rules of pet behavior for inside and outside—just like with your child. You can restrict your animal to certain parts of the house—he doesn't have to roam freely. Set limits: no jumping on furniture, no jumping on people, and no rough play. No begging. Quiet at mealtime.

Animals that behave badly should not be tolerated. Either you correct the behavior or, different from children, you find a more suitable home for your pet. First try to figure out why your animal is misbehaving. Maybe your puppy is wild because no one takes the time to be with him. Maybe he's alone all day and craves human contact. Maybe someone is abusing him in your absence.

Analyze the situation. Try to figure out how to give your animal what he needs. You might have to make some changes at home to spend much more time with your pet. You might have to rearrange your schedule or hire a trainer or midday caretaker. Animal behavior, just like human behavior, is complicated. Apply SECRET to your pet—know what works for you and make appropriate choices, be composed, respect his needs, and spend time with the pet.

Know that sometimes household pets become vicious. It's true. Sometimes they bite—even maim and kill. Certain breeds of dogs are predisposed to be aggressive, some animals develop senility, and some are just mean (just like people). Whatever the reason, there is no room in any household for a vicious pet—certainly a contradiction in terms, if there ever was one. An animal that threatens or attacks a person has to go.

Believe it or not, this can be a difficult decision for some families. The dog who is older than your toddler—sort of your first baby—may resort to biting your child when teased or poked. Your pet may be turning old, blind, or arthritic, and his only defense is to strike out. This animal needs a new home, because he might really hurt your child. Or he might have to be put down. The limit involved here is yours. You have to recognize any risk and act upon it. Don't make your child a statistic—a victim of an animal bite—especially one you anticipated. Before you regret anything, make a change.

I hospitalized one toddler for a bad, deeply infected hand wound—a bite from his own "pet." He was lucky it wasn't his face—or an eye. Still the family was most reluctant to make a change with their very old, practically blind dog. The choices can be hard—but as a parent, you are obligated to protect your child.

Don't get me wrong—animals are wonderful. But sometimes we neglect our children in favor of our pets. Don't let this happen. Scars from a bad animal bite are not only physical, but emotional as well. Don't do this to your child or pet.

HOUSEHOLD CHORES

Throughout this book, I have recommended that you involve your children in the running of the household by assigning simple, doable chores. Even from early childhood, children can be taught to pick up their toys—to help clean up a mess. That doesn't mean you expect them to pick it all up or do a perfect job. But it's very appropriate to involve them in part, and really a mistake not to. You can make a game out of it. Picking up and doing chores can be fun. Your child doesn't have to know it's "work." And it certainly shouldn't be punishment.

Chores and jobs are what make the world go 'round. Someone has to do the shopping, cooking, cleaning, laundry, and yard work. What about the animals, the appliances, the cars? Who does what? Who fixes what? There are probably over a hundred—if not a thousand—different household jobs that need attention during the course of a year. The truth is, there is no free ride.

Just as we have a responsibility as parents to provide for our children, we have a responsibility to delegate to them some job-sharing. In a gentle, consistent way we need to teach our children their responsibility to participate.

We, as parents, are not our children's slaves (we've said this before)—we are their parents. Our duty is not to wait on them hand and foot—no one should—but to teach them to be independent and self-sufficient. Involving our children in chores helps them to achieve those goals as well as to appreciate that honest-to-goodness work is part of running a household. Make the chores age appropriate, and stroke your children when they follow through with a job well done. When not so well done, work with them kindly and calmly to improve upon their efforts. Emphasize the positive—remember, you want to build confidence and a sense of success. Leave time to move slowly. Don't be in a hurry, and don't be compulsive. (Remember SECRET.) Be careful not to overreact to a less-than-perfect job, but encourage gently to do better. "Oops—a few papers you missed—let's pick them up together now." Then move on.

Household chores need to be clearly defined, with no confusion. They need to have a beginning and an end and should not dominate the household. A teenager should not have to spend her entire weekend tied to the house. Remember, she is one of many sharing the load, not the only one. Assignments need to be fair and open for discussion, and they should rotate. There should not be gender issues. Both boys and girls can do the same tasks. Hopefully, as parents, we model this, too. Take turns, everyone, with cooking, cleaning, doing the laundry, and mowing the lawn. Physical strength would be the only limiting factor—otherwise, there should be equitable distribution. Respect your child's other commitments. Leave plenty of room for homework, outside jobs, and team practices—and don't forget about fun.

I remember when one of my daughters went to college and had to show her roommate how to operate a washing machine. Or the college roommate who visited with us one snowy winter day and admitted to never having shoveled snow, despite the fact that she grew up in a northern climate. These young adults were perhaps more guests in their own households than active, participating members. I don't think that's really fair to the rest of the family. (Children should be treated like guests once in a while—but not always.)

So put your kids to work, a little bit. This is not child labor—it's teaching responsibility and respect for honest work. No job is too menial or trivial—they all need to get done. A job is a job, period. And they all should be done well, with a sense of purpose and pride.

MANNERS

Not to demand strict etiquette, nor to bring back the white gloves, but I think it's time to make room for some basic, simple manners. Please and thank you have a place, as do handshakes and deferring to adults. Manners need to be formally recognized, even resurrected, as having worth in and by themselves. Manners represent a kind of personal and social behavior—really a code of ethics. They need not be artificial. They are a way of showing respect to one another—as we ask and respond politely. Having good manners means being comfortable with all people—extending a friendly handshake, looking someone in the eye and saying hello. It places worth on every person; it means being nice.

What kind of example do we set for our children, and what expectations do we set for them? Are we polite and kind to everyone? To each other? Or do we treat some folks better than others, select out by rank or title? We must watch that, as we expect our children to behave and develop good manners, we show respect and kindness universally to all we encounter. Respect (part of SECRET) knows no boundaries.

There is no room for rudeness to anyone, anywhere. Rudeness is unacceptable at any level. It presupposes a hierarchy, with us on top. What right do we have to presuppose that? Wherever we are, we face life together. We need each other—all persons—to accomplish the tasks at hand. In the office, how far would we get without a complete staff? Don't all folks deserve respect for a job well done? What about in the home—how do we treat each other?

Remember that no job is without merit (see "Household Chores") and that all jobs are just that—jobs. Someone has to do them, be they dirty, messy, or simple. As we teach respect and kindness at home, we must make sure that extends out into the world. Remember the inherent worth of each individual, and know that people bring merit to their work, not the reverse. So be polite to everyone. Everybody deserves respect.

With elders, teach your children to hold doors, move chairs, and order their food last. Teach your children to stand when an adult enters a room and to recognize that person. This is nothing more than common courtesy, and it takes almost no time, just practice. Teach your child how to shake hands—a very simple task. Realize that some children are more comfortable than others doing it—some are truly shy. But work with them all—give them reassurance and confidence and watch their social skills mature. It's so easy if repeated over time. Let your children learn from early on (preschool and school-aged years), and it's a "piece of cake."

Teach your children to write thank-you notes, an art we as a society seem to be losing. Again, it only takes practice. Often, we spend more time harnessing our children to write those notes than they actually spend writing. Make sure that you write notes, too. They don't have to be lengthy—just a brief correspondence, a thank you, an acknowledgment of a gift, kindness, or favor. There is something more permanent about a note than a call. Yes, the call has merit, but sometimes a written card carries much more meaning. Don't strive for perfect grammar, spelling, or penmanship—just a finished product. The grammar and handwriting will improve with time. Let your child develop comfort with the written word—again, this comes with practice. Provide the pen and paper—make it easy. Even sit down and write your notes with her, then make an expedition out of going to the post office. Make it fun!

In all seriousness, I worry about our lack of manners—any callousness and unkindness that we, as a culture, might model. We must make sure we set limits on ourselves, at home and at work, and then, of course, on our children. We do have the opportunity to exercise control here.

Reading Together

In this age of television, video, and computers—with so much to see and do—are our children reading? Does your child ever pick up a book? Are you taking the time to read to her, and does she see you read? These are simple but very important questions—think about your answers.

If your answers are yes—terrific! Well done! But, if not, you must take *and* make time to encourage the reading of books and magazines in your household. Is it too easy for your child to flop down in front of the tube (see "Television," Chapter 14)—it is easy for us as parents, as well. It can be so automatic for your child to just pick up the telephone and spend hours talking about nothing (see "The Telephone," Chapter 14)—what about you? Then, there's the computer and many other distractions. How does your child spend her time, and what about you, the parent? What kind of role model are you?

I am amazed at how few school-aged children read *anything* over a summer vacation. When I ask my patients about summer reading, I usually get a muffled, kind of embarrassed response. Many, if not most, kids don't read! That's at least two months of lost time—and loss of skills for that child. Ask any teacher. A child who does not read over the summer often returns to school in September at a lower level of reading than when school ended in June. A skill unused is a skill lost, just like anything else. And the child who can least afford to slip behind is exactly the child who will. Furthermore, it is the rare student who ever reads anything above what is required. What about your child?

It is important for your child to develop her reading skills, because, like it or not, she needs to know how to process information, develop a rich vocabulary, and develop writing and communication skills to be the best that she can be. Reading is still the core for these tasks. Take your toddler and preschooler to the library, and read to her. Let her share in the picking out of books. Let your school-aged child read to you—remember this at bedtime (see "Bedtime," Chapter 5). Let your older child and adolescent share some of her reading discoveries with you. It does *not* have to be the classics—just anything. Even trade magazines! Reward your child for her reading with a sticker chart or a list prominently displayed in the home. Make sure *you* read, as well—again, you are your child's role model. Let your child snuggle up with you with her book when you have yours, and read together. Plan reading groups over the summer vacation to share books and stories.

If your child is having difficulty with reading at school or at home, make sure her teacher is aware and is working to support your child in her efforts to learn. Know that not all children are automatically ready to read at age six. Maybe things will click for your child at another age, perhaps sooner, or maybe later. For sure, if there seems to be any delay or difficulty, be on top of it. Ask for an evaluation. Don't be shy. Your child may have difficulty with word or letter sequencing and need special help. She may not be able to focus, for whatever reason. You need to know. Take the time to be informed and to follow up.

And then, once in a rare while, we see children who actually read too much. In truth, I can't believe I'm saying this—but if you are cultivating a real bookworm who sits and devours a pile of books every day, with no other outside interests, make sure this child has a little balance in her day as well. Encourage participation in other activities, preferably with peers. You don't want this child to isolate herself and miss out on social development.

In summary, reading is basic to all of communication, no matter how technical we have become. Don't miss the opportunity to spend enriching time with your child in books. Read to and with her, always.

WINNING AND LOSING

Our culture is a very competitive one, with winning a high priority and losing representing a kind of failure. "Did you win?"

we often ask, instead of, "How did you play?" A bad win is better than a good loss. Some people will do anything to get a win—stretch the rules, even cheat. What kind of message are we giving to our children? The winners of the World Series and Super Bowl are the heroes.

One challenge we all face as parents is to teach and show our children that it's *how* the game is played that is important, not always the win/loss column. I don't mean that the score is insignificant—not so. But I think sometimes, if not often, we are too concerned about the final score and less so about the playing. There has to be balance. We need to teach and show our children not only how to win graciously, but also how to lose with honor—how to play with dignity. A game well played is a good game. An honest effort is just that. Sulking, screaming, throwing of racquets or clubs or balls, swearing on the playing field—these are absolute nos. There is no room for a bad sport—a "spoiled brat," if you will. If your child cannot behave, remove her from her arena—immediately—and deny her further play until she reforms.

There are more important things than winning. If comportment is bad, correct it. Do so early. Your child may be a rising star, but she still has to behave herself. You still must expect good behavior. No better time to make that clear than right from the start. Who is in charge—and what are the priorities? Make sure that you're an appropriate role model—no screaming, yourself.

Why is it that the players on the professional golf tour are so well behaved? Simple—the tour demands respectable behavior and, oddly enough, gets it. Children know how far to push—be it on the tennis court or at home. Don't permit rude or inappropriate behavior in either.

Teach your children honesty above all else. If a line call is marginal, call it in favor of the opponent. Leave no suspicion for cheating, for matters of integrity. People will remember your child's suspicious call long after the score has been settled. Know that a bad reputation is very hard to overcome—don't risk it. Integrity is not a win-lose issue and, once lost, is very hard, if not impossible, to regain. Finally, you have the right and responsibility to insist upon honorable behavior—with respect for fellow competitors, as well as officials involved with any competitive play.

Remind your child that the athlete who comports herself properly can direct all of her energies into her play—and not at a bad call or a lucky shot. She will be more focused on her game rather than on an official or a piece of equipment. She will probably have more success with her game because she is less distracted. Is it any coincidence that there are many benefits to good behavior?

9

Difficult
Issues

When it comes to facing difficult or complicated situations, all of us are vulnerable. It's no one's fault when things don't turn out "right." Things happen—we simply don't control life. People get ill, even die. Problem children—not just your slightly rebellious teenager, but children who have serious behavioral and emotional issues, even severe pathology—do exist, and they deserve special attention. Likewise, issues of chronic illness and injury, change, children with special needs (preemies, twins and triplets, the physically and emotionally impaired), even child prodigies and gay children, all warrant special discussion. These issues can be especially difficult and affect us all. Sometimes things go unexpectedly or wrong—they just do.

We, as parents, may work very hard to preserve the rules and limits we have chosen—to be kind, show respect, and value each other. We give of our time generously. We maintain calm and composure. We love and hug our children. We honor SECRET. But sometimes our own resources get tested beyond our capabilities, particularly when we are stressed. It's easy to show a kind, enthusiastic face and to be a good role model when life is wonderful.

There is little challenge to being Pollyanna when we meet with constant success—when everyone is thriving and when our children are happy, fit the mold, and play by the rules. But what happens when life isn't a bowl of cherries? Just as we need to monitor our children's behavior, we also need to listen to ourselves. We must watch that we don't expect too much from anyone—our children or ourselves—especially when confronted with frightening and/or complicated decisions. Don't set unreal expectations for anyone, child or adult, particularly if dealt a difficult hand. Honor yourself; listen to and take care of yourself, just as you would your child. With difficult issues or times, strip back to the barest necessities. Limit yourself to do only what you can and/or must.

Chronic Illness

Many of us are healthy, with active, robust bodies. Thank goodness! Our children usually grow well, usually thrive—that's what they are supposed to do. They should develop physically, intellectually, and emotionally—follow predictable, normal paths of development. They should go to school, play sports, participate in all kinds of activities, and have a good time.

We don't expect to be confronted by serious illness or injury—not in ourselves, and certainly not in our children. We don't expect to be threatened by chronic disease or disability—not from a young person. Some of us even take our own health and our children's health for granted. The truth is that just as there are many of us who are well, there are also many of us who are not.

Illness and/or injury invade many, many families at different levels. Whether it is strictly a physical illness such as cancer, mono, or asthma or mental illness such as depression, schizophrenia, paranoia, or a blend, like alcoholism, illness takes its toll on families, not just the affected individuals. Whether it's you or your child, as a family, you face illness together. Only if you have been there do you know how it feels to be frightened for your child or for yourself. Illness can paralyze us both physically and emotionally. But it can also push us to reach new levels if we refuse to let it get us down. The limit here—we can't let illness beat us!

We are all mortal, but we do not expect to face our own mortality or even illness in our young adult years, and certainly not through our babies. We don't expect to deal with illness on a day-to-day basis. Illness—be it the daily reminder of cystic fibrosis (CF), hemophilia, sickle-cell anemia, or diabetes—changes things at home. Everyone in the outside world, including our friends and acquaintances, doesn't have to do daily chest physical therapy—but you do if your child has CF. Nor does everyone else have to monitor bruises (for hemophilia) and blood sugars (for diabetes) multiple times daily and/or give injections of clotting factor or insulin. Unfortunately, we can't change the fact that illness exists. But what we can and must do—for the mildly ill, the chronically ill, even the terminally ill—is make life as normal as possible for you and your child.

As disruptive and debilitating as illness can be—and no one would deny the pain and suffering that many endure—we still need to work together to keep life as sane as possible. We must work hard to acknowledge and respect each other—to still be polite and caring. We still need to set and maintain limits—to reward appropriately, not over-reward. We have to recognize needs beyond the illness—needs for human contact, for reminders of "normal" daily living. The ill child or ill parent is still a participating member of the family, and as he or she is able, we must allow for that participation. Don't count your child out, just because he is sick. He gets a vote, too. He gets to go places—it just means more planning. No matter how ill, he or you still deserve respect. Don't leave your child or yourself in the cold because of illness. Don't let that illness control your lives. An ill or disabled person is still that—a person who definitely feels emotion. And illness can make anyone even more vulnerable to feelings. Be open to those feelings—make time, really extra time, to share them.

Set no limits on time together; reduce or remove outside stress, just as in the newborn period. Illness or injury will mean more work for everybody. Divide up the tasks, but at the same time, keep them simple. It will help everyone. Remember, again, you are still *people* who have an illness—you are not the illness itself. But at times, depending upon your individual situation, the family focus will shift—as it should with a crisis. But we hope for a return to more normal living as things resolve.

Know that crisis comes with acute events, like a hospital stay. An admission even to a "routine" floor—not just the intensive care unit—is a major event for any family. Someone is sick or impaired—too sick to be at home. When a family member is in the hospital, the rules change and bend. Clearly, everyone is focused on the patient—and should be. But that shift does take its toll. Everyone else's needs are postponed—appropriately, but it can hurt. It's an unreal life, having someone in the hospital. Life temporarily freezes. Time has no meaning; rather, it is marked by the admission date and then by the discharge. Worry, concern, and memories of prior "near misses" all play havoc on you.

It is important to recognize that the world cannot absolutely stop when a family member is in the hospital. Despite a shift in priorities, we have to work very hard at taking care of ourselves—still!—and our other children. Be open about everyone's feelings; don't close anyone out. Spend time getting your own food and rest, and make sure you spend some time with your other healthy children. Bring them to the hospital, and do go to their soccer games, as well. Remind them that they are loved, too. Give them some goodies of their own if the hospitalized child is receiving a lot of gifts. Try not to breed resentment or jealousy toward your ill child. It may sound unreasonable, but it happens. Then, when discharge does take place, it will be easier to resume some semblance of a normal life at home.

Life in the hospital leaves memories and scars—fears and worries that don't just go away. Both you and your children—especially the patient—may leave the hospital with unresolved feelings. You all got through the immediate crisis that precipitated the hospitalization, but now, with discharge, feelings you have suppressed have a way of penetrating as you let down your guard as the crisis passes. The "what ifs" have a way of haunting us all.

It is very important—almost crucial—that you as a family have time to restore yourselves after someone has been in the hospital. Life does not just pick up where you last left off. It is forever changed. Limits on your time and energy need to be set and honored. Do what you have to do—nothing new or extra. The limits here involve keeping a lid on your own lives. You are tired. So let the neighbors cook and clean; let your friends do the carpooling. Take advantage of offers to help. Remember *self.*

It's worth recognizing that, when most patients are discharged home, they are only better, not completely well. Usually discharge is planned as soon as home care can be safely and conveniently arranged. This puts an extra burden on you, the family, to provide and continue special care and treatment begun in the hospital. But remember, your energies and emotions need attention, too. Get rest when you can. Get nursing and/or home health aid to spell you. Don't try to be all things to all people—you can't. Don't forget yourself.

Chronic illness or permanent disability (brain injury, cerebral palsy, paralysis) places daily demands on a family—sometimes enormous demands, with no end in sight. Whether the result of a birth trauma or congenital malformation, or an illness or injury sustained later in life, the demands and changes brought on by any chronic condition are often overwhelming. We wish that we could change certain situations, but we cannot. But we can support each other through difficult and heartbreaking times. Be available to each other—set no limits here. Get as much help as you can. Try to maintain calm.

"Problem" Children

Many children, if not most, respond to rules and regulations with compliance, even enthusiasm. Most welcome the limits we set because they provide structure to their world. However, there are always those few children who cannot or will not follow the rules. It's not always clear why—and it's not necessarily anyone's fault—but it does warrant discussion. Whether or not it is our failure to really follow through with our rules and our warnings, or whether it is an indication that our chosen rules are inappropriate, whatever the reason, we should step back and reassess when things are not working.

Take a look at your home life, and try to evaluate it objectively. Is it a happy place? Is it full of love and support—are you relaxed and calm? Make sure you're really spending time with your child. Remember those limits we have to place on our own selves (see "Schedules," Chapter 10)—are you available and modeling good behavior? Don't forget to honor SECRET, and try to uphold those elements of control. Are you recognizing your child's needs?

If life at home is not going well, it is a signal that you need to get help and need to make a change. The bottom line is that you have to come up with a new and better plan. If there are frequent outbursts of uncontrolled behavior on anyone's part (yours or your child's), something has to give, or things will just get worse.

The family that lacks order needs help—not as an admission of failure, but rather as a call to sort out the mess. Messes happen to all of us. When a child is struggling with limits, then the family struggles. There is no such thing as an isolated child—he does not live and function in a vacuum. So, for the troubled, unhappy, or noncompliant child, the family needs to get involved. You need to get help with family dynamics—help to direct behavioral changes for everyone.

For the child who does not or will not obey or comply ever, look for an explanation. You may find one, but maybe not. Maybe, as previously discussed, your child is unhappy with you or with his home life. Maybe he's confused or worried about your loving him. Maybe he is miserable at school, and he is trying to tell you this through his behavior at home. Or perhaps your child has been abused, and now he is frightened. This may be your child's way of calling attention to himself. Don't punish or correct automatically—rather, look for the source of the misbehavior.

A child who cannot conform—who acts out—this child is rarely a real troublemaker by nature. He was not born mean. Instead, he probably has a more difficult time controlling his own impulses. His mechanisms for self-control may be less developed, leaving him more at risk for "bad" behavior. The child who is causing a disturbance may be just bored or truly emotionally impaired. Or maybe he is incredibly bright and has nowhere else to direct his energies. Again, it's not his fault. But you need to ask why. And you might need professional assistance such as an evaluation with a psychologist, social worker, or physician to sort things out. There is no stigma in that. If there is a behavioral issue, look for the cause. Children who behave badly may be confused or unhappy; they are not simply "bad" children.

Ignoring a child with behavioral issues only makes life—school, social gatherings, family life—more difficult as life becomes more complicated and the demands for self-control increase. Ignoring a child who appears unable to honor rules and regulations is doing that child—also his family, and eventually society—a disservice. His problems will not just automatically go away. He needs help—and needs it now! Furthermore, his home and school settings will be happier, calmer, and more supportive if we can understand the child better, structure his home and school environment appropriately, and work to direct his energy and behavior more positively.

Know that we *can* restructure a child's environment to help him function better. We can make our homes neat and tidy. We should work hard to preserve predictable routines with meals, homework, and chores. At school, look for the teacher who recognizes your child's needs, and place your child in that teacher's classroom. Control your child's schedule, get extra help at school (even a tutor), and eventually you will help him make progress with rules and regulations. You can and must spend time with your child as he works through conforming, and you must praise him for any improvement. The payback is increased happiness (everywhere) and improved self-esteem. Learn your child's cues—keep things simple and very concrete, eliminate sources of confusion, be it complicated instructions or background noises, and leave extra time for everything—and do get help.

I resist the word "chronic" when referring to behavioral issues. Somehow the word "chronic" implies unfixable. But truth be known, there are some children who always need a very strictly controlled environment with very explicit rules in order to cope and behave. But even the "difficult" children can do very well—

or at least better—if we are truly sensitive to their needs. Some do need medication to assist them—don't deny it to them. And remember that any child with long-standing behavioral issues needs an opportunity not only to be evaluated once, but to be reassessed over time.

Several disorders or syndromes can masquerade as behavior problems. Attention deficit disorder (ADD), a well-recognized syndrome characterized by impulsivity with problems of focusing on and completing tasks—with or without an element of hyperactivity—often presents as a behavior issue. Much researched and highly publicized, this syndrome is finally receiving the attention that it deserves. Many children—and adults too, for that matter—are inappropriately labeled or misdiagnosed as having behavioral problems, when the source of the problem is not the behavior itself, but rather an innate attention problem. Treatment is available—be it structure and/or medications—and, again, can make the difference between success and failure in these individuals. Furthermore, it can have long-term impact, extending into adult years. Don't be afraid of this diagnosis—or any other diagnosis for that matter—particularly if your child fulfills the identifying criteria. A diagnosis can help to direct treatment, and that can be a very good thing. In the end, work in earnest with the best professionals to come up with a workable treatment plan.

Finally, with any behavioral issue, make sure you know your child and that you are not relying too much on professional help to fix a problem. Just as schools cannot and should not replace the home, doctors, psychologists, and counselors are not parents. Make sure that, in the busyness of your day, your child has not been excluded from your priorities. You may be providing all the physical and medical comforts he needs (maybe more), but he might plain and simply want only *you*, i.e., your time and presence! You will and can make an enormous impact and difference. The recommendations made by the professionals will need hard work and implementation. There is rarely a quick fix. Are you willing? The limit here is on you. How far are you willing to go for your child? After all, you are his parent. Don't forget he needs you!

In general, a severe behavior issue is a complicated one that in most cases must involve a professional evaluation, even a team approach. Depending upon the age of your child, not only family input, but school and physician evaluations need to be obtained. It is everyone's responsibility to optimize the conditions for living and learning for every child. You, as the parent, will ultimately make an informed decision on a treatment plan. You will learn a lot yourself as you advocate for your child and then make provisions that allow for him to do better. In short, you must take charge here.

CHILDREN WITH SPECIAL NEEDS

We have already touched on issues of chronic illness and difficult behaviors in the preceding sections. Certainly these children have very special needs of their own, and I don't mean to exclude them from this category by making a new heading. However, I do want to extend the discussion to include other children who also have very special needs—and whom we may have missed.

Whether it be illness or injury, behavior problems, or other syndromes, children with special needs do change the complexion of any family. Brain-injured babies, children with Down syndrome, floppy infants—their needs are much more complicated than those of more "normal" children. More demands are placed on the family to provide for these children—be it everyday needs like feeding and sleeping (which can be very complicated) or routine tasks like bathing and toileting. Just going to the doctor's can be a major outing—not to forget all those other subspecialists, as well.

Yet these children still have the same human needs for love and support. They, too, just like the ill or disturbed, are individuals with their own merit and worth. And despite whatever disability or syndrome they have, they still have purpose. A premature infant with problems of developmental delay, twins and triplets who demand double and triple from their parents, the learning disabled child, the blind child, the child with a congenital heart problem—these children demand something extra from their parents and the family. Working with children who have special needs usually involves many professionals and a complicated treatment plan. Sometimes it means meetings, reports, and even hospitalizations.

It is vitally important that as we focus on the medical or physical needs of these children we not deny them the care and tenderness every child deserves. But in terms of setting limits, we have to be very careful about ourselves and not try to do too much. You cannot be all things to anyone—even less so with a child who has complicated special needs. It is absolutely necessary that we recognize our own limits and get help to fill in the gaps.

Advocating for a child with special needs is complicated and can be very exhausting. As much as society would like to provide services, it is not always able. Just finding equipment such as a wheelchair can be very hard. Locating an aide—if twenty-four-hour care has to be provided—can be a full-time job. Much falls upon the family to research and evaluate. Expense is often a real concern. Talk to other families with similar problems. Find medical centers with a large resource base that can help you. Find support and get occasional relief. Don't accept the answer no—at least, not in the beginning. Be creative—find an ally (doctor, nurse, social worker) who can help you advocate your child's case. Don't give up—and try to maintain that sense of calm, even humor.

Change

Life is never constant. Just as we may think we have everything under control, change inserts itself into our lives. Change brings on new horizons and new opportunities and forces us to put aside some of the old. Change can be healthy, forcing us to adapt and expand in ways we never thought possible. But it can also be threatening or destructive, taking away security and even our loved ones. Change that is unpredictable and never even imagined happens.

Whatever the source for change in a household—be it birth or death (of a parent, sibling, friend), change in marital status (separation, divorce, remarriage), or a move (by choice or not)—

change always brings on an element of stress. Whether the change is welcomed or not, things will be different. Life will not be the same. Either the players or place will be altered, giving a new face to the household. Expectations may change (if only a little), as well as relationships to one another. Hopes and dreams will shift—up or down—with the risk of being fulfilled or not. Initial excitement might be only temporary, with disappointment to follow.

Now more than ever, despite any change in a household, the basic rules and limits must be upheld. More than ever, children need to know that the rules have not changed. In spite of even a drastic loss or upheaval, some things have to remain constant. Every child needs to know and needs to be assured that certain things are inviolate. Love, respect for one another, acceptance of each other—these are the rocks of the household. Despite some change, there has to be some stability. Yes, this seems a contradiction in terms, but it is a truth, nevertheless.

How can we assure a child that love and kindness remain? By open communication. We may lose control of our life plan, but we shouldn't lose control of each other. If the framework goes, then why not everything else? It is incumbent upon those left behind—the widow, the newly separated parent—to maintain the limits set before the disruption. If, despite a move or change in employment (both of which can be very traumatic), the hardcore structure remains, you can survive change. The limits you have worked so hard to establish—from courtesy to each other to behavior at meals and bedtime—these must go on. Don't change the rules of operation just because life is different. Coping is much easier if there is some sameness. You are still the same people—and your children need to know that. The principles of SECRET—remember yourself, be composed, respect each other, spend time together—these should not change as life around you does.

For the family that was in trouble before change interrupted their lives, change can precipitate crisis. Look at and listen to each other. Even with a strong foundation, families may shake. With a weaker base, the walls can crumble. Know when you are in real trouble, and seek help from family, friends, or professionals.

Change is greatly underestimated as a stress in our lives. Acknowledge it as such, and work together in meeting the challenges that change brings.

When Things Go Wrong

Life with all its uncertainties does dole out certain unpleasant, unexpected, and difficult moments. Try as we might, we cannot shield our children from unhappiness or unfairness. We cannot keep disappointment away. We have no control over illness, peer groups, team selections—even school and college admission policies. We can't always make everything right—some things are just not fixable. And there are times when we cannot even be there to help.

As parents, we want to and need to prepare our children for everything—and that means the bad as well as the good. We want to build a foundation for success, but one that can also tolerate disappointment, even failure. As we prepare our children to make choices, we do need to let them accept the consequences or outcome of their actions and decisions. Handling success as well as defeat (no matter how minor or major) is a significant lesson in living. Be it winning or losing a competition (see Chapter 8) or simply not fulfilling one's aspirations (getting a C, instead of an A or B; not being chosen for the spring play), accepting that disappointment, although hard, is part of life. We cannot shelter our children from the outside world; we cannot control decisions made by an outside authority. We have no choice about major illness or injury. There are certain things we have to accept.

When things go wrong—where are we as parents? Are we available—at least in spirit if not physically present—to help support our children with their disappointments? Do we give time and space to acknowledge their feelings? Make sure that you maintain calm, even in the face of challenge. Keep home sacred— a place where your child can come to vent, to cry, to renew or retreat. Don't get too busy in your own world—or too wrapped up with your own disappointment or worry—and fail to recognize the needs of your child. Be on guard. Make sure you don't limit your attention and affections and cut out your own child.

If you have been successful in giving time and love, setting limits and upholding them, and communicating to your child how you feel and what you expect, yet leaving him room to be his own person, then you can struggle through the hard times, as well as the good. Are you a survivor? If so, show your child how. Help him to be one, too. Then you have done the best you can. No one can ask for more! Keep your priorities in line, and remember SECRET. When things go wrong, you still have each other. You still have your inner strength to carry you through. No one or nothing can take that away.

THE VERY GIFTED CHILD

Many children develop physical and/or language skills far ahead of their peers. Walking and climbing at age seven months, speaking sentences at age twelve months, playing tunes on a piano at two years—well, I get nervous. These children are the exception—and that may prove to be more of a burden than a talent.

Exceptional children have exceptional gifts. They learn and achieve faster and attain higher levels than their peers. They are always a step ahead, if not many. They excel—and do so naturally. As infants, toddlers, and preschoolers, we marvel at their early achievement, not knowing what lies ahead. That gifted athlete might be Olympic caliber—and if so, that will demand enormous commitment and sacrifice by the whole family. The child who reads at age two or three—our genius, if you will—may have trouble waiting for his slower peers once in school. He may be very bored in a traditional school structure yet may have trouble with social skills. The piano prodigy with a temperament driven to practice and perform still needs to go outside and play. The very gifted child has a special set of needs that have to be worked through.

It is important that all children develop globally—not just in the area of their gifts. It is always a challenge to provide broad-based opportunity for development—but, I think, more so with the very gifted child. It is important that he develops other interests and skills and not neglect the rest of life.

It is also important that we not push any child too much in

his area of excellence—that we still allow him to be a child. Don't automatically move your very skilled reader up to the next grade, where he will be the youngest and probably the smallest. He may be intellectually mature but not socially adept—and certainly not physically ready for the bigger kids. His age peers will know he is different—maybe even think he is odd—but they know that anyway, no matter what grade he is placed in. And there should be no hurry to getting through school. What's the rush? There is so much more to learn than just book knowledge. Try to look at the whole picture. There is no advantage to starting college at age fifteen or sixteen—that's just too young!

The very gifted child is sort of the odd man out and will demand special time and attention in any setting. He is so bright and talented, that a new emphasis will have to be placed on the *quality* of his learning, not just the quantity—wherever he might be. Designing a special program and/or curriculum will be a necessity, regardless of his grade placement.

So work to support and cultivate your child's gift—but with control. There will be time enough for pressure in later years. Don't set expectations far too high early on and make everyone unhappy. Allow your child space to pursue his gift, but be very sure to not let his gift dominate his life completely. Also, leave room for failure or burnout, hard as that may seem. Know that failure for the very gifted is a real stumbling block.

You, as the parent, can work to control your child's world—and work you must. It won't always be easy, but you can make an impact. Talk to other parents of gifted children. See what has worked for them. Seek out the right teachers at school—those with the "right" temperament and skill to direct and excite your child. Make sure your child's teacher recognizes his gift. Involve the school administrators, if you have to. Get help, if you need it. Try not to get frustrated—although it happens. Be open. And make changes, if things are not working.

Being the parent of a gifted child requires restraint, as you try not to show off your child to the world. Of course you are proud of him—you should be. But at the same time, a little humility goes a long way—for both you and your child. Try not to put him on a pedestal—that's a pretty high position. Let him enjoy a special, but not inflated, status. There is more to life than his gift, as important as it may be. Putting all your eggs in one basket is risky—beware!

Exercise some self-control yourself by being very available. Take time to direct your child appropriately with skilled teachers or coaches. Be involved—supervise.

THE GAY CHILD

Gay adults were once children, too. They didn't just turn "gay" automatically at age twenty-one—or whatever age you choose. Feelings don't just appear and develop suddenly. Quite the contrary—they are usually years in the making.

This is a difficult subject for some, but one that needs to be addressed. Where do gay children come from? Again, what did you, as parents, do—right or wrong? What kind of message did you give your children? What happened? Honestly, nothing!

People come in all kinds of shapes and sizes; they also vary in terms of sexuality. This is fact. They are made this way—it is the way of nature. Throughout history there has always been a homosexual orientation for some—males with males, females with females—in all of humankind. Trace different cultures and you will find evidence for homosexuality since the beginnings of time. Pick a number—somewhere around 9 to 10 percent of our human race is said to be homosexual and always has been. So why are we so surprised by homosexuality? Are we homophobic for reasons that are unclear? And what can we do to diffuse this phobia?

What can we do for the teenager whose sexuality is developing on the "other" track or who is uncertain? He senses something is different. His peers may be heavy into heterosexual relationships, but that is not his inclination. Quite the contrary—he is attracted physically and emotionally to a schoolmate or teacher of the same sex. But the vibrations he gets from peers and family make him feel awkward or wrong—even deviant. Signals from us and others can be powerful, giving a very dangerous message. They can even push a child over the edge—drive your child to drugs, even suicide! He may turn to hiding his true feelings—the "closet." He may go out on dates to "fake it." But in truth, he is greatly conflicted—and may be very disturbed. How can we help this child?

First of all, it is important to realize that same-sex attractions do not necessarily mean that your child is gay. Same-sex attractions and same-sex "idol worship" are also a part of normal heterosexual development. Sexuality is complex, with social and genetic components as well as elements of maturity. Your child may just need to wait.

But as with all issues, discussion and communication have to be open and honest. If you are uncomfortable talking about issues of sexual preference with your child, find someone who is not. This is a perfect place for your family physician to become involved. Feelings, as we mentioned before, are real and should not be denied. If your child has a homosexual persuasion, there is nothing wrong with him. That is the way he is made. You, as a parent, have done nothing wrong—unless you have denied him the love and support any child should have. You cannot reject your child because of his homosexuality. That is your problem, not his. This may be a very bitter pill for some parents to swallow, but swallow they must—and with dignity. You cannot make your child into what he is not, at any level. Support your child, as he may be going through a very hard time trying to sort it all out. You all will be better off. Respect your child—don't forget SECRET.

10

External
Pressures

Like it or not, there are always external pressures affecting our families, impacting our ability to parent and to set limits: not just the "difficult issues" of illness, injury, or change, which we have already discussed, but the ordinary, everyday issues like schedules, school demands, peer pressure, and even carpools, sports, or exercise programs. These are usually things where—when push comes to shove—we still have some choice. Illness is often beyond our control—but not so the carpool. Peer pressures will influence our teen children—but again, we're still the parents. And when it comes to schedules—who sets them up, anyway? Look at what's driving our lives. Are these external pressures real or artificial and of our own making? One more time, who's in control?

The elements of SECRET can still be applied. You must know your*self*, especially as you meet with outside opinions and forces. Where do you draw the line for behavior? What are your expectations? Be clear. Exercise that *calm*—particularly when you might be bucking the system, the odd man out. Be rational and thoughtful. *Respect* those around you—your children, folks in the community, friends (yours and your children's); make room for discussion, flexibility, and understanding. And of course, consider *time*—a limited resource that must be divided appropriately, not stretched.

Our children need to be prepared for life outside—where our walls do not extend, where we have less control. How should we handle their schedules, or ours? How can we optimize school and peer relationships? Look at what happens when we travel. What about a visit to a neighbor's, friend's, or relative's—or an appointment at the doctor's office (I couldn't resist)—or even a bit of shopping at the mall or dinner at a local restaurant? How do we and they behave?

Your child needs and should demonstrate appropriate behavior at all times. This means that we need to extend the model of respect and kindness that we have established at home to include the world around us. Our children need to see us being fair and courteous to all people, so we can expect the same from them. Again, no matter who or where, every person deserves our respect. Calm and consideration—don't leave home without them!

Now let's look at those outside pressures and make sure we— not they—are in control.

Schedules

A discussion of schedules is really a discussion of time management more than anything else. For what do our schedules do, if not manage our time. The issue is, what drives our schedules?

How busy are we? Chances are good that many of us are just too busy. Our children, the household, outside work, volunteer projects, home entertaining, maybe some exercise class or regular sport activity, something creative (music, art)—the list goes on. And maybe you're doing some home remodeling, as well. Looking at your schedule—everything has value. But how did your list get so long? How did you get so committed to so many things? As a composite, it can be too much! Does it leave you time to enjoy and appreciate life—and especially, to appreciate your child or children? Has your schedule taken control of your life? Beware! Don't get overcommitted. Learn to say no to those many requests for your time. One more committee assignment, one more worthwhile project—leave it for somebody else. Where are your priorities? Be honest. Do you spend most of your waking hours *not* with your children—and is that what you had intended?

Sometimes the stress of parenting is not really the parenting, alone. Rather, it is parenting plus everything else. Is there no room in your week to spend the time you should—you want—with your children? Are you stressed because your schedule is too full, leaving little if any space for quality time with your family? Stress is not a good thing and can permeate families. It can ruin happy times—it can cripple you. If the stress is from outside, nonvital sources—truly your own doing—get rid of it. Make changes. It sounds simple. Just try it. Is the grass really greener on the other side of the fence? Take a gamble and see. Quit that job—be it volunteer or paid; cut back on something. Take a "sabbatical" at home with your children. Do something creative, not necessarily goal oriented. Paint, write, read—and share these activities with your child. Let her paint and write, also.

Don't have so many deadlines. Whose deadlines are they? Does it really matter whether that project gets done? You have to set limits on yourself—leave room for unstructured play and spontaneous outings (just as you did for the toddler). We've said this before, but it's so important.

Are you a slave to your schedule—to your income, to your home or yard? A slave to your child's school fund-raiser? Once this event or project is over, then what? Then there will be time—maybe. Remember, you don't get time back, ever. If you miss an athletic event or a special occasion with your child—or just a walk to the park on a sunny day—you don't get it back. A moment in time is just that—there are no second chances.

So do what you must, but be definite about those "musts." Leave spaces between commitments to regroup. Also take time to feel the difference between a crowded schedule and one that is free. Which feels better for you and your family? You do have choices. Hopefully, you really are in charge!

Know that with each added child, life at home becomes more complex. One child is usually pretty easy to accommodate—two, a little more difficult. But three or more can become very complicated, especially if your schedule is already crowded. Getting children from here to there—even the doctor's, not just gymnastics and music class—can be a test to anyone's managerial skills. And the more you have to juggle, the more the stress. Who is going to take Sally, Mary, and Billy to their after-school sports, all in different places? Who is going to take care of the home front after school—supervise the homework and fix a nutritious dinner (not just another take-out meal)? And finally, what happens when someone gets sick—parent or child? It does happen. There has to be room for flexibility. Things do backfire, despite our best efforts.

Make sure in planning your family or in bearing your children that the numbers aren't going to exceed your ability to provide, not money, but *time*. If so, you must reassess. Do you have time for your children? Many parents, previously at work in the business or professional world, choose to stay home with the birth of that second or third child. It just gets too complicated and even too expensive working outside.

Now look at your child's schedule. Remember, don't overload your preschooler, your school-aged child, or your teen with too many activities. Just as we adults need time and space to gear down, children do, too. Keep some afternoons and weekends free—allow for spontaneity. Help your child deal with unstructured as well as structured time. Don't automatically sign up your child just because every other child is doing "it" (be it dance or scouts or baseball). Be very selective about the extras, and you will get more mileage out of them. You and your child will run less risk for fatigue or burnout, and your child will be healthier, both physically and emotionally. You, too, will be less stressed if there are fewer carpools, fewer demands on your time. After all, you still have to schedule meals, snacks, and school activities—or, at least, make some kind of arrangements. And if there are too many other activities, you're sure to have conflicts—and that only breeds stress. Parenting is a full-time job. But don't make it an "overtime" job—where the payback is *less*.

The take-home message is simple: Limit outside activities. Do some extracurricular activities, but *not* all. Plan and choose with your child. Let her participate in the selection process. Respect her need for rest, and choose carefully. Have basic ground rules. For instance, how about a maximum of two or three activities per week for the school-aged child? If one activity turns out not to be fun, change it at midyear, but follow through for that half year at least. For the teen, school will probably dictate the schedule—make sure there isn't a varsity sport, spring play, and yearbook production all at the same time. Something will give, and it may be your child—or you. Watching your child be stressed is stressful in itself. If she is happy and relaxed—not pushed—chances are good that your child and your household will function much better. There should always be time to "smell the roses." If not, reassess. Don't let everyone's schedule run the household. Who or what is in charge?

PEERS

A peer is an equal—one with the same rank and title. We think of adolescents with their peers—their "equals"—meaning age mates, fellow adolescents. But don't forget that toddlers and school-aged children have their peers, too. It's just that the pressure of the peer group is paramount in adolescence. And not uncommonly, parents and peers are at loggerheads with each other—true rivals—during the teen years.

As parents, we invest much time in setting limits—being kind and courteous to each other, showing respect, developing manners, and establishing rules. We spend years modeling acceptable patterns of behavior, hoping that our children will mimic them. Then, all of a sudden, we happen upon adolescence—and out of the blue our children begin to model their peers' behavior—which may be completely contrary to ours. (See Chapter 7.)

Welcome to the reality of parenting! Try as we might, the influence of peers on our growing children is very strong—and by adolescence, often stronger than what we wield as parents. We have to do a certain amount of letting go with our children. That usually hits home with the adolescent peer group. We have to give our children space to make choices, to choose their friends. Like it or not, as much as we parents control, we also have to give a little slack. Your success as a parent may depend upon how well you maintain this delicate balance: you versus the peers. Separation is a normal part of maturation. It is part of the identity process, if not the identity "crisis."

Recognize your child's peer group (at whatever age) as having merit; affirm it, but also leave room to both approve and disapprove of what your child (with or without peers) is doing. Remember—per our previous discussion on teens—keep the lines of communication open. Leave room to both agree and disagree. Be very clear about how you feel, and leave room for your teen to react—with calm. Listen to each other. Don't forget about love being unconditional—and no matter what, always be available for your child. You can set some limits—for example, where your child goes and when. But you cannot mandate everything—only discuss. You cannot select her friends. Do stick to the tenets of SECRET as best you can. Let your teen (and we've said this before) count on stability in you.

Remember to let your child make decisions, as long as they are safe ones—and then let her deal with the consequences. And on issues of safety—and here's a true reality check—even then, you have to give a little. Driving, parties, overnights—there is always a bit of risk to just plain living. Drugs, sex, alcohol, cigarettes—what is the peer group doing? You can impose curfews, insist upon events being chaperoned, even know where your teen is, always, but even the most compliant teen will just get curious and stray. And (we've discussed this before) things happen. So be available and watch. Be at home—be involved. Talk! Recognize that your child's peer group has power; give it space but not complete reign.

Schools

Schools are part of our American heritage. Our children enter around age five or six years (see "School," Chapter 5) and graduate at age seventeen or eighteen. During those twelve or thirteen years of education, they will learn how to read, write, and analyze written material. They will be exposed to technology—math, science, computers. But they will also learn more than just the books.

Children at school must learn to function and participate in groups. They must learn to master certain social skills. They have to work with their classmates and their teachers. They have to get along with each other. They learn about give-and-take—they have to take turns. They will begin to assess their own abilities against everyone else's, no matter how low key the evaluation system may be (kids just know). They will learn to compete—be it in a classroom, on a playing field, or on the stage. They will have a taste of both success and failure—if not for themselves, at least for their peers. They will sample a lot of life—but mostly, they are preparing for life. The academic, physical, social, and personal skills that they acquire in school will launch them for future careers—prepare them for further educational and/or vocational training. In short, school is a very important component of your child's life.

When to start school and where to place your children are often-asked questions and valid concerns. The answers are sometimes hard and complicated, because it depends on the child. And it also depends on the options, if there are any.

First of all—and I've mentioned this before—there is no rush to enroll your young toddler or preschooler in school. Preschool or nursery school in the early years has its place, but it is not a must. Children enter school for all kinds of reasons—from a need for more social contact to giving Mom or Dad some time off. These are all legitimate; just be honest. There is no absolute time when a young child must begin school—because in fact, she may be better off at home. But when you are ready—whatever setting you choose—the most important thing about any school is your child and her teacher—not the walls, not the classroom size, not the age mix. Is your child happy? Is her teacher a loving, caring, sensitive person who will continue to model the behaviors you are working so hard to promote? Does the teacher play with your child—does she or he know her? There are so many questions, but it really comes back to the person in charge.

Make sure the other children are happy, as well as the parents. Test the mood—are the children wearing smiles? And check the school environment inside and out for cleanliness and safety. When your child goes to school you relinquish control to that teacher. Are you comfortable doing that? If so—great! If not—don't. If trust is in question, you must seek another alternative.

Many parents wrestle with the decision about when to start their child in school. A very smart child may appear more ready than others. Your child may be very verbal—even reading at age five—and may be bored at home. But beware! There is so much more to school than the academics. Know that the very bright child is often a bit socially immature, particularly as she gets older. Don't push this child just because she is bright. Don't make her the youngest, and maybe the smallest, in the class. Why not make her one of the oldest—and enable her to be more of a leader than a follower? Besides, what is the real hurry to growing up? Your child will probably live for ninety to one hundred years—don't rush her. Furthermore, no one will care if she's young for her class—not even for a second—when she's in high school and competing for any position. That's her problem, not theirs. So, my advice is, keep your bright child in her chronological age group. Work within the system to see that her bright mind is challenged and directed (see "The Very Gifted Child," Chapter 9). Don't push her beyond her years.

As your child grows, and she is mandated to attend school, it is important to recognize that you still have responsibilities for your child that extend inside the classroom walls. Yes, you do relinquish some control. However, you still are responsible for advocating for your child—particularly if she is unhappy or not doing well. Parent participation is a must—for who else will advocate better for your child? Take time—be informed. Get involved. Be a part of the process. Work within the system to find the best match between child and teacher to enable your child to grow positively. This is often a delicate issue, as all schools unfortunately cannot accommodate every single issue and every child, despite their intent. That's fact. However, without causing undue upset—without being a pain in the neck, just a squeaky wheel—

you, as the parent, do need to be involved with your child's school life. You need to let the teachers and principal know that you care, and that you will work with them (not against them) to find the best fit for your child. Teachers and principals are generally very reasonable and knowledgeable people; they will support you.

Sometimes, the child who has no "special needs" gets lost in the system. The child who is easygoing, causing no disturbances—who is neither especially gifted, nor a behavior problem—this kid often gets moved around with the pack. He or she might be just a number—not a problem. Make sure that this doesn't happen to your child. Is your child being "sacrificed," if you will, because no one is advocating for her? Remember, every child has needs—some are more obvious than others.

For the child with special needs, your town and state should offer special programs that will provide for your student. You might have to fight the system to get the services you need, but don't give up. As with any child, try to optimize the school setting and teaching staff. Ask for and get the evaluations that are indicated. More than ever, be involved. Involve professional counselors—even doctors—to help support you.

As your child grows, it may become apparent that school is not her bag. Or, more to the point, your present school setting is not a match for her. As a parent, your responsibility is to monitor, watch, and study your child—not in an overbearing way, but as a caring, informed father or mother who can assess your child appropriately. Make no mistake—this can be very painful. If your child is more suited for vocational or nontraditional learning, do your best to provide for it. This takes enormous time, energy, emotion, and, sometimes, money. And still, there are no guarantees—there never are. Your options may be limited.

If you live in one town, but your child's friends are in another, she might be better off making a change. You might have to fight the local school boards. But know that social acceptance is as important—if not more so—than academic match.

If you have a long legacy at one school (i.e., *all* the Smiths went to St. Charles) and people expect your child to succeed automatically, but she isn't, you have to consider a move. You may have a few extra hurdles to climb—like your family's opposition. You might have to "buck" the system if your child is unhappy and/or unsuccessful. But here's where you have to recognize (again!) your child's individuality. We keep coming back to this point: Your child is unique and no one's clone, so do work hard to find the right place where she can thrive.

If you have an unhappy school situation and cannot change it, then work within the system to make changes or exceptions. The squeaky wheel does get the grease—just don't get too squeaky. Let your child know that you care and you are working to improve the situation. Recruit her and do take advantage of professional counselors for ideas and help as well. The bottom line is, do the best you can with the resources you have. You have a job here.

Sports and Exercise

Everyone needs regular exercise. Healthy bodies need challenge; hearts, muscles, and bones need to be used. Although exercise comes more naturally for some than others, we all need it. And whether it be a desire for a good physique or a natural drive for physical activity, some folks are more driven to exercise than others. Some are definitely more coordinated than others. Exercise and sports are fun and easy for some kids, but not for all.

Regardless of your child's inclination (and yours) to exercise, he or she must. Our lives are generally too sedentary, which is not good for our skeletons, our digestive tracts, our hearts and circulation, or our minds. Lack of exercise is unhealthy. Physical fitness is a priority!

Believe it or not, children (and adults) are happier when physically challenged. They eat better, sleep better, and concentrate better. They even get along with each other more easily. Pent-up energy is untapped and undirected energy—it needs to be funneled properly. Standard physical education programs—two to three meetings a week in the gymnasium—try as they might, are not sufficient. Children absolutely need to work hard physically— they need to get their hearts pumping, and they need to sweat and build muscle tone. Twenty to thirty minutes of sustained physical challenge three times a week should be the minimum goal for every able child (and adult, as well). A regular exercise program—and it can be individually designed—needs to be implemented for all children. This is an ambitious goal, but a desirable one! Speak to your schools—your doctor—and start somewhere.

Look at your day and at your child's day. Does she sit in a chair for hours? Is she driven everywhere, in bad weather and good? Does she use an elevator even to go up only one flight of stairs? (What about you?) It seems like such a waste! How about taking the stairs or walking to a friend's house even if it's cold outside? Without packing more or too much into anyone's day, make exercise a priority. If your child needs encouragement, do it with her. Again, be a role model. Don't just drive your child to the track or the pool to watch, but actually join in and exercise with her. It can be a lovely way to spend time with your growing child, and you too can benefit.

As we encourage fitness and participation in physical activity, we need to monitor for overuse—and of course, be aware of abuse. There has to be a balance between mental and physical activities—not too little of either, not too much. The athlete who is participating in multiple sports at competitive levels, with practices daily—watch that this child isn't overchallenging her body. Remember, your child—even your teenager—is still growing. Her bones have yet to achieve adult density. Her joints are flexible, but not as strong as they will be. She can push, but watch that she does not risk chronic or serious injury by pushing too hard. Knees and shoulders can be damaged from overuse. The concept "play through pain" needs to be tempered, really reevaluated. When the body hurts, the pain is its signal to stop! Pain means rest until the pain goes away. Playing with an injury puts your child more at risk. Clearly, there are choices. Make sure your child's coach and trainers have their priorities in the right place. Speak to them. Make sure adequate supervision is available for all practices and games. Sports, particularly when competitive, are a wonderful opportunity for your child to test her mettle. They are physically and mentally challenging and a healthy release for both body and mind. There's a valuable lesson in the give-and-take of team play that will serve your child very well in later years. Just don't overdo. Your child has a long life to lead, with years of sports to come. Don't ruin her body now! Take time to monitor and respect your child's limits! (For further discussion, see "Sports," Chapter 7.)

CARPOOLS

Carpools have a habit of dominating suburban life, especially during the school years. So many places to go—how do you get your child from here to there? How and with whom do you need to coordinate rides? Are you a slave to the car?

Starting right off in the toddler years, if not at birth, planning any outside activity often involves transportation—particularly as we spread our geographic boundaries. If you have complete flexibility and access to a car, you can go anywhere at any time. But if, like many of us, you are pulled in different directions and have to provide rides to two places at once, the ever-present carpool may be your only way out. Or you might want to travel with a friend and/or save gas.

Carpools are a boon to the busy parent, as they provide safe and convenient transportation for those outside activities. But you still have to have some rules. Make sure anyone driving your child is experienced. A new driver is more risky. Don't let young teens or baby-sitters who are new to the road—or maybe new to our country (not everyone drives on the right side of the road)—drive your children.

You want a safe driver—most assuredly—but how can you guarantee this? This can get ticklish. How do you ask about safety? Perhaps questions about speeding tickets and/or accidents can be addressed, but a better test is to drive with your driver. Arrange to be a passenger. Plan an outing together—go as a carpool. After all, your child—your most precious possession—is going to be entrusted to this unknown driver. Do your homework. Do a test drive. Take time to check things out.

Make sure the car is never overloaded. Everyone, without exception, needs to have a seat belt on. Don't pack the kids in like sardines in the interests of convenience. If you do—or if you allow it—you are making a *big* mistake. Make sure your carpool driver isn't trying to meld more than one carpool into yours—you'd be surprised.

Plan plenty of time for pickup and delivery, and make sure your fellow carpoolers are doing the same. If it's a ten-minute drive to school, and your child gets picked up eight minutes before the school bell rings, you *must* say something to that driver. Just by the clock, your driver runs the risk of driving too fast—speak up!

When doing the pickup yourself, make sure everyone is ready at the appointed time. If not, you must talk about it. It is not fair for one person to keep others waiting. If one cannot get his or her act together, cancel that person out.

Make sure your carpools are flexible. Life with all its unpredictability brings last-minute changes. If you suddenly cannot drive, are you comfortable calling someone else? It never hurts to have an acceptable backup driver, if your schedule is inflexible. But think about that ahead of time. Also, discuss what to do if no one is home when you are delivering. Obviously, you would never leave a three-year-old in an empty house. But it is better to discuss this up-front. Of course, when you do drop off a young child, *always* make sure he or she is safe. A simple hand wave from the receiving parent is all you may need. But don't assume that because the child went into the home all is safe and well. Regardless of the child's age, wait for some signal—use that hand wave or a flick of the house lights.

Arranging carpools can get dicey: Some families want in, others want out. Some can only drive on certain days. Feelings get hurt, believe it or not. Your people management skills can be pushed to the limit as you try to put together a schedule. Working with children can be hard—working with some adults, sometimes impossible. If the carpool is more of an issue than the activity, perhaps you have the wrong pool or you need to reevaluate the activity itself. Don't let carpools ruin your life. Maintain a sense of perspective—that's the limit you need to honor.

One last word about the car radio: "Mom—don't talk, and for goodness sake, don't sing." Somehow as our children get older, they want us to vanish into thin air. We are allowed to drive the car, but we are supposed to remain silent, not touch the radio dial, not play our music, and never, ever, sing along. We can chauffeur, but as a mute robot. OK, we won't ask stupid questions—but we can speak and expect civil, polite conversation, which includes us adults. Make that clear. Don't be put off by your child. Who's in charge? With regard to the radio, perhaps make a compromise. Find a blend of music that both you and your child (usually a teen) accept. OK, no Bartok—but not necessarily hard rock. The radio dial does *not* belong to your child. Just as your house is your home, the car belongs to you. You set the limits. You can be gentle—"No, I don't think so."

Whether you sing or not first depends upon your voice—but I don't see anything wrong with a little humming if everyone else is singing. Now really. We are not out to embarrass our children— but our children need not ignore us nor be rude. The car can be a microcosm of the world—be in charge. Expect a little respect for and from everyone, keep it calm, don't be in a rush, and maintain control—remember SECRET.

Traveling

Traveling is supposed to be fun. But there is nothing fun about being trapped in a car with a screaming toddler who only wants out. Who gets to drive—and who is the lucky parent who gets to sit in the back seat and try to keep this monster happy?

Travel—whether it be in a plane, bus, or car—requires preparation. Even the quick trip across town to visit Grandma needs a little planning. Or at least you need to keep something on reserve to grab at the last minute. Remember that bag of goodies (see "Behavior," Chapter 3) we talked about for the toddler. Keep one in the car—or at least have your child's tote bag ever ready. A fifteen- or twenty-minute drive can easily expand into an hour. All it takes is one stalled car. If that hour happens to be mealtime or sleep time (and you forgot the binky—one reason to get rid of it), the extra forty-five minutes may be very unhappy. No one likes to listen to a tired, hungry, crying child. Spare yourself and your child this misery. Travel with food (preferably dry), a spill-proof drink, a soft blanket, a sturdy book, a stuffed animal or doll, and some music or story tapes. Keep napkins and wipes, even diapers and a change of clothes in the car. Like a scout, be prepared! If you live in a cold climate, have blankets and boots in the spare compartment, always; make sure you can cope with exposure if you have a breakdown.

Travel with money. It sounds obvious. But throw in enough cash to cover gas, food—even a speeding ticket, depending on where you're going. Keep your gas tank full or at least never below a quarter full. Again, this sounds obvious. But you don't ever want to be caught on a roadside out of gas with a small child. Then you have two things to worry about—your car and your child. Even if you're in a hurry or running late, stop for gas. It takes a few minutes and may save you many more, not to forget the associated anxiety. No one will fault you for stopping for gas—but who really cares, anyway? So what if you're a little bit late. Again, who's in control? And where are your priorities?

When traveling a long distance, you may want to pack a special trifle, a little gift or surprise for your child, something to break up the trip. You can even wrap it up. Save it for a change-over or the midway point—or keep it in reserve for when everyone's antsy. Anything from a comic book to a new coloring book and crayons, a small hard-covered book, or a matchbox car. It can be a diversion for both you and your child, a real lifesaver if things are dull. Know that if you always pack a little something your child will come to expect it—but that's OK. In fact, it can put a little extra excitement in your traveling.

Picnics along the way at a roadside stop with favorite sandwiches and yummy brownies can be a treat, if you're not in a big hurry to get to where you are going. If your route is scenic, plan on a stop beyond the halfway mark. Find a picnic table by a stream, and don't be in a rush to eat and run. Let your child help plan the picnic—it gives all of you something to look forward to. Make traveling itself—not just your destination—an adventure. As always, the process can be fun as well.

Airplane travel has its pluses and minuses. You can get up and walk around, but you are still confined to that cabin. For the young child, again, pack lots of fun things, even a few new ones. Make sure you have at least the equivalent of one meal with you.

Airline food, although improved, often does not appeal to young children. And, if your toddler isn't traveling with a ticket, no meal will be provided for her. If you think of it, you can request a child's menu for your school-aged child, but you or your agent have to call the airline ahead of time.

As your child gets older, think about keeping a diary for all your travels. It doesn't have to be complex—just a brief notation of where you've been and some of your thoughts: "It was fun— it was cold—I got sick." This shouldn't be a task-oriented project, but something the family can do together to remember your adventure. You can be the scribe and let everyone contribute. You'll cherish these memories in later years.

When you are traveling—even across town—bring your daily medications. When you are traveling long distances, bring whatever you *might* need. If your child has asthma and you use a nebulizer (occasionally or regularly)—bring it. It can save you a trip to a local emergency room if she requires a breathing treatment and is otherwise stable. (Obviously, if you need the services of an ER, you go.) If your child has any chronic illness, talk to your doctor about what provisions you should bring. Depending upon the remoteness of your destination, you will want to be oversupplied, not undersupplied. Occasional medications like antibiotics or steroids need be considered. Don't forget about basic first-aid items—bandages, first-aid cream, acetaminophen, an antihistamine, even ipecac for poisons. If there is a risk of serious allergies in anyone or if you're hiking into wilderness, consider having a source of epinephrine for anaphylaxis, a severe allergic reaction. (Epinephrine is adrenaline and can reverse this life-threatening event.) Talk to your doctor about appropriate provisions. A well-stocked first-aid pack is a very good insurance policy. Don't leave home without it!

Traveling should be fun. If you're yelling at everyone whenever you're in the car, make some changes. Rearrange the seating; take turns with the front and the back. Keep the trips short, or break up the long ones. Don't feel pressured to make record time. In fact, plan on extra time for stops or detours. If you have two fidgety kids in the back seat who are not inclined to sit still and who get bored, it's an automatic for trouble—split them up.

Watch for the wrong combinations with your children. Some kids feed off each other's misbehavior—really a guarantee for trouble if you're not careful. Keep a variety of toys and distractions coming. Be relaxed; remember SECRET—plan your travel, enjoy it, make room for everyone's needs, and take time to make it work.

Play road games—look for letters on license plates and road signs. Keep track of the different states. Play car bingo—there are packs for traveling. Sing songs and rotate tapes. Make it fun, and your travel will be much more enjoyable. You might even look forward to a trip together.

A fun, relaxed trip is also a safer trip, because you, the parent, can concentrate on the task at hand. Be it driving or keeping your child quiet, you can do anything better when you have provided for your child.

SHOPPING

When shopping—be it for groceries or clothes or appliances—plan on enough time to accomplish your chosen task, and then add extra time for your child. She may see something of interest, not necessarily for purchase. You may want to window shop or stop at the pet store and check out the new puppies. Make shopping fun. Remember to set an example. Be courteous to the staff. Be a role model of considerate behavior. There should be no whining from you or your child—and certainly, no stealing. Be honest. Pay for that doughnut or bagel she ate in the shopping cart. And do limit the number of items she can choose—keep it to one or two. Don't go home with every brand of sugar-coated cereal (if any) just to keep her happy. Again, who is in charge? Choose and set a pattern, and then hold to it.

Have you ever been shoe shopping the week before Labor Day—just before the reopening of school? Everyone, myself included, seems to cram into the local shoe shop that week to outfit their children in new footwear. All of a sudden, fall is here. Watch and listen as those children and their parents make the final decision on what to buy. Watch that poor, friendly sales clerk be reduced to mush by a screaming, misbehaving child and an indecisive parent. The whole store is in an uproar. Children *can* learn to sit still and be patient. You can talk to them and amuse them during any wait, but always reinforce good behavior. Be patient and courteous yourself. No running around wild, and no hysterics! Decisions are not life determining, especially when it comes to shoes. If your favorite shoe is unavailable, disappointment needs to be handled appropriately—no tantrums. Make this a pleasant experience, even fun. But only the disciplined child—again, who's in control?—will make this a fun time. Otherwise, havoc takes over, and a very poor precedent for behavior will be established.

DINING OUT

From an early age on, it makes sense to take your child with you when you go anywhere. Expose her to travel, take her shopping, and go to your local restaurant (not necessarily fancy)—teach her how to behave in all kinds of settings. Make her comfortable through familiarity.

Here are a few tips. First, try to avoid taking your child (of any age) anywhere when she is overtired or too hungry. Keep her fed and rested. If you're going out for a meal, and it's not fast food, think about giving her a light snack at home beforehand. Keep her tank full. Restaurants can be crowded. What if you have to wait for a table and/or the service is slow, and you end up waiting beyond that threshold of no return, beyond hunger? You're courting disaster. Your child will explode. Pack little snacks, just in case. Order small portions, and request that when your child's food is ready, it be served immediately. Bring crayons and a coloring book or paper and pencil to pass the time having fun. For the older child, you can always play tic-tac-toe or hangman, make boxes out of dots, or play another paper-and-pencil game while waiting.

Let your child order what she wants—don't be too concerned about the perfectly balanced meal. Keep her happy—this is a special occasion. When you order, show respect and courtesy to the person taking your order. We've talked about this before: treat all people—and this includes service people—with the respect they deserve. A waiter or waitress is doing a job. Help him or her. Speak politely and say please and thank you. Help your child do the same. Watch yourself and listen to your own tone of voice. Know that your child is watching you.

Expect your child to sit in her own seat quietly, not disturbing other patrons. Keep her engaged in conversation or activity. Allow no throwing of food, no screaming, no running around tables, and no ruling the restaurant. This behavior is disturbing to everyone else and also dangerous. Hot foods get spilled and burn. Realize that the other patrons didn't come to listen to your child act out. Don't impose your child's bad behavior on others and ruin their meal.

If your child creates a disturbance, remove her from the scene. It is time to go home! This is a limit you *must* observe. A noisy child is not cute. Later, with calm, you can discuss what went wrong and try to do better next time. As always, there should be no yelling but composure on your part. Know that sometimes it's not the child's fault; rather there may be too much confusion or too great an expectation. Sometimes the child's been set up. But make it very clear that bad behavior is unacceptable.

Shopping and dining out, just like any trip or excursion, should be fun. Set the stage so that you and your child can enjoy your time together, wherever you are.

VISITING

Just as for shopping or traveling, take your child visiting when she is best prepared. Take her along when she is well rested and fed—when she is happy. If she's tired or hungry, it is much harder to maintain good behavior, no matter how popular (or unpopular) Auntie's may be. Particularly with a small child, observe the traveling rules described earlier. Have a bunch of play things and a snack (even a change of clothes and any daily medications) when you're going out. Be prepared for staying longer than planned—maybe Grandma needs you there to run an unexpected errand or help with a meal. Maybe your friend is in a crisis and would really appreciate a visitor for longer than a quick drop-in. Respect your friend's needs but also your child's.

Observe the same rules of courtesy outside, as well as inside, the home. As in the restaurant or the store, make an effort to say please and thank you; show appreciation. And most important, give your child an opportunity to adjust to a new setting—to play and relax. Don't rush the visits.

Remember to check safety conditions. Make sure that other homes and yards are safe. Where does Grandma keep her medications? Probably on the kitchen table, within reach of your toddler. Move them! Remember to watch your child, especially if she is young. Your host may not be aware of the inherent dangers in his home, so you must be on guard. Never assume anything. Don't let your child out of your sight in an unfamiliar setting. Be vigilant, just not neurotic. Your home may be childproof—but not your friend's or neighbor's. Ask about any particularly valuable or dangerous items—it's better to know about these up front. Take precautions with unfamiliar plants, heirloom pottery, cleansers, swimming pools, and so on.

Once in a while, visits anywhere are a complete failure. Perhaps the host was not prepared for a busy, active, even moody toddler (or teen). Despite your best preparative efforts, there was no space for her, nor acknowledgment. Or your child failed to cooperate. Well, it's time to go home. Regroup before coming back. Maybe it would be easier for you to be the host rather than the guest.

Sometimes our children—whether on purpose or not—insult or hurt the feelings of our hosts. Maybe Auntie Sue was too forceful in her affections and your child was not quite ready to accept her. Small children accept adults on their own terms. You cannot force a relationship with a child—young or old—ever! You might be able to fake it a little with a teen, but never with a preschooler. Children are very definite about whom they like. Usually, it reflects not only acceptance but a degree of trust and comfort. Let your children warm up *slowly* to friends and relatives. Visit often and casually, and let your children set the pace.

When friends or relatives visit you, welcome your guests with genuine warmth and caring. (See "A Warm Hearth," Chapter 15.) And remember (we all need reminding here) that, as we make an effort to treat our guests with special consideration, might we direct some of that special treatment toward our own family and selves? Again, who is in charge? And what is driving us? Know that there is nothing wrong with treating our family—our very own children and spouses, the people who mean the most to us— like guests, at least once in a while.

THE DOCTOR'S OFFICE

I cannot resist discussing the doctor's office—but this could just as easily represent the dentist's office or extend to any professional setting. Believe it or not, limit setting even extends to the doctor's office. Most patients and their parents do a wonderful job of cooperating here. In fact, most are unusually patient and very willing to wait when office hours are overbooked and waiting is a fact. (For this, I am sorry and working always to make changes myself—setting my own limits!) Most parents and patients are very supportive and helpful in planning treatment.

But, I have to say, not all. So—to some parents—I urge you, please help the doctor and your child by being firm with your child when you come to visit. Not only do we ask that you respect our toys and equipment, but we need your help and support with all procedures. Even with routine examinations such as ear exams, throat cultures, and injections—we need your help. It's true, these procedures plainly and simply can hurt. As a physician, I do all I can to minimize any discomfort and to limit the intensity and duration of pain. But often I (and we, generically) need help from the parent in holding a child—reassuring that child that this is a necessary but time-limited event. The parent who is unable to hold and support his or her child makes my job harder as a doctor and, more important, makes it more difficult for the child. That parent is giving very mixed messages to the child—i.e., that he or she is afraid to be here, too, or doesn't believe or trust in what I'm offering. The parent who is firm and supportive of me, the physician, enables me to be more gentle and efficient—gathering or giving only what I need and then moving on to something more pleasant.

To the parent who promises, "No shots" or "No ear exams"— please don't do that. First of all, vaccine schedules change, and, in fact, your child may be due for a vaccination, even if she is "up to date." Better to promise nothing and let the doctor advise you and your child in the office. Ask your doctor right away—"Are there any shots today?" If so, get them over with. Then, no one is caught in a lie—no one has to break a promise.

With regard to ear exams, just because your child may be coming in for another complaint—for example, a rash—please don't assume the ears won't need to be examined. As a pediatrician, I feel very strongly about examining more than just the skin when a child presents with a rash. The body has many parts, and they relate to each other. Even a limited exam for a brief office visit needs to include the heart, lungs, abdomen, skin, throat, ears, and neck. If your child has had chronic ear problems and is being seen for something else—what a great opportunity to check on those ears in a more normal situation! Of course, judgment calls and bargains are made with children individually—particularly, with those who have been traumatized by previous exams. But if I can make one request: please let the doctor make that contract with your child—and together we will have more success at building a trustful relationship.

Seeing children in the office—particularly over time—enables your doctor to help and advise you on behavioral issues, as well as the immediate physical concerns. Take advantage of his or her expertise—ask questions, seek advice. Don't be afraid to ask sensitive questions. If there isn't time in a scheduled visit to address all of your concerns, there is always time for a follow-up phone call or another visit. Just listen to yourself, and make sure you are addressing your parenting needs. Make sure your physician hears you. There are no limits here.

11

Special
Events

A brief word about special events—vacations, birthday parties, and holidays. Try to *keep* them special—that is both a challenge and a goal. Try not to overdo.

Don't let vacations get spoiled by unrealistic expectations that can never be fulfilled. Enjoy being together and having a break from routine, if nothing else. Do get rest and relaxation. Keep a lid on birthday parties and holidays. Special events should be times of gathering and celebration that the family welcomes—but only if they are kept special. Enjoy them and don't let them slip away.

In terms of limits, watch that special events do not get out of hand. Try to orchestrate ahead of time; plan and be in control. Think SECRET. Keep the purpose of any celebration as the focus, not the specifics.

VACATIONS

Vacations, like travel, are supposed to be fun. They are supposed to be a time for rest, relaxation, and, hopefully, renewal. Vacations are a time for families to gather in a special spot for unencumbered time together—for play!

But just because you may be away doesn't mean limits and behavior standards stay home. Quite the contrary. The rules of the household should carry over into vacations and give them structure. Respect, manners, and patience should never take a vacation. Abuse, be it verbal or physical, has no place at home—so why ever on a vacation?

The together family has a together time—it works. They know the rules and limits—what the expectations are. It is no surprise that the disorganized family remains disorganized when away, just like when at home. Nothing changes. If your children run the household when at home, what's to make them change when on vacation? If they act spoiled and misbehave at home, don't expect that a change of scene will work magic. In fact, they can become worse. A midwinter jaunt to Florida to go to Disneyworld can be a nightmare for the family in chaos—eating in restaurants, sleeping in strange places, spending money. If your children get carte blanche at home, they will expect nothing less when away. In fact, the sky becomes the limit as the "I want" and "I deserve" thinking takes over. Make sure SECRET goes with you. Take SECRET on vacation as well.

In terms of the specifics: Before going on vacation, look at your itinerary and look at everyone's needs—parents' and children's. Try to think ahead of time what you want to do and what you can and cannot do. Make some plans, but don't plan every second; leave room for free time and flexibility. Schedule tours or special events early on, as well as later—spread them out. Do a little homework if you're visiting a new area. Find out what is the most fun and most special. Contact a travel agent, the resort, or family and friends.

If you have to watch your spending (and I don't know who doesn't), try to figure out how many meals out you can afford and how much money is available for side trips or sporting events. Let the family know that you can do some things, but not all. And tell your children why. You have no obligation to give your children everything. In fact, you do more harm than good with total lack of discretion. Being honest about what to expect can save future disappointments. Teach your children that money doesn't grow on trees—not to be cheap or punitive but only to be realistic. Learning and appreciating value comes in many ways. Certainly knowing that things have a price tag is *life*.

After assessing costs as best you can, try to put a little extra money aside for the unexpected—the unanticipated "must do." A slush fund, if you will. Not an emergency fund, but something for that special item or event you knew nothing about. If the money's not spent, you can use it for another dinner or souvenir or maybe a contribution for your next vacation.

Sometimes giving your children some money of their own to spend is a valuable experience. It forces them to make choices, with your guidance. It empowers them. You just have to be careful in directing reasonable spending without encouraging miserly hoarding or unchecked extravagance. If you use money wisely, that will give your children a very good start. So have a good time.

If while away you would like and/or need some time separate from your children—if this is important—arrange for sitters and tell the children now. Prepare them ahead of time. Let them know that this is your vacation, too. Don't forget about *self*. Vacations are for everyone, including you.

One last word—sometimes trips to exotic places are simply not within the family budget. If so, don't go! If a vacation costs too much in money and/or anxiety, it's not worth it. Remember, there is nothing wrong with a "vacation" at home. Talk to families who have done it. A week at home with lazy mornings, local outings, relaxed schedules, and time together can be just as restful (if not more) than an elaborate, expensive trip. It's the frame of mind that is important. And if you're like most people—have you really explored your hometown area? Probably not.

BIRTHDAY PARTIES

We mentioned birthday parties previously, but I think they deserve a special discussion. First of all, thank goodness birthdays come only once a year. They can get out of hand very easily and lead to more unhappiness or disappointment than no party at all.

Watch that your parties are not overdone. Watch the buildup, and then don't go overboard. Show your child that there are definite limits—to parties as well as life, in general. The important part of the party is getting together and sharing the moment with family and friends—that's it! It's not to outdo the neighbors with clowns, ponies, and puppet shows. It is not to set a record in presents. It's as much a family celebration as a time to honor your child. It is not a time to be greedy—to blow your credit card limit, to buy out the toy store. Let your child learn that early on. Let him help you plan a party—favors, cake, even some homemade decorations. Let him include special friends, but it doesn't have to be the whole class. Don't kill yourself with fancy cooking and planning—you'll only end up being fatigued and stressed, and the kids don't really care. Make it fun for everyone, and everyone will be happier. Keep it simple. Choose a theme that's fun and easy, then toot the horns.

Holidays

Holidays are special occasions—days set aside for families to gather, time to celebrate and to remember. Gifts may or may not be involved—at Christmas yes, Thanksgiving no. There may be a religious theme or a national theme to your gathering. It may be a time to reflect upon the memory of a historical figure—Martin Luther King, George Washington. Or it may be a time to reflect upon sacrifices made by the war veterans and war dead.

Whatever brings you together, holidays are supposed to be a special time when families can break from their daily routine and share a moment. They are similar to vacations but more thematic than pleasure oriented. Holidays are *not* for shopping—not a time to outdo each other. Rather, they are a time to remember what we are all about.

Limit setting has a place with holidays, as we must work hard, sometimes, to keep the emphasis in the right place. Do you take time at Thanksgiving to give thanks for your freedom, for the right to gather as you please? Or are you more focused on the turkey or the football games? It's not that you can't enjoy the latter—but where is the primary concern?

At Christmas or Hanukkah, is the family focused more on gifts rather than the meaning of the holiday season? And are the holidays so commercialized that you no longer enjoy them? (What a terrible indictment!) Make sure your children are not so caught up in the receiving of presents that they forget how to give. Is the spirit of the holiday season lost as the busyness of preparation takes hold?

It is very important to set the right tone for any holiday—certainly, one of reverence, not just complete and utter frivolity. It is important that our children share in the meaning of each and every holiday—that family traditions develop and then get perpetuated. Let your children contribute. Let them think of ways to celebrate appropriately—be part of a ceremony—be part of the giving. Help them to share with others less fortunate. Teach them a responsibility to include and give to those who have a harder life. Cook or serve a turkey for the homeless; send a gift to a less fortunate child. Give your child a sense of the world beyond himself. Keep the holidays special, not just selfish.

As you gather, remember to love each other and delight in just the sheer gathering. Give hugs—say "I love you." Welcome those who have traveled, and take time to appreciate everyone. Hold hands at table—offer a blessing—keep the holidays "holy," as they were intended to be. Remember SECRET—know what works for you, be calm, respect each other, and take time to make your holidays memorable.

12

Work

Work means accomplishing a goal-oriented task—everything from washing the dishes to fulfilling employment obligations, from completing committee assignments to raising our children. We all work!

As parents we work very hard as we raise our children to become responsible, happy citizens. Certainly, that's our biggest and most important job. It's a forever job—once a parent, forever a parent.

But in addition, you may have other work, over and above your parenting responsibilities. And regardless of your situation, work involves certain issues. In terms of setting limits, maintaining a balance between or among your jobs is one of the biggest challenges. And yes, again, SECRET has application, as we seek balance for ourselves, and ultimately, our families.

WORKING OUTSIDE THE HOME

As much as we work at home as a parent, some of us are also working outside. Whether it be for pay or volunteer, work at another site can provide income as well as something to claim as our own, something to balance out the stress of our parental duties. It can give us mental and emotional satisfaction, over and above the demands of parenting.

But we do need to be careful. Are we presuming that we use neither our brains nor our educations at home? Parenting is not mindless work. Hardly! Don't forget that raising children and managing a home are as challenging as any job. But, in truth, sometimes the demands of parenting seem ordinary, and sometimes we parents feel trapped. People on the "outside" appear more stimulating and more well rounded. It's true, home life provides less adult contact and the rewards are sometimes less tangible—but nevertheless, the rewards are our children.

We have to be careful about making judgments—about ourselves as well as others. Parents working outside the home *can* have it all—satisfaction from family and career. But there are never any guarantees, and there may be a price to pay. Certainly the opportunities for men and women to mix and match families and careers are numerous. However, the challenge is in finding the correct balance—an ever-present dilemma. The balance between home life and the "other" job is not easy to achieve and can be very difficult to maintain, particularly as the parenting demands change over time.

For starters, arranging child care—finding (and keeping) the right baby-sitter with the love and flexibility that you want and need—and then extending yourself beyond your home responsibilities but not overextending, while remaining calm and available—these are the real challenges. The elements of SECRET still need to be honored—limits need to be set. The mood at home and your own energy levels need to be monitored. This is not easily accomplished.

Many parents, particularly mothers, take on a part-time schedule at work to permit more time and flexibility for home. But watch that part-time doesn't grow into part-time "plus," approaching full-time—with full-time duties still present at home. Be careful about ending up with two full-time jobs, trying to do it all. Truly, is that what you wanted? (Not to forget a little time for recreation and/or creative outlets, if that's important.) Again, who or what controls your life? (See "Schedules," Chapter 10.)

Now, a few tips. When working outside the home, try to keep home and career lives separate. When you're at the office, concentrate on the tasks at hand there. Likewise, at home, focus on your family. Leave the office at the office. Try not to bring work home—or at least minimize its intrusion. A little bit of sharing is OK, but don't let your professional life dominate your whole day and invade your family life as well. Otherwise, you will sacrifice family time that you won't get back.

Leave plenty of time for transition when leaving one site and entering another. Remember the time element of SECRET—leave time for you and your family. Don't schedule too tightly, particularly at work. Don't try to cram sixty minutes of work into thirty minutes of real time. It's probably better to plan on seventy-five minutes, anyway, to leave room for those interruptions, the so-called "unexpected." If the unpredictable is the predictable, then factor it in—or you'll always run late. Leave a time cushion for your exit for home—for example, thirty minutes of extra, unbooked space to finish whatever, to get yourself home on "real" time, as promised. If you really have to be gone by six, plan on being done by five-thirty. Otherwise, you will fall behind and your credibility will be at risk. (Are you always late?)

For any parent working outside the home, without blurring boundaries, think about bringing your child to work once in a while. Let her see you function professionally. Let her come to the office, shadow you for a few hours, and use and/or wear any of your special equipment. Let her have lunch with you, particularly if there is an office cafeteria. Let her meet your buddies. Let her know how proud you are of her. Show your child off to your colleagues. Even give her a sense of the schedule and pace you maintain, and she will appreciate better your time away from the household. She may even become more proud of you—"You should see what my Mom or my Dad does." If possible, as she gets older, allow your child the opportunity to think through a work problem and propose some solution. Sometimes children are very perceptive. Allow for some input, and then reflect upon it in a very positive way—"Well, that's a really good idea; I never would have thought of that myself." It never hurts to stroke anyone! Just keep your work life in its appropriate space.

Share your work experience with your child's class or play group. Arrange to go to school one day and let the children have hands-on experience with the tools of your trade. Teachers welcome parental involvement. What could be more natural than doing some teaching yourself? Not only will you be helping your child understand your work, but now she can show you off to her peers. The relationship between you and your child will become stronger, just through sharing.

Now what is the risk of "having it all"? All of us have to be very careful to make sure that our professional careers do not deprive our children of the time they deserve and need. It is so easy for our own lives to get out of whack, for us to think that if things are out of kilter today, we can correct for them tomorrow (or next week or next year). Or we can just buy our kids off!

Watch that you don't lull yourself into thinking you can do it all—and then find you cannot. Ask your children how they are doing—*and* how you are doing. Ask their teachers, their sitters. Step back and feel the emotional climate in your home. Take a day off and hang around the house—what does it feel like? If good, then OK. If tense, make some changes. Remember, time gone is time lost.

Working at Home

Again, for the record, remember, we all do work at home. As parents, our roles require work every day—from sunrise to sunrise, or sunset to sunset (depending on how your day goes). There are no days or nights off—we are always "on call." We need not ever feel the need to apologize for not pulling in an income—for not having another title related to formal employment. After all, isn't "parent" enough?

But for those parents who do "other" work at home—be it volunteer or for remuneration—make sure that the "other" work doesn't take over and change the atmosphere of your home. Home is a place for the family, for the nurturing, caring for, and disciplining of its members. It is not supposed to be a place, primarily, of employment, although it may function as one at certain times of the day or week. Home is a place for quiet but also for activity and, occasionally, noise and commotion. It is a place, presumably, where other children are welcomed—where the focus is the family.

If your home has a dual role, watch and monitor where the emphasis falls, i.e., on either family or work life. Is the family able to be a family? Are you able to make a ruckus, or does a little confusion disrupt and then ruin the "other" work life? If Mom or Dad needs space and quiet to write, teach music, practice medicine, or study a law brief—is this only a minor inconvenience or a major burden? Certainly, in the context of setting limits, it doesn't hurt to have children attend to someone else's needs now and then. But if the complexion of the family is altered significantly because of outside constraints, perhaps this needs to be discussed. At least some conversation should take place to air feelings and needs. That is only fair. If playmates cannot come over because Mom or Dad is always working, something is wrong.

Working out of the home has its definite conveniences—reduced overhead, no commute, and availability—but it also has its disadvantages. For one, you never escape that work if it's only a room away. It can nibble away at you continually. If clients or patients know you work at home, the phone can and will ring for business purposes day and night. Is that OK? Or is it *not* OK? It may be hard, if not impossible, to make a break.

It's just like everything else—who or what is in charge of your life? If you set up a work space in your home, you have to place some kind of limits on it or it will run and ruin your life and that of your family. Separate the work space from the living space—shut the door, limit your hours, and set up a separate telephone number with an answering machine. What you gain in time and convenience can be lost if your priorities get out of whack. You do not want to sacrifice your family for your job. Be careful. Let your home be a home—let the other work take a backseat.

The At-Home Parent

So often I hear a parent say, "I don't work—I stay home." Well, as previously stated, let me be the first to tell you that all of us work—whether or not we have responsibilities or jobs beyond our parenting. Remember, we all parent. Usually what is meant is that this parent has no "other" job.

As the pendulum swings back and forth—as dual-career families try to balance the needs of their children with the demands of other careers—it is becoming clear that parenting really is a full-time job. Whether you, the parent, or a substitute provides some or all of your child care, parenting is still an all-consuming responsibility. Furthermore, it is also becoming clear that staying home with your child has merit—and there is worth in your being a parent only.

The at-home parent has a long list of job assignments—from shopping, cooking, and cleaning to organizing schedules and doing volunteer projects. You will be challenged to be creative, to use your powers of ingenuity. Your education is not wasted as you teach your children what you know and learn together what you don't. You are always being a role model and teaching them something. Furthermore, you still will have to work hard to make each day special for you and your children. And you will also have to work hard to limit your day—not crowd it with too many other items. Every child has multiple needs, and each day is an unknown.

When you're at home, word gets around. Every organization in your town will want a piece of you and, at times, even get pushy. (That lucky professional parent who can say "I cannot!") Watch that you don't overcommit to activities. Make sure your time at home with your child is not time on the telephone organizing the book fair or getting support for a new referendum. Are you around—but really not there? Watch your own limits, even now.

Presumably parents stay home with their children because they want to. Also, it is more convenient and safer, and it may be less expensive (i.e., no day-care expenses). But there are trade-offs. First, if you are used to bringing in an income—no more.

And that may force a change in your lifestyle. Second, the opportunity for adult contact and conversation will be less. You'll have to work to gather and socialize with other at-home parents and their children. Your feeling of self-worth may be affected, although it shouldn't be. You may feel "I'm only a Mom—or a Dad." Well, how about dropping the "only"?

Being a Mom or a Dad sounds very important to me. And how about your child? Isn't she delighted that you are home? Isn't after school easier and more pleasant? The pressure of arranging getting from here to there is no problem. You're already there.

The at-home parent need not ever apologize to anyone for staying home. Instead, how about a little bragging? Turn it around and let folks know how much you enjoy being with your child. Don't feel embarrassed or feel awkward about giving your child the best start you know how. What could be more important? You're lucky if you can stay home. Be proud of it!

13

A b u s e

Abuse is inexcusable wherever you come from. I don't think anyone would disagree. There is no room for abuse—be it physical, emotional, verbal, or sexual—it is entirely unacceptable. The problem or challenge is in breaking the cycle. Maltreatment of anyone has no justification—and certainly, as we set limits on our children, how about ourselves?

Think about SECRET, especially the principles of calm and respect—again, there is no place for abuse. Even with substance abuse, again the challenge is to break that chain. It only destroys lives.

VIOLENCE

Weapons and physical abuse inflict pain, trauma, and injury at an immeasurable cost. How can we put a price on the loss of a life, the wounding of a limb, or the crushing of a spirit? How can we permit ongoing abuse of our children or of ourselves?

The world is not always a pretty place. Our lives have their ups and downs, sometimes with more downs than ups. Things happen despite our honest, hardworking efforts to do right and to maintain control. All of us have a threshold limit beyond which we really lose it—*all of us!* There are times when we all break down and maybe take it out on someone else—our spouse, our colleague at work, or our children.

What I am trying to say—and I have said it before—is that we have to know when we are losing it. We have to be mature and wise enough to know when we are about to fly off the handle or "melt down." We have to know ourselves. (Remember *self* in SECRET.) We have to know our *own* limits before we hurt someone. Because that someone is often our children. They are usually smaller than we—they're vulnerable and often have to pay for our failure or unhappiness.

We can dominate our children physically and emotionally. We can strike out at them and not get hit back. We can lash out with a weapon or our tongue and remain lord and master without obvious repercussions. No one tells—it's the family secret. Curiously, the bond that ties us to our children (and vice versa) is complicated. Despite our hurting or beating a child, he or she still seems to hide from others what we have done. It's almost as if they cope by denying the abuse. "If I don't talk about it or think about it, maybe it will go away." Or maybe they don't want to admit to our failings.

Whatever the reason, children are being abused. It is for us adults to protect all children—to build a space where hurt cannot invade. But we can only do this if we consciously watch ourselves and those around our children and make it very clear that abuse is not tolerated. We cannot play into a disguise in our homes. We cannot pretend it is not happening. If you or your spouse is hitting your child, *stop* it—and seek professional help to resolve the problem. Speak up and out. Take the time and courage to undo the wrongs and set them right. Just as we teach our children not to hit, we need to teach ourselves. Limit setting really does apply to us as parents.

We've said it before: we cannot hit just because we've had a bad day. If you've been fired, don't come home and hit or malign your child because you're upset. It isn't his fault. If you didn't get that contract that you worked so hard to get—for payback, don't abuse your child, physically or emotionally. He didn't lose it. Remember, your child is on your side.

Even very successful parents who appear to be emotionally stable abuse their children. It doesn't take a whole lot to tip any of us. We all have our limits. Despite advanced education and knowledge in the field, even those who know better lose it, too. Now step back and think about someone who might be less stable, more fragile—someone who has been previously abused, who is really down and out. Is it any surprise that he or she may strike out? It doesn't ever make it right, but maybe we can understand a little better where different folks come from. We have to work together to support everyone in an effort to replace child abuse with family support—coping mechanisms, backup child care, anything to ensure a safer and happier childhood.

But what to do if you're losing it? First, get space. Allow for a cooldown. Go out for a long walk, preferably brisk, or a hard run. Get some exercise; let off steam in a physically acceptable way. Call a friend. Share your sorrow and disappointment through the right kind of words and tears. Talk to your pastor or your rabbi. Find or start a support group. Get some counseling.

If you had a bad day, come home to the love and refuge you have built. Come home for support, not revenge! It's OK to let your kids know that you had a rotten time at the office. I can promise you that they know it anyway. Just by your body language, even without your spoken word, they know something isn't right. Tell them you're in a bad mood, and let them see that you can handle disappointment without striking out. Give them a hug. Show them that even when you're down, you've still got each other. Share your life with them—but, and here's the catch, don't burden them with your worries. If your career is at risk, don't make your children lose sleep over the next meal or paycheck. Let them know that you will make it through. Hopefully, you have been able to build enough trust in your household to know you will eventually prevail. If not, and tensions are very high, think about calling a supportive hotline or getting that counseling to weather this period. But don't hit!

And don't shake your baby either. "Shaken baby" syndrome is caused by bleeding into the brain, the result of violent shaking. Brain damage, even death, can follow. *Never* shake a child. If you feel like doing it, get someone else right away to take your place as a caretaker. Call immediately for help.

Emotional stability for us and our children develops over time. It doesn't just grace us automatically. If we are in charge of our lives and doing a good job of directing and taking care of both ourselves and our children, the climate in our homes should be right. But if we are overworked, overwhelmed with hurt or pressure, or driven "to distraction," then our children will suffer. We talked previously about watching our schedules and monitoring time—we really have to watch our lives. Make sure our attempts to "get ahead" are not for the wrong reasons. Do we really need five bedrooms in a house? Does it matter what kind of car we drive? Where are our priorities? Make sure that our "things" are not more important than our children and are not causing tensions. Don't work for more, and then get less.

Remember that words can be just as damaging as your arm. Verbal abuse leaves scars—just not on the skin. Words say a lot—sometimes too much. Watch your tongue. Bad or mean words set a very poor example and a terrible tone. Clean up your act if you or anyone slanders, demoralizes, diminishes, or gossips about another person.

Weapons have been discussed previously (see "Behavior," Chapter 6). Let me remind you that the home is no place for weapons, no matter what your feelings are about the right to bear arms. Too many children are dying from home "accidents" that are really preventable injuries. Adults are not controlling what weapons they possess—it's not working.

I haven't yet mentioned the topic of sexual abuse, but it is a topic that cannot be swept under the carpet. Sexual abuse, just like physical and verbal harm, is wrong! It is a violent act with no justification. The consequences are severe—emotional and sexual dysfunction, not to forget the risk of disease and pregnancy. No one has the right to violate anyone, much less a child.

Scary as it may seem, most children who are sexually abused

are hurt by someone they know. This is fact. Implicit in this is that someone they trusted has violated them. In terms of limits and controls, be vigilant about who is with your child and under what circumstances. This includes adults and teens and even pre-teens. Be open to your children, always, about the inappropriateness of anyone's touching or fondling their genitals or private areas. Make sure that children know that if they have been violated they are not at fault. They are not guilty of anything. Instead, be proud of them for coming forward (encourage that). Praise your children for being honest and exposing any misdeed. Support them in their efforts to do what is right—for themselves and for other children, as well. No stigma should ever be attached to the abusee. Get help and see any abuse incident through to its conclusion. That is your responsibility, and for the good of your child (and all children), it needs to be done.

SUBSTANCE ABUSE

Another abuse taking its toll on our children is substance abuse. Not just crack cocaine, but legal drugs like alcohol and cigarettes. Here, as parents, we can have real impact—being a good role model, setting our own limits—to keep our child's environment safe and healthy. Drugs in any form are dangerous and addicting. We are all vulnerable and easy targets when we are a little bit down.

Starting with our child's conception, we need to eliminate our own intake of alcohol, illicit drugs, and tobacco during pregnancy, as they can all have dramatic effects on the fetus. We need to take care of ourselves. The scary thing is that we never know when and/or how much use will affect our babies. It is safe to say that *no* use is the best control. No alcoholic beverages during pregnancy, no cigarettes before and after the baby is born, and no cocaine, ever. Know that it's not necessarily drug or alcohol abuse, just exposure, that can leave our babies damaged. Know that after birth, the environment in which we place our children has its consequences, too. Tobacco smoke puts any child (or other person) at much greater risk for respiratory illnesses and asthma—and sometimes this can be life threatening. It may sound unbeliev-able, but it's true. And any drinking or doing of drugs clouds our judgment and affects our parenting skills.

Substance abuse costs us plenty. It hurts our children and costs us lives. The intoxicated person behind the wheel of the car—and this may be you—puts everyone on the road in danger. The depressed parent at home, nipping at the bottle, is not a qual-ity care provider. We may think we have it under control, but no one who drinks during the day does! The bottle may be hidden, but the impact of daytime, uncontrolled drinking is enormous. Think of the child having to apologize for his drinking parent. What kind of message are we giving? Do we say no to drugs for our children—but say it's OK for us adults? We're supposed to be mature and, therefore, have it under control. But often we don't! Even if you are a "social" drinker, watch it. Are you depen-dent upon that drink at night—and it's becoming two and three?

It is very hard to recognize any problem in ourselves. But, and I plead with you—if you drink, talk to your own doctor. And if you cannot get through the day or night without liquor, you have a problem. Alcoholism is an illness, with a very definite genetic heritage. If your parents drank, you're automatically at risk. And if you do, that places your children at risk, too. Alcoholism can be treated, but the first step of treatment is recognition.

Our children know that we are not perfect. And if we drink, they know it all too well. We owe it to ourselves to seek help and support before something really wrong happens. Our children are entrusted to us—we need to honor that trust and make sure we are not abusing it. Who's in charge here?

So keep the slate clean. Don't get drunk, ever! It is not amus-ing. Don't smoke—it can make your child ill, either immediately or later on. Don't do drugs. Learn as the children are learning at school how to say no. And get support for yourself—none of us can do it alone.

14

Modern Technology

The world of technology is not only at our doorstep, but inside our homes. It is virtually impossible to escape the magical three: the telephone, television (including videos), and the computer. These systems have expanded our horizons as they educate and inform us, but they have also invaded our homes, almost surreptitiously. They greet us in the morning, interrupt our meals, become sources of friction ("It's *my* turn—you had yours"), and complicate bedtime ("It's my favorite show").

Was life simpler before television? Before the telephone? Before the computer? Maybe or maybe not—but we can't turn the clock back. Instead, what we need to do for ourselves and for our children is to appreciate and use all these instruments of communication wisely—and not let *them* run *us*.

We still need to leave time for quiet, time for reading, time to be together. With so much making a claim on our time, we need to be ever more vigilant on how we spend it and make quite sure that unstructured time remains (see "Schedules," Chapter

10). With complex communication networks, let's not forget about communicating with each other on a personal level. I'm afraid the vigilance required here will only get more demanding as the possibilities for telecommunications expand.

Application of SECRET—setting limits—still has a place. Know what works for you—calmly establish rules and limits about the use of telecommunications. Respect each other's need for time with and without electronic resources—make time with and without. So let's look at the magic three.

THE TELEPHONE

In our world of mass communications, the telephone has become an increasingly complex piece of equipment. I resist the word "important" because I think sometimes its value is overrated. We have come to depend upon the telephone but perhaps become too dependent. We no longer write letters; we call. Likewise, our children have learned that it is easier to phone than write. Why struggle with a letter when we have a telephone in every room? Conversations give immediate answers—no more waiting for responses. You can even fax anything—articles, reports, legal documents, whatever you want. The phone is like being there (and will be more so when telephone video becomes routine).

Phones are omnipresent—home, the office, the car, the airplane, the golf course. There is no place that is sacred. Portable phones will and do travel. And at times, they become intrusive—almost running our lives. What happens when the phone rings? We usually drop whatever is at hand, run to answer the phone, and ignore whatever is going on around us. For some reason, the phone always takes precedence over everything else. Why? I mean, if by some chance we miss a call, won't our answering machine, with all its capabilities, record the message for us anyway? Still, we don't want to miss anything, so we pick up. Nothing can wait.

And then, because everyone needs a phone (do they, really?), we run multiple lines into the house. We have his line and her line—different rings, different phone numbers. And then there is call waiting—where even our phone conversations are interrupted, coincidentally, by the phone itself. Conference calls enable us to speak to several people at one time.

Now really, who or what is in charge? I hope it's not the telephone. Has the world of communications taken over our lives? What would happen if you didn't automatically answer the phone every time it rang? What if you missed a call—even disconnected your answering machine? Have you ever taken the phone off the hook? Now I don't want to inconvenience any caller, but I think my point is well taken. If you miss an important phone call, I bet the caller will try again.

Make sure the phone system isn't running your life. Set limits on its use—for you and your child. For example: No phone calls at mealtime. No late night phone calls—set a curfew (10:00 or 11:00). Sit and have a quiet dinner or conversation with your child. Let the phone ring! Have a quiet time together at bedtime. Let the phone ring! Let your child see that she is more important than AT&T. The person at the other end of the line can wait. Truly, how many of your calls are really emergencies and need immediate attention? We are so used to getting immediate responses—are our expectations a bit unrealistic? There are more important things than answering the telephone. Make sure you set limits on your priorities—for you and your child.

With regard to phone lines—do your children really need their own phones? Monitor their phone use. Again, who is in charge? "Mom, I'm on the phone." Well, maybe it's time to get off! Do you ever hear yourself or your child say, "I've got to go?" Beware of your school-aged child or teenager spending hours on the phone talking to the same children she saw all day in school. What do they talk about? Has the boy-girl thing exploded so that everyone is calling everyone else to see what everyone else is thinking and then repeating that loop? Make sure that phone time isn't cutting into family time, homework, and practice. Who is calling, anyway? Make sure you know.

As a parent, you do need to watch phone use and set limits if it is being abused. Look at both yourself and your children. Don't accept calls at certain times and hours. As long as you are clear, your child will learn to honor the limits you set—and so will her friends.

TELEVISION

How often do you or your child turn the TV on? How many hours does she sit watching, mesmerized by the "box"? Watch out for channel surfing. Monitor yourself, your child, and your sitter.

Television is a fact, just like the telephone. Its presence in our homes is a given. In our modern world of communications, where would we be without it? It provides news, sports, entertainment, and teaching. It takes us all over the world, to places both tropical and Arctic. It expands our own horizons, as it introduces us to cultures and animal habitats only a few can see firsthand. But that's the good news.

The bad news is that the average child spends more time watching TV than in school! Through television, children are exposed to violence, sex, and drug use. Just watch! Television is very powerful—really persuasive. If "they" are doing it on TV, it only takes a small leap of faith to transfer "it" to the real world.

The bottom line is that television needs to be monitored, right from the start. When we talk about setting limits, here's a prime target. Even for the very young child—the infant and toddler—there are age-appropriate programs that certainly have merit. But even these can be abused. There are programs with songs and stories for preschoolers, programs for education, and even programs for your parenting needs. But beware, television is only an aid to parents—it is not a replacement. It is not supposed to do your job.

The television entertains—and it does that very well. It's fun to watch—and should be in small doses. Certain times of the day it can even rescue you. There is nothing better than a little music or story-telling at the predinner "witching" hour when everyone, including the parents, is tired. But recognize television for what it truly is. It is *not* going to prepare your child for Harvard. In fact, it can sabotage your efforts to truly educate your child if the television takes the place of your own reading and working with your daughter. Your child will learn her ABCs even without television when she is ready. I can assure you that it doesn't really matter if that is at age two or four or five! It's the overall readiness and maturity that are important when it comes to learning—not just the recognition of letters.

How many times a day does your child have to watch the same show? Well, that should be self-evident. Only once! Only one viewing per day should provide what information you are looking for. Children propped up in front of the "tube"—almost hypnotized by the same show running over and over again—that is not quality time. Your child is wasting time she could be spending on something else. Chances are good she's "spaced out"—overdosed on TV—anyway.

It is for you, the parent, to limit the amount of TV time in your household. Watch, first, that you as a parent are not an automatic button pusher. Remember that you are your child's role model. If you're glued to the television, your child will probably follow your lead. Does the TV go on early in the morning and stay on all day? Is it more background than anything else? Is your child even watching it? So make rules.

One hour of TV time a day of age-appropriate programming seems more than enough. And then leave some flexibility for special events. Some of the movies and holiday specials are just that—"special"—and can be enjoyed even by the whole family. Likewise, be selective about what qualifies as "special," and make sure that you, the parent, agree. Watch with your child—be together.

Do *not* place a TV in your child's room. What does she need it for anyway? She does not have to have constant access to the tube; she does not need to watch all of her programs always. Where is the priority—and who's in charge?

As children get older—and it doesn't take long—the issues of sex and violence on television are dangerously real. Without a doubt there is an excessive amount of both on television—and again, it is up to you, the parent, to know what your child is watching and set the guidelines. Bloody killings, torture, intercourse—I think no one would argue their inappropriateness at any age. But do you really know what your child is watching? Is your school-aged child left unsupervised after school? Or does she go to someone else's house where the TV is open game? Again, you have to monitor your child's unstructured time. Perhaps there needs to be more structure planned ahead of time, if your television is having too much of a presence. Ask yourself these questions, and be honest. Know that there is a place for TV for us and for our children—but determine that place ahead of time and then hold to it.

The soap operas are popular with the teens. They hold an almost cultlike allure. Make sure there isn't more emphasis on them than homework.

In addition to the scheduled programs, video has invaded our homes. Like TV, it is both a boon and a curse. There is just that much more to watch! Again, video is for entertainment—and that's OK, as long as you use it as you should. Occasional videos are fun, but do not allow sequential, constant viewing of videos. Don't be the most frequent user of your local video store. Be selective. And then watch your own use, as you monitor your child's.

Parents often ask what to do with the children when the television and video are off. Well, you can play a game or read a book; consider writing a letter. This is the place for that quality time with your child. It is a time when you can explore together, get some hands-on learning. Get down on the floor—all of you. Play with puzzles or shapes and colors. Take time to go to the library or local museum or zoo. Make sure you are not so rooted in a schedule of meals, naps, and television that you are shirking your parenting responsibilities and then missing out on valuable time together.

What did children do before television was invented? They played games. They read. They went outside, ran around, and played hide-and-seek. Why can't children do that now? Is television replacing spontaneous play and after-school snacks in the kitchen? Check it out. Is television more important than friends or family? If so, I would suggest making some changes.

Watching television is passive, not active play. It has a limited value. It makes no demands on the viewer—makes no challenges.

Don't get deluded. Be vigilant about the TV, and know that you *can* turn it off.

THE COMPUTER

The use of personal computers, laptops, and all other forms of communication and information systems is expanding rapidly. The world of technology—fax machines, E-mail, the Internet— is growing and changing so fast, it's impossible to imagine where we will be in years to come.

Our children are growing up in a very media/communication-oriented world, with new technology replacing old on a daily basis. How will they handle the volume of information they need to know to communicate and succeed? And then how will they adapt to the constant change that is taking place?

First, there is still a need for basic knowledge. Regardless of our technology, children must learn how to read, write, and deal with numbers. We, as parents, must still work hard to make sure these basic skills are learned. Don't ignore the three Rs (reading, writing, and arithmetic) in favor of the computer. Make sure your child has these fundamentals firmly mastered. Work with your children at home—put aside specific time if necessary. Make sure the classroom at school also emphasizes these same skills.

Furthermore, now more than ever, your children need a very solid foundation in math and science, upon which so much of our technology is based. No longer can children go through school avoiding these areas. Both boys and girls must build a strong foundation in these areas, upon which they will superimpose computer skills. Then they will be empowered to better meet the challenges of their generation.

In truth, we do need to expose our children to the use of computers, even if we are somewhat phobic or totally unskilled ourselves. We just shouldn't overdo it. We may be anxious about the new technology, but we cannot afford to pass that on to our children. Because children learn new languages with ease, the computer is effortless for them. It can become a great source of fun—with games, puzzles, and communication all limitless. But just like the telephone and television, as well as other products of our mechanized world, the computer has its limits. Remember, the computer does not replace dealing with people—it provides no face-to-face social contact. It does not replace the spoken word. Computer use can be very isolating, as children spend more time at the keyboard than with other children. Furthermore, it gives no exercise—the body is not moving, except for the fingers and eyes. (Watch for carpal tunnel syndrome and eye strain.) So just like other products of our civilization, the computer has a very definite, even expanding place, but its use should be monitored. Make sure your child is not sacrificing time with peers and time outside glued to the friendly computer.

One further word—when considering an investment in a computer system, you will see that the price tags are steep. Try to buy knowing that your system, no matter how up-to-date, will become obsolete. Try to allow for flexibility and/or adaptability— talk to a consultant. Talk to a teacher or professional in the field. Consider purchasing secondhand equipment—you can get some good buys. Whatever you buy, help your child become familiar with your system, as a building block for more. The world of electronics and microsystems has no boundaries. Through basic education and familiarity with computers, you can empower your child to be part of this frontier. But do some appropriate limit setting.

15

"Pearls"

For lack of a better term, I wanted to wrap up with a few "pearls" to put some closure on this topic of limit setting. Ultimately, as we have already discussed, limits we set on our children are really those we set on our own lives and then model consistently. It's not always easy to set limits—sometimes it is not fun. The joys and challenges of parenting are real. But I honestly believe that, if we work hard, establish and maintain calm, spend time with our children, limit our schedules, and define codes of behavior, then we will meet with more success and pass on proper standards to generations to come. Our children will be happier, knowing what limits have been set. They—like the well-disciplined athlete—can then focus on the tasks at hand.

For the last time, let's review our acronym SECRET. Remember your*self*—find what works for you and hold to it. Work hard at keeping your cool, maintaining your composure, being *calm*. *Respect* your needs, and *respect* your child's individuality and need for space. Spend *time* being a parent—real time, not just an artificial marking of time.

Your Child Is Special

I've mentioned this before, but I think it worthwhile to say it again. Each child is special—one of a kind. You probably saw it from day one—even as a newborn infant, your child had a special and separate quality.

It's probably a good thing that we are all different. How boring if we were all the same! Imagine all being athletes or musicians. Imagine all being the same size or color. Instead, what a richness we bring to living in our being so varied.

One major challenge as a parent is in recognizing that each child is, in fact, different—and each requires a slightly different set of parenting skills from us. A quiet, sensitive kid will buckle with even a harsh word, while a stubborn, physical child will demand more. Each child needs to be recognized for his own needs and demands. Resist comparing one child with another—don't benchmark siblings. It is important that we not fault or blame a child because he is less "adaptable" than others. Rather we must recognize a different makeup. The standards of behavior should be the same—we still need discipline and order—but how we achieve those goals will vary slightly for each child.

As our children grow (and I have mentioned this before), there will often be conflict as they develop their own identities. Your child will need space to make his own decisions—he will need your permission to make choices. You will have to give him room to make mistakes. We need to recognize that our children are not you or me—let them follow their own paths. Our children are not our carbon copy. They have their own dreams, which are not necessarily our dreams.

Don't pin all your hopes on your child—don't sacrifice everything for him. That's a pretty big burden for your child. What sacrifices you make, do so graciously, not with resentment. Try to maintain balance within the family. Let your child know that you are accommodating him, but don't make him feel guilty.

Remember that, as you adjust for each and every child, you are showing respect by accommodating individual needs. It is an art form, developed over time with lots of patience and attention to fairness.

HUMOR

When things go badly, do you still have your sense of humor? Or did you never have one to begin with?

Humor is one of those delicious gifts of life. A smile, a joke, a laugh is fun—and wonderfully therapeutic if the chips are down. Certainly as a parent, caught in some of the more mundane tasks of parenting—from diapers to carpools—maintaining a sense of humor can be the difference between sanity and collapse. Sometimes you can even find something funny about a poopy diaper or a messy kid.

Our lives as parents are complicated and often difficult. Our children bring joy but also sorrow and hurt and worry. We were never promised a rose garden, and by golly, sometimes we do not get one. But humor can carry us through many trying moments—and can serve as a lesson to our children. If we can smile or laugh in times of trial, hopefully they can, too. If a hint of a silver lining really lies inside every cloud, let it shine. If our inner selves are preserved despite challenge, grief, or disappointment, then perhaps theirs will be, too. Consider how you cope with stress.

Once again, who or what is in charge of our lives? Who sets the limits—our life circumstances or some inner strength or spirit? Without waxing too philosophical—humor can save us. Humor does not mean silliness—it means the capacity to laugh. It is a showing of hope in spite of circumstances. Don't let anything take this away from you and your children.

PROMISES

A promise is a promise is a promise—it should be something inviolate, even sacred. It means that whatever you say is true—that whatever agreement you have made, you will uphold. It is an absolute with no misunderstanding. "I promise to . . ." means you *will*!

In setting limits for our children, we set limits on ourselves. When we mean to do something, we do our best to do it. But when we promise, it raises the expectation for fulfillment. It guarantees a job will be done, a trust will not be violated. How better can we develop or destroy faith in our developing children than by honoring or denying a promise!

Teach your children that a promise is a most special kind of oath. Show him through your actions that there is the highest level of commitment when a promise is made. A promise is not a flip, light agreement, but rather a holy vow, if you will.

Promises, agreements, contracts—they all need to be honored. Make sure your child learns this early on. Share with him the making of a promise and then honoring it. Make absolutely sure that you follow through on *all* of your promises—or don't make them. If you cannot be sure, then don't promise. Your child will learn to accept that. Promise only what you can, and be up-front about that. You cannot promise that the sun will shine tomorrow—you have no control over the weather. You cannot promise to earn more money—things happen. You should not promise to be home at a certain hour unless you know, unconditionally, that you can. Let your child learn the difference. You can promise to do your best and not necessarily guarantee the outcome, but this is a more sophisticated promise, for the older child. The bottom line is to promise only what you can deliver—and deliver what you promise.

QUALITY TIME

Several times throughout this book I've mentioned the term *quality time*. It's a phrase that is loaded with good intentions but, in fact, often deceives us and our children. Quality time with a child means a special moment or an hour or day together that is truly good—memorable—fun—for *both* participants. It is worthy of separate discussion because quality time is so important. How do you spend time with your child? When and where? Who decides?

Quality time happens. It cannot always be programmed into anyone's day. You cannot dictate "quality time," although you can try. Instead, you can and must leave time (even open-ended time) for things to happen. Those outings—those times coloring on the floor or doing puzzles—you *do* want to leave space for these events. Allow space and time for spontaneity—for "quality" to happen. But to force the issue of quality will sabotage your very goal. You cannot demand "quality"—it has to evolve. Let it.

A Warm Hearth

Your home is what you make of it. It doesn't have to be magazine material. It doesn't have to pass the white glove test. But what we do want to strive for is a warm, welcoming atmosphere where family and friends want to gather. Home should be cozy—the hearth should always be warm. The cookie jar should be full—a meal always ready to throw on the stove. The atmosphere and the people who fill a home are what's important, not the belongings.

It takes time and work to make a *home* out of a house or an apartment or wherever you live. Know that your presence and your special touches can transform any space into a home, if you make the effort. It takes time and constant attention. It's not something frivolous, but basic. You and your family need to feel good about your space, both corporate and individual. Special pictures, blankets, and pillows can really make the difference. You need to be able to relax in and use what space you have. Don't overdecorate and then not use it. Don't save it. (For what, anyway?) Know that you and your children don't need to be overindulged (don't seek prize-winning decor, unless that is important to you). You just want to be where the action is.

Keep your home neat, but not necessarily spotless. Keep it clean—but a place where spills can take place and a broken dish is not the end of the world. Children do need to pick up, and this includes their rooms (see "Behavior," Chapter 6), but out of respect. Help them do it—even make it a time together. And make sure that, with your efforts to maintain cleanliness, you don't overdo. Don't make your children afraid to make a mess. And don't spend more time cleaning than playing. Furthermore, in times of stress (the newborn period, hospitalizations, and so on), let your house go a little. Let those standards slip some if your priorities have to shift.

The feeling you bring to your home is what is important. Is there love, tenderness, and respect? Or is there tension, unhappiness, and worry? We rarely have complete control over our lives, so despite our efforts to maintain calm, pressures may invade. All I can advise is not to let those pressures control you. Keep the warm fires burning—stay in charge of yourself. Pass this on to your children, and you will have given them a real gift. Keep the peace at home, always.

The limits we set for our children are really those we place on ourselves and then model for them. If we can love, they will. If we are kind and patient, they can learn that, too. If we can maintain control no matter what life throws at us, they will be better able to handle the unpredictable. All this we try to do at home.

A home where violence and bitterness take hold is not a home, but rather a prison. Watch that you work hard to prevent these villains from entering. Seek help from family, friends, or professionals when you need it. Don't deny or hide problems; face them. Make the changes you must, though painful they may be. We're all in this together. Enjoy the precious moments we do get, and do delight in your children. Recognize them for the power and beauty they have—launch them for the road ahead. Make home a happy place.

Remember SECRET: Take care of yourself, be calm, respect everyone, and take the time to smell the roses!

Who's in charge? Hopefully, we are! Keep the hearth warm.

index

SOUTHEASTERN COMMUNITY COLLEGE LIBRARY

3 3255 00064 3891

2